SUCCESSFUL SCHOOL MANAGEMENT

Roger Smith

CASSELL

For my parents, my wife and all my children

Cassell
Wellington House   215 Park Avenue South
125 Strand   New York
London WC2R 0BB   NY 10003

British Library Cataloguing-in-Publication Data
A catalogue record for this book is available from the British Library.

ISBN 0-304-32945-2 (hardback)
     0-304-32947-9 (paperback)

Typeset by Saxon Graphics Ltd, Derby
Printed and bound in Great Britain by Biddles Ltd, Guildford & King's Lynn.

CONTENTS

FOREWORD

The 1980s and 1990s have witnessed unprecedented changes to the education system. These have had a dramatic impact, particularly in relation to:

- schools' relationships with parents and the community;
- the funding and management of schools;
- the curriculum;
- the assessment of children's learning.

It can be an extremely daunting task for student teachers to unravel the details and implications of these initiatives. This Introduction to Education series therefore offers a comprehensive analysis and evaluation of educational theory and practice in the light of recent developments.

The series examines topics and issues of concern to those entering the teaching profession. Major themes representing a spectrum of educational opinion are presented in a clear, balanced and analytic manner.

The authors in the series are authorities in their field. They emphasize the need to have a well-informed and critical teaching profession and present a positive and optimistic view of the teacher's role. They endorse the view that teachers have a significant influence over the extent to which any legislation or ideology is translated into effective classroom practice.

Each author addresses similar issues, which can be summarized as:

- presenting and debating theoretical perspectives within appropriate social, political, and educational contexts;
- identifying key arguments;
- identifying individuals who have made significant contributions to the field under review;
- discussing and evaluating key legislation;
- critically evaluating research and highlighting implications for classroom practice;
- providing an overview of the current state of debate within each field;
- describing the features of good practice.

The books are written primarily for student teachers. However, they will be of interest and value to all those involved in education.

Jonathan Solity
Series Editor

ACKNOWLEDGEMENTS

The author would like to thank the many people who have contributed directly and indirectly to the thinking that has culminated in this book especially all those anonymous course and conference members who have helped, often without knowing it, to shape the ideas expressed here. It would certainly be impertinent and unjust not to acknowledge the debt owed to all the authors listed in the references at the end of the book and especially to Jonathan Solity for the original idea and for the support and encouragement he has offered during the writing.

I am also grateful to the ever-patient staff of Milverton Combined School and all the lecturers and students I have worked with at The Open University and The University of Warwick.

All of these colleagues have helped me in many different ways but, in the end, I accept full responsibility for any errors which may appear in the book.

INTRODUCTION

The management of schools is concerned with the organizational arrangements which enable a school to function effectively. This has become an increasingly complex process, largely because schools are multi-faceted institutions with a changing population of teachers and pupils and an ever-shifting range of structures and processes that must be put in place to make them work successfully.

The main function of schools is to make sure that teaching and learning take place in the most effective way. In managing schools, systems have to operate so that a whole range of social, intellectual and emotional activities can evolve and develop (Playfoot et al., 1989). The speed of recent changes and the scale of demands made by the legislation of the late 1980s have increased the difficulties faced by those who manage schools. More than ever before they have to work within a context of: diverging views on what is and is not effective education; major and constantly shifting curriculum changes; a high incidence of unsatisfactory buildings; frequent staff shortages; and doubtful public confidence.

ALL TEACHERS ARE MANAGERS

This book is intended to offer an introductory overview of some of the main issues in school management. In one sense this may mean that by presenting views and analysis on many different aspects of management it will be fragmentary. But there is one central theme running through each chapter, which is that all members of a school community have a role to play in its management. No one is exempt and no one should assume that they have no part to play in the development of the structures and processes that make any school function as an effective institution. All teaching jobs contain at least some element of a management function, so it can be argued that every teacher is a manager and that the whole school can only operate sensitively and responsively if all the staff are involved at all levels. ILEA's *Improving Primary Schools* (1985) recognized, at least in one level of the education system (and there is no reason to believe that this cannot be applied to secondary schools), that there was a need for all teachers to be involved in working with colleagues and advising them on many aspects of school structures, systems and organization. With this in mind it needs to be recognized that the more teachers at all levels in a school's hierarchy who have had management training of some kind, the better.

THE FUNCTIONS OF MANAGEMENT

Everard and Morris (1985) offer suggestions as to what management in its broadest sense is about. They argue that its five main functions include: 'setting aims and objectives, planning how a goal shall be achieved, organizing available resources (people, time, materials) so that it can be economically achieved in a planned way, controlling the process (i.e. ensuring that the goal is achieved) and setting organizational standards' (p.5).

Throughout this book the assumption will be that in order to plan, organize, direct and control these broad management functions, and to meet the needs of all their learners, teachers, governors and parents, schools will be more successful if they depend for their effectiveness upon co-operative activity in which leadership exists to foster team work, facilitate problem-solving and focus the 'team's' attention and enthusiasm on working together to ensure continuous improvement of the teaching and learning process.

With this in mind each chapter is intended to help teachers and students recognize that there are ways in which schools can be managed so that their goals are clear and everyone is aware that they have to take some leadership responsibility at some time and participate actively in the management of the school. Teams need to exist to support each other within an atmosphere where different opinions are respected and relationships and communications are such that optimal performance is gained by people working together co-operatively.

The general point being made is that of one form of 'collegiality': the idea that 'involvement, co-operation, participation, delegation and effective communication are more likely to enable schools to achieve their objectives' (Bell, 1989, p.128). The framework within which this happens, however, is of relatively specific management tasks.

AN OUTLINE OF CHAPTER CONTENT

Each chapter attempts to break down the school management into these 'specific' areas, recognizing that even with this kind of division there are many complex sub-headings to be considered and many areas where an inevitable overlapping of ideas occurs.

Chapter 1, 'The school as an organization', concerns itself with the structures that are needed for a school to function and examines teams and team-building, decision-making, job descriptions, directed time, responsibility allowances and the organization of the school day.

In Chapter 2, 'School ethos and whole-school aims', the whole-school dimension is discussed by reviewing aims and mission statements, the school development plan, external relations with parents, the school and its immediate community and its links with the governing body.

Chapter 3, 'Management roles', deals with those roles that have to be considered by both headteachers and teachers. They include leadership, change agents, motivators, facilitators and those roles that are specifically related to curriculum co-ordinators.

These roles become more precise in Chapter 4, 'Managing the curriculum and the classroom', which is more to do with what the teacher does in the classroom and concentrates on such areas as differentiation, match, classroom management, planning the curriculum, assessing and recording and reporting to parents.

Obviously there are constraints placed on schools and certainly the successful management of 'Finance and resources' (Chapter 5) does, to some extent, determine what can and cannot be attempted. A great deal of school management is not only about managing finance but is dependent upon the level of financial resources that is available. It is important to know more about the school budget, how spending is prioritised, what decisions are taken about spending, how the curriculum is resourced and how all spending and resource allocation is related to the School Development Plan.

Chapter 6, 'Appointments and staff development', stresses the importance of human resources and the need to have clearly defined appointment procedures and interview systems, as well as processes designed to help induct newly appointed teachers.

It is these same human resources who are involved in 'Communication'. In Chapter 7, its importance is stressed because everyone who works in schools needs to know what is happening. Lines of communication need to be appropriate within the school but it is also useful to be able to define how the school will develop its external links with parents and the wider community.

Chapter 8 considers 'Appraisal', which has to happen in all schools. It is a legal requirement and the chapter examines the process of appraisal as well as self-appraisal and self-evaluation. It also develops ideas about reaching agreement on what to appraise, how to utilize classroom observation, the appraisal interview and what development and follow-up is necessary.

If self-evaluation is to have a role in the appraisal process, then 'Developing relationships with colleagues' (Chapter 9) is important because individuals have to be able to function both on their own and as part of a team. This means they will need advice about assertion, team membership, professional attitudes and behaviour, working with colleagues and how to help make meetings more productive. Teaching is recognized as a difficult and potentially time-consuming job.

Chapter 10, 'Stress and time management', suggests how teachers can function badly in both these areas and examines the advice that is needed on various aspects of stress, including the signs to look for and how to avoid it as well as how to prevent time-wasting by developing strategies for using time well.

Schools are becoming more public arenas, and more and more demands are being made on the relationships between schools and their 'clients'. Chapter 11, 'Accountability and the inspection process', discusses the new methods of inspection that started in 1993 for secondary schools and in 1994 for

primary education and recognizes the need for schools to be prepared for what is an inevitable part of their development. This
chapter also recognizes the importance of discussing accountability in terms of who is accountable to whom, what inspectors
will look for and how schools can prepare for an inspection.

MANAGEMENT AND A SENSE OF DIRECTION

Taken together, the chapters should enable more teachers to be
more successful within the management and organization of their
own schools. The cliché 'A little knowledge is a good thing', is
partly appropriate in the successful management of all schools.
More necessary, however, is that many more teachers of whatever
status need to know what school management is about because
there is the growing need for whole schools to have a sense of 'corporate' direction. It is said that Columbus, when he set sail on his
epic voyage, was not quite sure where he was going. When he
arrived he did not really know where he was and when he
returned to Spain he did not know exactly where he had been.
Schools must not only have a sense of direction but must be able
to articulate what it is to everyone who has a vested interest in
the school's success. There is a need to know what kind of school
leaders, managers and teachers are needed to ensure that it is
effective.

It is certainly true that the major part of successful management involves several quite complex issues, which must include
formulating a clear vision, ideally one that has been reached collaboratively and shared by the staff; an open school culture in
which professional collaboration is at a premium; conditions of
work which allow for active reflection and close scrutiny of
teaching and learning; an acceptance of professional accountability; and last, but certainly not least, strong, purposeful leadership which encourages a commitment to learning on the part
of the teacher as well as the pupil.

In forging ahead, not many schools will have the epic quality
of the voyages of Columbus, but if they are staffed by knowledgeable 'managers' they should certainly move forward within the
minefields of educational change more thoughtfully, and with a
deeper and more innovative strength of purpose and direction.

CHAPTER 1

THE SCHOOL AS AN ORGANIZATION

CHAPTER OVERVIEW

In simple terms, schools are organizations where teaching and learning take place. Where people are working together within a finite space with restricted funds and material resources, however, there have to be structures and methods of organization. This chapter briefly examines two ways of looking at organizations: the hierarchy/collegial and the results/relationship continuum. Within these broad issues there will be fuller discussions of the culture and cohesion necessary to facilitate teams and team-building, how such groups function, where the individual fits into the group and the skills that are necessary to manage groups and teams.

BASIC ORGANIZATION

Schools are full of management structures which exist across the broad spectrum of primary and secondary education and which, though common to almost all schools, are the internal responsibility of each individual school. Others are imposed

1

either by national initiatives or by more local demands such as LEAs and the school's immediate community. The list could be endless, but Table 1.1 suggests some of them.

Table 1.1 Management structures within schools

Internal structures	External structures
Class groupings	Numbers on roll
Registration groups	Admission numbers
Subject groups	Salary scales
Year teams	School budget
Departments	Leaving ages
Responsibility allowances	Statutory length of the school day
Timetables and room allocation	Governing body
Meetings	Methods of appraisal, etc.
Committees	
Working parties, etc.	

It should be immediately obvious from Table 1.1 that there is a certain amount of interdependency between those structures controlled internally and those imposed from outside. For example, class groupings, registration groups and subject groups will be partly dependent on the number of pupils on the school's roll. The number of teachers paid above the basic pay spine and the number of teachers within each department will be closely linked to salary scales and the amount of money available in the school budget. This budget and the amount available to the school is very largely dependent on the number of pupils on the roll. The timetabling of lessons, subject grouping and room allocation will be affected by the number of teachers, the number of children and the length of the school day.

This suggests that what happens inside the school is dependent on the interrelationship of different structures. When they all come together to produce an effective organization what can and does happen has to rely on certain factors that are often outside the immediate control of the school. It is important to recognize, however, that in schools it is more common than not to find people (i.e. mainly teachers) working together to make educational sense out of such structures and organizations. While they may work alone as individuals in specified classrooms, the school itself cannot and will not function as a series of isolated people. There must be a sense of balance between the individual and the organization that allows both to succeed. As Day *et al.* (1989) suggest, these needs may be different and sometimes conflicting.

The crossover point as illustrated by Table 1.2 is where groups exist to create working teams with specific functions. It is important to recognize that there is movement in all directions across this organizational dimension. The school obviously cannot function without teams of individuals, nor can the individual work and perform effectively without a successful team that exists within the whole organization.

Table 1.2 The organizational dimension

Individual	Group	Organization(s)
Head	Classes	Nursery schools
Deputy	Years	Primary/secondary, etc.
Teachers/pupils	Departments	Schools within specific
Allowance holders	Committees	areas
Parents/governors	Working parties	
Caretaker	Year teams	
Secretary	Key Stage teams	
Technicians		

This link between the individual, the group and the organization could be extended to include a wider network of influential groups including LEAs, teacher unions and the DFE. But however far we extend, managing schools has to be about individuals working together and this is where we have to examine different ways of organizing schools.

HIERARCHY AND COLLEGIALITY AS TYPES OF ORGANIZATION

Although schools have many similarities each is also unique. One part of their organization, however, is that of the hierarchy of headteachers, deputy heads, heads of department, etc. Where this kind of structure dominates there is likely to be, as Bell (1989) suggests, 'more directing, controlling and commanding' (p.128). Because of the nature of the structure, this

bureaucracy

will come from the top of the pyramid and be directed downwards and because the organization is one of directives there will be less room for discussion and debate; although this kind of hierarchical chain of command does not necessarily stop colleagues working together, it makes it more difficult. Collegiality, however, is more about professional colleagues being involved, and co-operating, participating and delegating within a structure where working as a decision-making team is seen as important. A simple way of illustrating a hierarchical pyramid is shown in Figure 1.1.

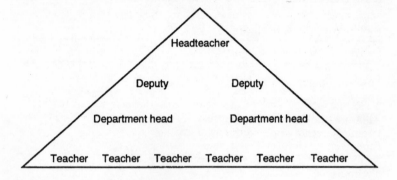

Figure 1.1 Hierarchical pyramid

Obviously this kind of structure would be inappropriate in many schools, especially small ones. One could question whether it is appropriate as the dominant organizational structure in any school, but it is the case that some schools will be more hierarchical, others will be more collegial and others will successfully combine the two. They will all, however, be organized in such a way that they will try to achieve effective results and make every effort to maintain good relationships between those who work in them.

THE RESULTS/RELATIONSHIPS CONTINUUM

While it would be the aim of every competent manager to merge both the achievements of results and the maintenance of good relationships into a coherent whole where they would be equally successful, it is not always possible to do this. In fact it is often very difficult to be both concerned with results and to be equally concerned about people. Adair (1983) suggests that schools and those who work in them have three sets of needs that shift and change in terms of priority but need to constantly inter-act. They are (1) the criteria of the task which requires results; (2) the needs of the staff team as a whole; and (3) the needs of individuals within the staff team. Whatever type of decision-making structure is established, it can determine where the school stands on a results/relationships continuum. Tannenbaum and Schmidt (1973) recognize that within an organization such as a school, this continuum has at its two extremes an autocratic and a democratic structure.

Certain processes take place between these two 'opposites'. In many schools, both individuals and teams would operate at one or several stages of this continuum. This is illustrated by the following discussion of the different stages, which not only moves from the two extremes but suggests various methods of staff involvement and certain ways of taking decisions.

Results			Relationships
Autocratic	Paternalistic	Consultative	Democratic/collegial
(Tell)	(Sell)	(Involve)	(Co-determine)

At the autocratic end of the continuum, *telling* is the most favoured method of managing the organization. Thus orders are given and the expectation is that they will be followed. As we move through the different stages, the next step involves a cer-tain amount of dialogue in that there is an attempt to *sell* ideas to colleagues by persuading them to accept some of those ideas. This involves some discussion which rarely goes beyond agree-ing with the ideas being put forward. *Involving* colleagues, how-ever, is more about consulting them about new ideas, changes in direction and different ways of working. This type of consul-tation begins to move the organization towards a more collegial structure. At the end of the continuum the management processes must involve consensus and recognize that colleagues need to be able to *co-determine* what happens in the school.

5

This type of structure calls for many meetings, and teams of teachers would take most of the decisions. Many effective schools will operate along the full length of such a continuum and by doing so will be able to create a decision-making structure and a management organization that is capable of initiating effective results as well as motivating staff and developing sound working relationships.

FURTHER CONSTRAINTS ON THE TYPE OF ORGANIZATION

Both the hierarchy/collegial and the results/relationship continua are important in that they suggest constraints within which schools function. As such they will feature in other chapters, but there are two further factors affecting the school as an organization which need mentioning here. These are the size of the school and its culture.

Size

It could be suggested that the larger the school the more the structure tends to be hierarchical. Departments, teams, sub-committees, etc. feature more in large schools, both primary and secondary, than in smaller primary schools. However, collegiality (as defined in the Introduction) need not be confined to small schools. Obviously the larger the institution, the more formal and possibly hierarchical the systems and structures have to be to enable the organization to function as a whole without fragmenting; however, there is no reason why involvement, co-operation, participation and delegation should not exist within those 'fragments'.

Culture and cohesion

According to Playfoot *et al.* (1989), 'Culture is often a product of history, the buildings, and patterns of interaction. Culture also reminds us that what matters most in a school is how *people* relate to one another. Schools have a subjective interpersonal dimension' (p. 38). This 'culture', described by Reid *et al.*

(1987) as the 'school ethos or school climate' (p. 20), is discussed elsewhere in this book, but it is important to recognize that it can reflect how the school is managed and how individuals and teams can function within its organization. Culture can and does influence how teachers and pupils work together by establishing conventions such as teaching styles, the openness of the school to parents, how correct attitudes and 'good' work are rewarded and how the symbolic rituals such as assembly, speech-days, etc. are used to influence the moral, spiritual and cultural development of pupils. People obviously play a major part in creating and developing the culture of a school but it has to exist within the boundaries of the buildings and the school's history and rituals. Issues such as lack of proper facilities, small or temporary classrooms, open plan areas, split sites, etc. can and do influence how the school develops. There are detectable social patterns and rituals over a period of time which influence how individuals and groups interact with each other and with the structures and processes of management. Traditions are visible in most schools, and what might appear to an outsider to be insignificant quirks of behaviour, such as who sits where in the staffroom, the rituals of the Christmas party and who has access to which store-room can, if unrecognized, often assume such large proportions that the running of the school can be affected. These traditions and rituals are part of a shared identity that is largely accepted, recognized and approved of by pupils, teachers, parents and governors. Deal and Kennedy (1983) suggest that the strengths of such a culture include the following characteristics:

- Shared values, i.e. 'how we do things round here';
- Recognized core values, e.g. lack of uniform, or strict uniform;
- Shared beliefs, i.e. 'why we do things as we do';
- Rituals of organization that reinforce core values, e.g. assemblies, speech-days, parent meetings, etc.;
- Balance between innovation and tradition, autonomy and authority, e.g. schools which rely too heavily on a single, rigid, unchanging tradition may eventually become so hidebound that they will find change difficult.

7

Managerial difficulties may well arise if staff fail to recognize, appreciate or welcome the kinds of rituals that are implicit in the educational philosophy of the school's culture. It is also true that 'shared beliefs' do not just happen in a school and exist harmoniously from then on. Wherever there are individuals, there are many different personalities and many different points of view. A successful management team recognizes this and by a process of high-quality leadership, consensus and compromise endeavours to create a strong, positive organizational culture that serves the needs of all teachers and pupils.

TEAMS AND TEAM BUILDING

Schools are staffed by people working to achieve certain results but, as has been suggested, working together to realize these results is not easy. Collegiality and team work do not just happen but do need to be present if schools are to be effective. Handy (1976) suggests several reasons why organizations use groups or teams of people rather than individuals. He includes:

- *For the distribution of work*: to bring together a set of skills, talents, responsibilities and allocate them their particular duties.
- *For the management and control of work*: to allow work to be organized and controlled by appropriate individuals with responsibility for a certain range of work.
- *For problem-solving and decision-taking*: to bring together a set of skills, talents and responsibilities so that the solution to any problem will have all available capacities applied to it.
- *For information processing*: to pass on decisions or information to all those who need to know.
- *For information and idea collection*: to gather ideas, information or suggestions.
- *For testing and ratifying decisions*: to test the validity of a decision taken outside the group or to ratify such a decision.
- *For co-ordination and liaison*: to co-ordinate problems and tasks between functions or divisions.
- *For increased commitment and involvement*: to allow and

encourage individuals to get involved in the plans and activities of the organization.

- *For negotiation or conflict resolution*: to resolve a dispute or argument between levels, divisions or functions.
- *For inquest or enquiry into the past.*

pp. 155–6

These criteria suggest that team-building should form an important part of a manager's role, especially when decisions need to be taken. If we accept Handy's main recommendations, a school without teams of teachers working together would be far less effective when taking decisions than one with a structure which values teachers' contributions.

THE MANAGEMENT OF DECISIONS

Team work is an excellent way of getting things done, but there has to be consensus among everyone involved that by working together better decisions can be made. As with the continuum from autocratic to democratic, it is possible to erect a similar structure when examining groups and teams taking decisions. This will involve examining seven distinct yet interrelated decision-making methods.

Decision by authority without group discussion

Here, the leader simply takes a decision and passes on the results to his or her colleagues. (This could be linked to the autocratic end of the autocratic/collegial continuum.) There are few advantages to using this method if team work and teacher involvement are expected. It should, however, be used for legally binding decisions or directives, e.g. compulsory teaching of the National Curriculum, adherence to health and safety laws, etc.

Decision by an expert

Here, someone with expertise related to the problem has total responsibility for a particular decision. This can be a useful approach after discussions involving colleagues, e.g. if there has been a discussion about the progression of skills in art, it might be appropriate for an art 'expert' to make a final decision as to what those skills should be.

Decision by averaging individual opinions

All members of the team are consulted, after which the leader decides what constitutes the average of opinion. This is a lengthy process and suggests that the leader is only a figurehead without opinions, who is only required to digest and summarize the decisions of others.

Decision by authority after discussion

This essentially means that the leader listens to opinions and argument but in the end makes up his or her mind. For those whose opinions are not accepted this can be off-putting, but in decision-making there has to be a leader who takes the final responsibility. However, this method does involve everyone and ensures that everyone's opinions are heard.

Minority decision

This is usually a delegated subgroup with decision-making powers, and will work if the whole group accepts that it is a process they agree with. Its main disadvantage is that the decisions that are taken may not reflect the views of the majority.

Majority decision

This is usually the product of some kind of vote, ballot or other method of finding out exactly what the majority decision is. The problem here is that there may not be a majority viewpoint. If this is the case, some other method may have to be adopted. If it works, however, it allows everyone to be involved and can lead to lasting change.

Decision by consensus

This involves agreement through long discussion and negotiation. The advantage is that there is 'real' sharing of ideas. The disadvantage is that of time. Although a lengthy and time-consuming process, it is very effective if difficult decisions that involve all the staff have to be taken.

Teams are built so that they can be effective at taking decisions, ensuring that the school runs smoothly and manages change successfully. There are ways of working together in order to make things happen and there will obviously be advantages and disadvantages in the methods suggested. When using any of them it is important to allow the circumstances behind the problem to be solved and the inevitable decision that has to be made to partly govern and determine which method will be the most useful, long-lasting and effective. A decision by a single authority figure, for example, will support and be supported by an autocratic management structure, but may also be necessary in the case of decisions about health and safety in a collegial and more democratic structure.

Consensus and majority decisions are effective when the decision has to be approved by all the participants in order to make it work. Many problems over teaching styles, curriculum planning and classroom management skills would benefit from the kind of decision-making processes where whole groups, whole departments or even, in small schools, whole staffs are involved. However, unlike authority decisions which do have their place in a collegial structure, majority decisions and consensus seem to have little place in the structures created within an autocratic regime.

HOW GROUPS AND WORKING TEAMS DEVELOP

If we assume that most schools employ more than one teacher, it would be logical to expect all teachers in such schools to agree that they and their colleagues work together, teach together and that they are successful in what they do. Macbeth (1989) argues that 'Without a central sense of unity, schools, like all other organizations, are no more than a collection of people who would rather be somewhere else because they lack effectiveness and conviction in what they are doing' (p.54). Unfortunately, where teams and groups get together to solve problems and

11

reach decisions, that is not always the case. It is equally true, however, that, as Macbeth argues, there is a high degree of consensus in an effective school and the ideals that the staff try to promote are supported and put into action by simple rules and clear procedures that are followed by all who work in the school. This will work if the procedures and decision-making structures are seen as necessary and appropriate by all the participants, but as Handy (1976) suggests,

> The problem is this: If groups or committees are convened or constructed for an inappropriate task, or with impossible constraints; if they are badly led or have ineffective procedures; if they have the wrong people, too many people, too little power or meet too infrequently; if, in short any one part of the model is out of line, frustration will set in and dissonance will be created.
>
> (p. 184)

As well as Handy's organizational problems, it is obvious but true that groups and teams are made up of individuals, and the effectiveness of such a team depends, to a large extent, on how well they can work together. Since the late 1980s the speed of educational change and its magnitude has been such that teams of teachers working to implement new demands have been essential. Handy (1976) recognizes that successful groups produce better ideas in that the ideas are well evaluated and thought through and that they usually produce better solutions than an individual on his or her own. Many schools have, as part of their responses to the challenges of the new education acts, created many different teams. It is important to recognize some of the problems associated with the formation of such groups. One way of doing this, suggested by Handy (1976, p. 171), is to look at the stages that groups of people usually have to go through before they begin to work together effectively.

The first stage is where group members get together and the group *forms*. Most groups form around one person who acts as a leader or because there is a problem that has to be solved. At this stage, most group members are anxious and over-dependent on the leader. This is a period of testing the water, as no one is quite sure what behaviour is acceptable. Group members are trying to find out what the task is, how they are going to go about it and what the expected outcome will be.

The second stage is common to all groups. It occurs when the members of the group or team do not get on and the group *storms*. At this stage there is usually a conflict between sub-groups within the team and sometimes rebellion against the leader. It is difficult to suggest obvious reasons why conflict and 'storming' occur in this way. There is certainly resistance to control, as if group members have to assert their individuality rather than succumb to the needs of the group or team. There is also resistance to getting on with the task, and at this stage it seems that most group members will feel that the task in hand has no interest for them.

During the third stage the group begins to draw together and gel. It *norms*, and a more cohesive pattern of behaviour begins to appear. This cohesion within the group will often mean that resistance is overcome and conflicts are largely resolved because there is a feeling of mutual support. It is at this stage that there should be an open exchange of views and greater co-operation in trying to reach sensible and valuable conclusions.

The fourth stage is reached when the group begins to *perform* and to move towards solving problems and achieving outcomes. At this stage there are few interpersonal problems. Members know each other well and there is a more flexible structure which enables the group to move forward. Solutions and outcomes emerge and there will be a constructive attempt to complete tasks efficiently and effectively. It should be recognized, however, that it is far from easy to reach this stage. Problems arise with group members who fail to contribute, who continue to see no meaning in the task and whose personalities are such that they clash with other group members. By verbalizing these views and attitudes there will be tension and acrimonious exchanges between group members. The quality of the group's leadership will be tested frequently as similar difficulties seem to occur in all groups and, because of these problems, decisions are often difficult to reach.

These stages are, however, relatively common within such groups and it is important for team leaders to reach the stage where outcomes are achieved, i.e. that decisions are taken as quickly as possible. Unfortunately, individuals within groups are not necessarily there to ensure that things run smoothly. Many have their own agendas, but it is important for everyone who does have a vested interest in moving forward positively to try to overcome individual prejudices so that decisions that are acceptable to all are actually taken. This will sometimes mean that whoever is chairing the meeting has to act decisively or it may mean breaking up the group and starting again with different individuals.

THE INDIVIDUAL AND THE GROUP

It is never possible to satisfy all the individual and group objectives simultaneously in most groups of people working together. Many individuals will try to promote their own interests at the expense of the group. Common interests, the needs of the school, or a mutually important job that has to be done usually make individuals sink their differences and work together. It is therefore important in the structure of all schools to make sure that meetings of teams do have a useful purpose and that the end product of the meeting or series of meetings will benefit individuals, the group or team and the whole school. Most successful and productive meetings should meet some, if not all, the following criteria:

- Any group meeting has to be in the right place at the right time.
- It must be held in appropriate surroundings.
- The content should be such that the whole group has an interest in the outcome.
- The basic organization of time, date and place of the meeting will have been circulated well in advance.
- There should be an accurate agenda.
- Starting and finishing times will be adhered to.
- The leader/chairperson will be efficient and effective.
- Each team member will be given the opportunity to express his or her views.
- No one will be allowed to dominate the meeting.
- Each person's contribution to the meeting will be listened to.
- The leader/chairperson will try to summarize what has happened in the meeting at fairly frequent intervals.
- Whatever decisions are taken will be made clear to everyone.

- Those colleagues who have been allocated certain tasks as a result of the meeting will know what they are.

Even when the *performing* stage has been reached and most, if not all of the above criteria have been met, there are still likely to be management problems in that decisions, changes of direction and important policies do not always sail smoothly across the stormy waters of people working together. Some groups of teachers will never reach the fourth stage. If this is the case it seems reasonable to assume that either the composition of the group is at fault or the subject under discussion is inappropriate. This may well have been the case since 1988 when legislation raised a large number of initiatives about which schools and teachers have since had to reach decisions. In any case, serious decisions need to be taken about whether the group should continue meeting. It is important to maintain both morale and momentum and to ensure that the task allocated to the group is still the prime objective and that the processes the group is using are appropriate. If the group ceases to exist or never develops then it will only become frustrated and, by its own ineffectiveness, cause a considerable amount of ill feeling.

THE CONTENT AND PROCESS OF WORKING IN GROUPS

We need to recognize that when schools work in a collegial and democratic way there are two major ingredients: *content* and *process*. The content deals with the subject matter, or the task allocated to the groups of teachers. Since the late 1980s, schools throughout Britain have been involved in some of the most radical 'content' reforms of the twentieth century. Much of this 'content' will have been common to all schools and includes the National Curriculum at different key stages, and the meaning of the different sections of the Curriculum, e.g. Statements of Attainment, Programmes of Study and assessment and moderation, etc.

The process, however, is concerned with the interaction between and moods of group members. It deals with such issues as morale, feeling, atmosphere, influence, participation, styles of influence, leadership struggles, conflict, co-operation, competition, etc. A similar content will generally exist in most schools. The establishment of the National Curriculum has ensured that there is a standard bank of knowledge to be taught and learned. It is the process which contains most management issues and whatever the basic organization, from autocratic to collegial, the effect of ensuring that the processes work will largely govern the success of the school's management. Eraut (1977) recognizes the dangers of neglecting the process when he suggests that it is wrong to assume that process skills already exist. If this assumption is made it is likely that the team will concentrate on ideas and decisions for implementation or change without providing any assistance with the process of implementation and change.

It has been suggested that everyone is a manager and should have an interest in the success of the school in which they work. Recognizing some of the ways groups behave when they work together will help to ensure success. Although this is fraught with difficulties, analysing what is likely to happen could help groups to function effectively. It will also help influence the processes involved, because it should be possible to know more about how the participants work together and what they do to either further their own interests or those of the group. It is useful to remind ourselves that groups working together are only effective if they produce results. Knowing who participates, who hinders the momentum, who leads and who is not allowed to express his or her ideas are some of the issues that are vital to the successful management of both the group and the school. Belbin (1981) suggests various characteristics of team members and, by examining how a group functions and who helps to move the group towards reaching decisions, it should be possible to discover the 'right' and most successful mix of individuals.

GUIDELINES FOR ANALYSING GROUP BEHAVIOUR

Who contributes

One indication of who gets involved in the group is the level of verbal participation of each individual. It is important to find out who participates a lot and why, as well as why someone else contributes very little. If, for example, it is because of fear, disagreement or disinterest, the group may under-perform because those who do not participate may have useful points to make. A compatible group should ideally encourage all its participants to contribute to any discussions and decision-making. This issue of participation is one that group leaders have to consider very carefully.

Who has influence

Influence and participation are not always the same. Some people who talk a lot may not always be listened to. Others who are quiet and speak very little can, when they do speak, capture the attention of everyone. In many ways this is influenced by power struggles and rivalry. Individuals with their own personal agendas may want certain things to happen. If this is the case then whoever participates may alter and change depending on who has influence at a specific time and who needs certain individuals to speak and support his or her particular cause.

The styles of influence

Influence can take many forms. It can be both positive and negative; it can enlist the support or co-operation of others or it can alienate them. How this happens within a group can be vital to that group's success. There will be autocratic colleagues who will attempt to impose their will on the group by passing judgements on others and blocking movement towards directions in which they do not want to go. There will be those who eagerly support everyone and everything and try to avoid conflict at any cost, and those who, by distancing themselves from the whole proceedings, influence others to do the same. The group may

17

also include the total democrat who tries to include everyone in the group all the time and by doing so slows the whole process to a tedious snail's pace.

Decision-making processes

Decisions are often taken without considering the effects on other group members. Some people try to impose their decision on the group and others want all members to share in the decisions that have been taken. This can cause friction and complications because group cohesion can be lost and inconclusive decisions taken. This is especially true if one individual 'self-authorizes' a decision without consulting others or a small group or clique get together and push others to agree to a decision. Consensus, while difficult to achieve, is one of the few ways of trying to satisfy the needs of all group members.

Maintaining the group

Getting things done, moving things forward and making sure the group is working together are important functions and if done well can improve morale considerably. If there are group members who perform these maintenance functions, then the group should perform smoothly as a team. This will work best if everyone is drawn into any discussions that take place and individuals feel able to express their own points of view. In order to do this effectively, ideas have to be rejected without demoralizing the individual and without losing the support of colleagues.

Group atmosphere

Observing teams and groups working together can reveal the atmosphere of the group. Some of the ways of trying to find words to describe such an atmosphere can be very subjective, but they include the following: friendly, congenial, interesting, calm and tolerant. To work best and to reach decisions effectively, there has to be a businesslike atmosphere where disagreements are never personal and where provocation and deliberate annoyance are kept to a minimum.

Who belongs to the group

Group members are often concerned about their degree of acceptance or inclusion in the group. Different patterns of inter-action may develop which give clues to who is accepted and who is not. Subgroups can form with conflicting interests and there may be those who are 'in' and accepted and those who are 'out' with views that are not considered important.

There are more suggestions as to how groups function in *The 1972 Annual Handbook for Group Facilitators*; however, analysing the behaviour of participants, while being interesting and necessary, is only a means to an end. The individuals who make up a group or team must be managed and, as Handy (1976) suggests, 'co-ordinated and their skills and abilities meshed and merged' (p. 184). Increased knowledge about the behaviour of individuals will enable more effective management strategies to evolve.

STRATEGIES FOR MANAGING GROUPS

At the risk of being repetitive, it is important to be aware that managing schools is largely about managing people. While lead-ership is discussed throughout the book, there are some specific examples of leadership roles in Chapter 3; however, even in the best led schools it is vitally important for everyone to recognize that the success of the decision-making processes and the work-ing partnerships of professionals will rely heavily on everyone being aware of their own contribution. A headteacher, head of department or chairperson plays a large part in making sure that there are effective and successful working practices. But there will be 'negative individuals' who specialize in blocking tactics and if they are not handled effectively the tactics they use will hinder the processes in which the group is involved. When this happens the move towards reaching decisions about the 'content' of the meeting will be slowed down or brought to a halt. Leaders of groups or meetings need to be able to recognize the common tactics which individuals use to dominate meet-ings and try to either stop decisions being taken or to persuade the group to take a particular stance. By recognizing such working

Box 1.1 Strategies to stop groups working

- The crisis-maker will build up an insignificant issue into a serious potential crisis in order to avoid thinking too deeply about the real problem to be solved or the real work of the group. He or she might be heard to say such things as, 'We couldn't possibly do that, no one would ever co-operate with us', or 'Do you really think that the inspectors/governors/parents will let us get away with that?'

- The rambler will specialize in trivia when talking at meetings. Rather than face up to particular issues, he or she will talk anecdotally around the subject or problem without really helping the group to work towards solutions or decisions. You might hear contributions such as: 'I met Bill the other day at a meeting I went to and he was saying that he was in a school where they were working on something similar...'.

- Some people create general 'enemies' to avoid being specific. This means that they invent situations which they believe they cannot do anything about. By citing abstract forces they try to prevent anyone else from doing anything. The enemies might be: they, them, the system, the LEA, the government, etc.

- The avoidance of issues exists when individuals pretend or suggest that certain areas under discussion or within the brief of a working party are unimportant. They might say, 'I don't really think that this is worth bothering about, let alone spending a lot of time working on it.'

- Some group members will have been at the school for a long time and will in one sense have a historical perspective of what can and cannot be done. They may rely on old rules of behaviour which are not at all helpful when dealing with current issues. You might hear them say, 'This is something that we have never been asked to do before and we shouldn't be asked to do it now.'

methods leaders will be able to develop tactics which will lessen the influence of such individuals or prevent them from having any effect at all. Rather than reading Box 1.1 and Box 1.2 separately, it would be more useful to look at each tactic employed to hinder groups and to try and find the most appropriate statement in Box 1.2 that would counter the blocking tactic and help the group move forward. If, as an example, I were to offer my own suggestion about which statement relates to which strategy I would link the 'rambler' of Box 1.1 to the response in Box 1.2 of: 'are you sure that this relates to what we are discussing?'. I would do this because 'ramblers' waste time, frustrate other group members and delay decisions. Asking them to think about what they are saying might focus their attention more closely on the subject in hand. You might see other links and combinations which you could use in the groups and teams in your school.

If teams have to spend a considerable amount of their time both listening to and taking note of some of the ways individuals will try to block forward movement then time will be wasted, decisions will neither be taken nor implemented and there will be frustration and ineffectiveness. Box 1.2 suggests some statements that will, if used successfully and appropriately, help to save time by limiting the success of any of the blocking strategies.

Box 1.2 Statements to counter avoidance strategies

- 'Are you sure that this relates to what we are discussing?'
- 'Could you tell us how this relates to the point we are trying to make?'
- 'How does this blanket and dogmatic rule help us in this situation?'
- 'Can you be more specific and tell us how what you are saying relates to any particular issues?'
- 'I am not sure that we all understand what it is you are actually trying to say.'

(Smith, 1990a)

By suggesting that decision-making, planning and the overall management of the school will benefit from colleagues working together in teams, we must not lose sight of the expertise and leadership of individual teachers. All schools will have general and individual job descriptions which allocate specific roles to teachers. Such job descriptions will often recognize specific qualities and talents which individuals can bring to the teams within which they work. This is especially true of those teachers who have moved through the teachers' pay spine and have been allocated extra points because of their expertise, their qualities as teachers or more usually because they take on extra responsibilities (DFE, 1993b). Their particular qualities can and must be allowed to flourish within working teams by allocating them status in terms of leadership and/or expertise.

CHAPTER SUMMARY

In this chapter I have suggested a number of ways of looking at the basic management structure of schools. It is important to realize that schools are complex organizations and that while it is relatively easy to pin down the content of what has to happen if they are to meet the needs of their learners, it is not particularly easy to recognize ideal processes that ensure success. There are, for example, self-inflicted structures imposed by what happens within the school. Alongside these are the external influences which have to be absorbed by the individual, the group and the institution itself, which means that schools tend to be organized hierarchically. This does not have to mean autocratic organization and there has been considerable discussion about the continuum from autocratic to democratic and certain aspects of collegiality. Whatever structure dominates – and it has been suggested that collegiality and effectiveness are close stable mates – there is a school culture within which 'things get done'. The most successful way of working, it was suggested, was in teams, and how teams work and reach decisions was considered at length together with the associated problems of individuals working together and finding the processes difficult. The democracy of such working groups should not, however, be confused with total equality. Everyone within a school should know what their role is in terms of what jobs have to be done. The pitfalls of individuals finding it difficult to work alongside colleagues have been addressed, but there are also issues of seniority and those who have extra responsibilities and are paid more than other teachers. Many of these complex processes are raised, often in more detail, in the following chapters.

FURTHER READING

Handy, C. (1976) *Understanding Organizations*. London: Penguin.

This is an important book, and while it was originally written for managers in industry, it is essential reading for anyone who works in schools and wants to be more aware of how institutions function.

Reid, K., Hopkins, D. and Holly, P. (1987) *Towards the Effective School*. Oxford: Basil Blackwell.

This book offers a survey and synthesis of recent research into effective schooling and presents strategies that can help make schools more effective.

Smith, R. (1990a) *The Effective School, Volume 1. Teachers Working Together: The Whole School Approach*. Lancaster: Framework Press.

This is one of a series of seven Inservice Training Packs for both primary and secondary teachers. The activities in them are useful for both individuals and whole schools. It examines in a practical and useful way the role of teams and how groups work.

CHAPTER 2

SCHOOL ETHOS AND WHOLE-SCHOOL AIMS

CHAPTER OVERVIEW

Schools and the structures and organizations within them need to be able to develop attitudes which will not only help pupils to learn but will show them the technique of learning and how to continue to want to learn. In thinking of 'ethos' we need to see schools in terms of their characteristics as social organizations. A school's organization and the way children are taught affect the success of that school and it is this ethos that can determine whether some are more effective than others. This chapter includes sections on positive and negative 'atmosphere', leadership and ethos, the role of both headteacher and governors in establishing ethos, and how a School Development Plan and aims statement can suggest what the ethos and atmosphere are likely to be.

SCHOOLS MAKE A DIFFERENCE

When members of the committee who later produced the Elton Report (1989) visited schools, they recognized the variations in 'feel' or atmosphere between different institutions and were convinced that 'some schools [had] a more positive atmosphere than others' (p.88). The report, which was commissioned by Kenneth Baker, the then Secretary of State for Education, addressed its conclusions on discipline to a whole range of people involved with schools, from parents to pupils and teachers. By giving it a somewhat universal appeal they hoped that there would be a greater sense of shared commitment to education and in particular to the standards of discipline in schools. They accepted that they could not attribute the differences in school atmosphere to the pupils' home backgrounds because almost all of the schools they visited were in what could be described as difficult urban environments. They concluded that these differences in atmosphere had a lot to do with what went on in the actual schools.

Rutter *et al.* (1979) had also reached tentative conclusions about the influence of schools well before the Elton committee, and suggested:

> It is not argued that schools are the most important influence on children's progress, and we agree...that education cannot compensate for the inequities of society. Nevertheless, *we do suggest that schools constitute one major area of influence, and one which is susceptible to change.*
>
> (p.182, my emphasis)

According to Rutter, the central problem was this:

> How was it that twelve schools set up to undertake the same task with children from much the same geographical area came to develop such different styles? Doubtless, part of the answer lies in the history of the schools and in a variety of external factors outside their control. *In addition, however, the schools' expressed philosophies and chosen ways of working were important.*
>
> (p.203, my emphasis)

Rutter's arguments suggest that while schools cannot wholly eliminate the effects of social differences between pupils, they can, through their own good practice, improve the standards of work, behaviour and prospects of all pupils. Mortimore *et al.* (1988) suggested what is now a fairly standard list of what managers need to be able to do in order to create a positive atmosphere. Their influential book, *School Matters: The Junior*

Years examined school effectiveness by carrying out detailed research in fifty schools in the now defunct Inner London Education Authority. They wanted to know the answer to a quite basic question: does the school attended by a child make a difference? They suggest that in order to achieve effectiveness and a positive ethos the following characteristics will help:

- effective and powerful leadership;
- the deputy head needs to be involved in all major decisions;
- all teachers need to feel that they 'own' those decisions that directly affect them;
- there needs to be consistency and continuity throughout the school, e.g. in terms of discipline patterns, homework policies, resource management, timetable structures, etc.;
- teaching sessions need to be structured, matched to pupils' needs, well paced and lively;
- the actual teaching should be intellectually challenging for all pupils;
- the environment of the school will be task- and work-orientated, i.e. every pupil will recognize that learning is the norm rather than the exception;
- there will be lots of communication between teachers and pupils both inside and outside the classroom;
- record-keeping and assessment are sensible and thorough and are communicated to parents when necessary in a way that they can understand;
- there is a positive climate where emphasis is placed on praise rather than criticism;
- control in classrooms is firm but fair, with children being treated as individuals;
- activities are organized to take place outside the classroom and away from the school. This is a means of offering pupils wider experiences and a way of putting the academic content of the curriculum into a different context.

The message to managers is unequivocally clear: they have the power through the efforts of the head, teachers and all those associated with the school to improve standards of work and behaviour and the life chances of their pupils. To do this, however, they have to both create and work within the 'ethos' or atmosphere of the school.

SCHOOL ATMOSPHERE

The Elton Report (1989), at the same time as suggesting that schools do make a difference, uses the nebulous yet useful phrase 'school atmosphere' (p.89). The report emphasizes that there were 'differences in their [schools'] feel or atmosphere' (p.88), and that 'perhaps the most important characteristic of schools with a positive atmosphere is that pupils, teachers and other staff feel that they are known and valued members of the school community' (p.90). They go on to suggest, fairly predictably, that schools can have a positive or negative atmosphere and equally that schools with a negative atmosphere will suffer more from bad behaviour than those with a positive atmosphere. Stating this may be obvious, but it is extremely important because creating a positive image and developing an effective ethos is extremely hard and involves time and commitment from headteachers, teachers, parents, governors and pupils. As we saw in Chapter 1, working together is not always easy. Working on the more 'abstract' concept of ethos which often involves conflicts of educational philosophy is even more difficult. What is perhaps easier to consider are those symptoms which suggest a negative atmosphere. They can and do include widespread litter, long-standing graffiti, teachers starting lessons late, teachers finishing lessons early, teachers ignoring bad behaviour in corridors and playgrounds, pupils regularly skipping lessons and getting away with it, pupils' work not displayed and the use of inappropriate punishment.

Many of these symptoms relate to the concept of schools as communities. A negative atmosphere largely indicates a failure to achieve a sense of communal coherence. In this kind of atmosphere staff and pupils are undervalued and teacher expectations may well be low. Where these negative aspects exist, the management of the school has to take steps to change the negative to the positive in a way that leads both teachers and children to value the school as *their* community. If this happens, and it is a difficult and lengthy process, they are likely to value it more and feel part of it. The Elton Report (1989) suggests that these management functions include: '...the quality of its leadership, classroom management, behaviour policy, curriculum, pastoral care, buildings and physical environment, organization and timetable and relationships with parents' (p.90). In other words, it contains a full range of tasks and issues. Turning the negative into positive in terms of practical solutions should involve schools in examining their policies in many areas and, where necessary, actually making an effort to set up structures and processes to initiate widespread change. Teachers, ancillary staff, classroom assistants and pupils need to be involved in such areas as the prevention of graffiti on toilet walls. There needs to be a working partnership. Pupils' opinions are also important and their views need to be listened to. Community involvement is necessary for all schools and ways need to be found to attract local groups into the school during evenings and weekends. Parents are in many ways the schools' clients and schools need to be accessible to them. Schools should also make sure that they tell their parents what is happening. If there are policies on bullying, parents need to know what their contribution might be.

LEADERSHIP AND ETHOS

It is certainly the case that if schools attempt to find practical solutions to what they perceive as issues contributing to a negative atmosphere, then the way in which a school is managed will be changed. It has already been suggested that this is not easy and can be a long, complicated and uncomfortable process. To do it well the first and most important requirement is a positive commitment to change by the headteacher (Mortimore *et al.*, 1988). The second is to carry as many of the rest of the staff as possible with them and to listen to suggestions. The conviction that change is possible and the ability to carry it through to create and maintain a positive ethos depends upon the quality of leadership and *the quality and involvement of teams, e.g. deputies, HOD, curriculum groups, etc.* (see Chapter 1). We must not lose sight of the fact that success can be enhanced by effective leadership but will only continue if we recognize and work towards encouraging the concept of teachers as teams of managers.

THE HEADTEACHER'S ROLE

Effective leadership tends to produce a positive atmosphere and a sense of security (this will be examined in more detail in Chapter 3). It is a difficult concept to analyse, in that there are two related aspects: the personal qualities needed to manage adults and the management style (see Chapter 4). However, as HMI recognized in *Ten Good Schools*, what 'good' schools have in common is 'effective leadership and a "climate" that is conducive to growth' (HMI, 1977, p.36).

Whatever role the headteacher assumes (see pages 31–34), it will be important because what he or she does will be central to creating the kind of positive ethos that will improve learning. Headteachers need to have an awareness of pupils' needs and be a curriculum leader and a forward planner. They also need to manage resources well and communicate their ideas to everyone who has an interest in the school. Their awareness of the need for continuous staff development will, through their skills of administration, go hand in hand with vision, foresight, faith and imagination.

The managerial 'environment' within which these roles exist can be related to the continuum illustrated in Chapter 1. At one end is the democratic style which can be seen as permissive to the extent that teams can operate in isolated 'democratic' groups without the strong overall leadership which is required to make sure that there is a whole-school approach. This can and does allow a fragmented, confusing and demoralizing sense of 'who is in charge' but it can also, with consistent, strong and involved leadership be extremely productive. On the other end of the continuum is the autocratic style in which decisions tend to be made without consultation with teachers. This can be demoralizing in a different way by denying teachers their professional competence as well as producing a lack of collective responsibility.

Purposeful leadership, while maintaining the professional involvement of teachers, is a careful balancing act and becomes even more of a complex tightrope when parents and governors are involved. But there needs to be an environment where the individual teacher can thrive and grow within a team which works to achieve success for everyone. Looking at the roles taken on by those working in school to develop a positive ethos in more detail may help in this elusive and difficult process. Macdonald (1974) sees these 'ideal types' in a slightly different way. He describes styles of leadership in three ways which are slightly different but certainly not too far removed from the autocratic–democratic continuum. They are: bureaucratic, which relies on concepts of service, utility and efficiency; autocratic, in which the key concepts are 'principle' and 'objectivity' and to a certain extent the 'responsibility of office'; and democratic, which relies on confidentiality, negotiation and the accessibility of information. Whatever the style of leadership, its quality and the role of the headteacher as a leader, it will have a profound effect on the ethos and culture of the school.

ROLES AFFECTING ETHOS

Getzels (1969), Shipman (1979) and Rutter (1979), together with Mortimore *et al.* (1988), emphasize the concept of schools as social organizations. They suggest that effective schools often see their educational objectives as applying equally to the fostering of an enthusiasm and interest in learning, of confidence and the ability to take responsibility, of adaptability to cope with life changes and of the development of personal relationships and individuality. They also suggest that the atmosphere of any school is greatly influenced by the degree to which it functions as a coherent whole, with agreed ways of doing things that are consistent throughout the school and which have the support of staff. Many of these roles, which include those associated with leadership but at the same time apply to all teachers, should help to reinforce their views because they move on from just conceptualizing what the school and those who work there should be trying to achieve, to suggesting ways of working and actual roles that need to be adopted. Here are some roles that may affect a school's ethos.

An awareness of pupils' needs

All pupils need to achieve success irrespective of their existing attainments, and no pupils should be made to feel that they are failing. Solity and Bull (1987) demonstrate ways in which children should be encouraged to see their progress in relation to their previous performance, rather than in relation to their peers. Thus the aim for children is to improve and appreciate that they are developing their skills and knowledge. The classroom environment is one which recognizes and celebrates success at every level. The 'coherent whole' of the school, both within classrooms in terms of processes and the differentiation of content and in the routines and structures of the school day, should reinforce success and celebrate each pupil's individual needs. Special needs policies are essential, as is back-up from external agencies and a commitment by the school to develop strategies for differentiating within the classroom for all ability levels.

Curriculum leader

The National Curriculum has affected what is taught, how it is taught and how work is assessed. Parents and pupils need to understand these processes and to recognize the positive side of the National Curriculum as well as the more difficult and contentious areas of SATs and school 'league' tables. The curriculum and the assessment processes need to be understood by teachers, pupils and parents. The organization of the school should make sure that Year teams, Key Stage teams, Subject departments, etc. all have a mandate to make the curriculum understandable and able to be assessed. It is a positive achievement for schools to be able to hold open evenings where parents can see pupils' work and discuss on an individual basis their children's achievements. There will have to be effective assessment and record-keeping for this to take place smoothly.

Forward planning

Teachers need to feel that they control what is happening in the school. As leader, a headteacher has to make sure that this is a managerial process. Teachers also need to play a leading part in

School Development Planning because they need to have a vested interest in creating and maintaining a positive and productive ethos. How decisions are reached is crucial in developing effective forward planning. Meetings (see Chapter 1, page 14) must be well-chaired with a set agenda, they must finish on time and be committed to taking and acting on decisions, imparting information and moving on to the next task.

Resource manager

Everyone working in a school must be involved in acquiring and sharing scarce resources. Teachers, governors and parents (usually through the Parent–Teacher Association) should be involved in choosing and purchasing many of the books, consumables, computers, audio-visual aids, musical instruments, etc. The allocation of resources must be seen to be fair, as this will have a positive effect on those using and sharing the resources.

Communication

Everyone who works in a school and, to a large extent the wider school community, needs to know what is happening. Obviously the detail and content will vary with the audience. Clear, lively newsletters will help parents understand issues involving them and the governors have a statutory obligation to issue information to all parents whose children are at the school. How this is managed is important. It needs to be clear, interesting and useful. Whiteboards, staffroom diaries, formal memos, minutes of meetings, staff meetings, etc. inside the school all help to maintain a manageable and important information flow.

Staff development

The quality of teaching and the quantity of ancillary staff are vital to the success of a school. What is taught and how it is taught, how classes are managed and what teaching styles are used will influence the ethos of a school (and see Chapter 5). What happens in classrooms is to a large extent governed by the skills and attitudes of individual teachers but they are affected and influenced by the styles of leadership offered by the school. There needs to be informed debate about classroom management and teaching methods involving all teachers and based on current issues and the school's needs. Governors and parents need to understand that what happens in classrooms is work-orientated and aimed at meeting the needs of all pupils in a non-threatening way. Once again, the school needs to communicate this to the governing body. There also needs to be a continuous stream of inservice training so that everyone realizes that their future development is valued. Using the school's own expertise and that of outside agencies will promote a positive feeling of growth and development. Informing parents and governors that this is happening will enhance the school's positive ethos.

General administration

Regular routines that enable the school to function efficiently have to be established. This kind of organization will ensure that teachers are not expected to handle too many administrative tasks. The school office has a secretary, bursar, administrator, etc. who will be able to use their expertise to keep the school's day-to-day management unobtrusive. The office staff do, however, have a part to play in creating a positive ethos. They are often the first point of contact for visitors and parents so they need to have the kinds of attitudes and personalities that show efficiency, friendliness and a knowledge of many wider aspects of the school's organization.

Vision

Effective schools will be aware of what is happening nationally and locally. They will recognize which events will influence what is happening in the school. (Table 1.1, page 2, illustrates internal and external structures.) Their success will largely be seen in the vision they project that avoids parochialism and absorbs all that is best in current thinking. Many of the concepts and issues surrounding 'vision' will be picked up in later chapters, but it may be useful at this stage to consider it in relation to its role in maintaining a school's ethos. Bennis and Nanus

(1985) have a useful and broad definition of vision. They suggest:

> A mental image of a possible and desirable future state of the organization...as vague as a dream or as precise as a goal or a mission statement...a view of a realistic, credible, attractive future for the organization, a condition that is better in some important ways than what now exists.
>
> (p.89)

Foresight

Schools have their own 'feelings' and 'attitudes' that set them apart and make them unique. The more positive everyone who works in the school feels about what they are doing, the easier it will be for those who manage the school to think ahead and absorb changes that relate to how they work and how the individual, the school and the community interact.

Imagination

Schools with a clearly defined ethos are more likely to be excited about moving forward and will be able to filter new ideas, take on board those that will help them continue to be successful and, by doing this, refuse to sit back and become complacent.

Associated with, and to some extent dependent upon, the success of these 'roles' are the important issues of a school changing and moving forward. Neither should happen without thought, care and discussion. Rather than being something that occurs almost at random, change needs to be planned to happen in a way that makes the school recognizably more effective. These kinds of forward movements which are a direct result of change can involve simple things such as improving the entrance hall, putting up more displays, preventing litter by providing more litter bins, etc. or they can involve the difficult and perennial problems of improving the school's stance on bullying, racism and gender issues. To be able to make such changes the headteacher and those teachers who are management leaders will have surrounded themselves with capable people with positive ideas who are approachable, easy to contact and not trapped behind office doors and desks.

PRAISING THE POSITIVE

A school which has a 'positive ethos' should avoid being defensive and negative about what it is trying to do. It should use all the marketing and media techniques at its disposal to publicize its successes and celebrate its achievements. There are crude performance indicators which describe a school's success, such as exam results, truancy rates, sporting successes, number of suspensions, number of pupils entering higher education, etc. All of these naturally belong to any debate about ethos, effectiveness and what makes a 'good', successful, positive school, but they do not adequately reflect the full range of achievements schools are developing such as their flexible teaching styles, the social development of each pupil, planning for both achievement and assessment and their team work which will make sure that change is both planned and implemented effectively. The danger is, however, that these crude methods cannot be adopted to collect evidence of anything more complex than simple statistics. What we need to recognize is that defining, recognizing and building up a positive and welcoming ethos is not a simple task. Many people are involved, both inside and outside the school, including parents and now, more than ever before, school governors. Unlike an industrial process, from which many of the indicators of success come, schools are, because of their diverse aims, extremely complex organizations. It is important, however, that everyone recognizes which tangible aspects of practice are to be praised. These may range from test and examination results through to how pupils move in and out of school at the beginning and end of the day. To make any kind of statement, a performance indicator can only be recognized as a measure of success if everyone sees it as such. Dennison (1990) takes a similar view when he suggests that a school needs to offer an education whose content and quality both meet and fulfil the requirements of what professionals think they ought to be doing, and satisfies the needs of pupils, parents and the local community. This is extremely difficult and must involve discussion and agreement. It will also partly depend on how the governors see their role and what effect they have on establishing the ethos of the school and the content and quality of the education offered.

THE GOVERNING BODY AND ITS ROLE IN ESTAB-LISHING ETHOS

Governors, headteachers and teachers need to have some shared understanding of what the school is trying to achieve and how it is setting about doing this. Although establishing a positive ethos embraces areas that will be examined in later chapters, demands that governors are involved in developing the school's aims and ethos by working out a development plan which should prioritize objectives will help the school to satisfy its aims and ethos. *The Education (No.2) Act* (DES, 1986) is quite precise in stating what the roles and functions of the governing body will be. In fact, as Bell (1989) emphasizes: 'The Act makes it clear that the whole of a school's work comes under the direction of the governors except where the Act assigns specific functions to others' (p.268). There are differences in the composition of governing bodies according to factors such as the size of the school, whether it is church-aided or voluntarily controlled and now, by opting out of LEA control, whether the school is grant-maintained. It is difficult to be exact about the proportion of parents compared to LEA appointments, church appointments or those from political parties. What is consistent is that more and more laypeople play a formal role in the management of schools and recent educational reforms have meant that the power of such groups as governors has increased. Because this is quite a recent change in status, relationships between teachers, headteachers and governing bodies can be strained and not as effective as they should be. If this is the case then all parties will have to review and evaluate their position with the functions and roles of the governing body. Obviously where this kind of relationship exists, the ethos of the school will not be a whole-school vision but will remain fragmented in the sense that the school's aims, philosophies and objectives will be misunderstood and misinterpreted. Kogan *et al.* (1984) found that governors worked within a framework where the local authority handed down functions, powers and modes of behaviour and the school's role was to help governors to almost internalize these functions. This meant that there was little sharing of vision and ethos because institutional boundaries were often so strong that the governor as a layperson was perceived as an 'outsider and a guest on the territory of the professional' (p.71). The reforms of the 1980s, however, have made this an untenable position. Governors cannot do what they have to do by being 'outsiders'. Democracy, accountability and notions of active citizenship are, according to Brehony (1992), some of the concepts relating to the status of governors in the 1990s. Baginsky *et al.* (1991) suggest that new legislation has given governors considerable power, not just over their schools but also over headteachers. If they exercise this power they will be able to exert a significant influence over leadership patterns, the headteacher's vision of the school and its ethos. Thus the distinction between the power of headteachers and that of lay governors is now extremely blurred. Deem (1992) recognizes the conflict which might arise when she suggests that

> a new breed of governor, typically a co-opted business person with financial skills, legal knowledge or managerial expertise is emerging with the onset of LMS...the beliefs and values of governors who hold 'schools are businesses' views may bring them into conflict with the values of their school.
>
> (p.211)

Similarly, the impermanence of a governing body whose members need only serve for four years may mean that being unclear about their role will only serve to increase their sense of impermanence. While the headteacher has responsibility for the teaching and organization of the curriculum and the internal management of 'discipline' in the school, the governors have a statutory right to be involved in any curriculum statements, syllabuses, schemes of work, policy documents, etc. Both parties need to work together and avoid destructive conflict because it is necessary to recognize that the duties of school governors, described fully in the Education (No. 2) Act (1986), the Education Reform Act (1988), Playfoot *et al.* (1989) and Smith (1992b), will and should enable them to influence the ethos and atmosphere of schools.

The duties of governors, however, are so onerous that they are almost impossible to execute independently. The school – and this will inevitably mean the headteacher – will need to offer advice and leadership where necessary. This is important because, by exercising their powers, governors can influence schools in different and diverse ways and a mismatch of vision and ethos can produce ineffective and destructive action. The boundary between the headteacher's job and that of the governing body has become blurred; yet it is important that appropriate structures enable both parties to exercise their responsibilities in a way that is compatible. If the governing body is going to take part in controlling and developing the ethos of the school, it is important that it has the information necessary to do the job properly within an atmosphere of trust rather than suspicion. Governors need to have access to the following information:

- the aims, goals and policies of the school;
- the catchment area and its effect on the school;
- the curriculum offered and how it is organized;
- the number of children on roll and future predictions;
- how staff are fitted to classes and curriculum areas;
- assessment and other results;
- the extent of success in achieving goals set by the School Development Plan;
- the background, qualifications and experiences of teachers;
- ideas for staff development;
- strengths, weaknesses and problems;
- how money is spent;
- the state of buildings and the school environment;
- the level of books and equipment;
- special events.

This information should not mean that the governing body is arbitrarily presented with certain facts and figures at certain times of the year. In a school which shares its management responsibilities with its governors they will have been part of ongoing discussions throughout the year either within the whole governing body or in subcommittees or working parties that have been formed to help formulate most areas of the management structures of the school. By being part of what is decided and by sharing responsibility for making sure that the organization works, governors should be able to feel that they can 'sell' the school to the community and by doing so help it to prosper, develop and move forward to more successes. In being part of the school's ongoing educational debate and in sharing the development of a 'coherent whole', governors are, both directly and indirectly, helping to develop the school's ethos. If they are helped to understand what the school is doing and why, their support will be extremely valuable because of the different kinds of expertise they can bring to the job and the different perspectives they will have. Problems will arise and tensions develop if their perceptions of effectiveness and their understanding of the school's positive ethos differ from that of the headteacher and teachers. If this were to happen, it would be necessary to use all the tact and diplomacy necessary to work towards a satisfactory conclusion that will benefit the pupils' education. These kinds of tensions could arise over relatively 'simple' matters such as the wearing of school uniform or the annual debate of whether the school should discuss with and ballot parents on the issue of moving the school towards accepting grant-maintained status.

For governors to play a full part in developing the school it is essential that they debate, help produce and evaluate both the school's Aims Statement and its Development Plan. Both these exist in all schools and are part of the policy document which contains the broad statement of intent, i.e. the Aims Statement and the forward planning decisions which will enable the school to move towards a confident future.

THE AIMS OF THE SCHOOL

It is important for schools to monitor their own needs. This can be done by periodically auditing the school's strengths and weaknesses. There are many ways of doing this, including examples in *Development Planning: A Practical Guide* (DES, 1991) and other published material such as GRIDS (*Guidelines for Review and Internal Development in Schools*) (NCC, 1989a). It is initially a time-consuming task but once it has been done it should be self-generating and in this sense it can be updated regularly to take account of new developments and changing priorities. Identifying and clarifying the 'state' of the school and recognizing its strengths and weaknesses has as its starting point the school's aims or values. Once these are established they create a general focus which can form the core of what needs to be developed. Box 2.1 illustrates an example of an Aims Statement and can be used to suggest some relatively obvious beginnings.

Box 2.1 An example of an Aims Statement

> The school will commit itself to creating a harmonious and stimulating environment, in which all pupils will be encouraged to achieve their maximum potential in terms of skills, knowledge and understanding. Each pupil will be offered opportunities to take decisions, use his or her own judgement, work co-operatively with others and develop as a confident individual. We aim to provide a broad and balanced curriculum which incorporates the requirements of the National Curriculum.

In the example given (Box 2.1), one of the stated aims is: 'Each pupil will be offered opportunities to...work co-operatively with others'. In the audit and during subsequent discussions about the writing of the plan itself, it would be inappropriate not to ask questions about how this is going to be achieved and what needs to happen in order to achieve it. Similarly, by using the same example, the Development Plan needs to demonstrate that concepts such as taking decisions and individuals exercising their own judgement will have to be part of the school's ethos. In other words, what the school says it is trying to do should be reflected in what it is actually doing.

The Aims Statement is the broad and general summary of a school's ethos. In effective schools it will have been communicated to the school and its community and yet it can only form the corner-stone of future developments if it is the beginning rather than the end of any audit or information-gathering exercise. Schools must take into account other external pressures and sources of information both nationally and locally. An HMI report or visit by LEA inspectors may also identify strengths and weaknesses. Other perspectives on where the school is now and where it needs to go all help determine the ethos. An effective school will value all these perspectives and should bear in mind what parents praise about the school and what they tend to complain about, what local residents think and what the pupils themselves are happy or unhappy about. What it cannot do is exist on its own. It is a broad statement of intent. The School Development Plan is the document which will create concise plans to achieve what the Aims Statement has broadly suggested.

THE SCHOOL DEVELOPMENT PLAN

A School Development Plan should not be devised solely by teachers. By involving parents, governors and pupils where appropriate the school is able to take advantage of wider expertise and knowledge. The more people involved, the greater the possible tensions and the slower the process; however, the end product will be owned by both the school and its community so its Development Plan is more likely to be accepted and made to work. It has already been emphasized that establishing a positive ethos must be part of the school's shared planning and it must result in recognizing successful and effective ways forward. This area of management needs to be part of the School Development Plan which, according to *Development Planning: A Practical Guide* (DES, 1991), 'is a plan of needs for development set in the context of the school's aims and values, its existing achievements and national and LEA policies and initiatives. Detailed objectives are set for one year; the objectives for later years are sketched in outline' (p. 2).

It seems unreasonable to expect a positive ethos to arise out of random events. There has to be committed and detailed managerial planning. The changes confronting schools are so many, happening so fast and are so urgent that they must be managed in a professional way. If random elements are allowed to be the main method of planning and decision-making, then they will inevitably become the 'norm' and everyone involved in the school will be so overloaded and confused by an unplanned mass of competing priorities that nothing of value will emerge and nothing that has been written in the Plan will be sustained.

Writing the School Development Plan

Writing the Plan can be made easier if it is based on the following structure, which is identified as a practical way forward in *Development Planning: A Practical Guide* (DES, 1991):

- evidence is collected which identifies the school's needs. This is usually done by taking an audit of the school's strengths and weaknesses;
- priorities are established from the audit, i.e. a list is made of what has been identified as needing to be done in order to continue the school's positive ethos or to improve it by more structured and organized planning;
- priorities must be made manageable in terms of time, i.e. if the school adopts a three-yearly plan and this seems to be a logical way to work then what is to be done in the first year has to be written in detail and in subsequent years sketched out in less detail, because much of what happens will also depend on the results of the initial year's work;
- the Plan has to be written for each year with detailed objectives for the first year and an outline for subsequent years. The following points have to be included:
  - The task, i.e. what is it?
  - What exactly needs to be done?
  - Who will be involved?
  - How much of the budget will be allocated to the Plan?
  - What are the implications for staff development?
  - What will be the outcomes?
  - How will the successes be evaluated so that the following year's detailed plan can be formulated?

It is not easy to suggest examples of priorities that will be relevant to a large number of schools, but there are certain 'common' areas such as those related to the National Curriculum that will have to be internalized. The most important issue here is the need to look at, discuss and evaluate a school's Development Plan bearing in mind the following issues. These can include: the curriculum in terms of the particular needs of 'subject' areas; staff development, e.g. classroom management and teaching styles; methods of assessing and recording pupils' work; improving the school environment;

communicating the school's aims and objectives to parents; special needs; staff appraisal, etc.

The processes behind the School Development Plan

The difficulties inherent in writing the Development Plan are not only that its instigators should get to grips with the real needs of the school but that the plan itself works in practice and produces the benefits it sets out to achieve. It is inappropriate, for example, to try to evaluate and rewrite the school's policies for all the core subjects of the National Curriculum within one year. It is possible, however, to evaluate and redesign policies and schemes of work in a single core subject, for example, English. To do this successfully the planning process has to work, and thus the Development Plan itself, according to *Development Planning: A Practical Guide* (DES, 1991), has to focus attention on the aims of education; to bring together all aspects of a school's planning; to turn a long-term vision into short-term goals, and to give teachers greater control over the nature and pace of change.

The benefit to be expected from a well-constructed plan that has involved governors and colleagues and which reflects the ethos of the school is a recognizable improvement in the quality of education the school provides for its pupils, not only in what they learn but also in what they are able to achieve. This, above all, is the point of the exercise. It should not only be the pupils who benefit from this kind of structured and careful planning. The whole process will help teachers by increasing their confidence, improving the quality of staff development, strengthening the partnership between teaching staff and the governing body and making it easier to report on the work of the school to anyone who is interested and who needs to know what the school is doing currently and what it intends to achieve in the future. If the headteacher and a few senior colleagues construct a plan which is then presented to the governors and the rest of the staff as the completed policy statement, it will be unlikely that such a plan will work and it may well be the case that in two or three years' time little of the Plan will have been implemented. It is important that as many people as possible are involved in creating the Development Plan. Success will depend on the quality of the planning process as well as the content of the Plan. Each teacher will need to play their part and, although the leadership of the headteacher will be vital (see Chapter 3, where management roles including leadership are examined more closely), governors and staff will need to develop an ethos of *working together to achieve the aims of the school*. This concept of individuals working together and the difficulties with teams is discussed at length in Chapter 1 and is the umbrella beneath which many other issues shelter.

CHAPTER SUMMARY

This chapter has concentrated on the school ethos. This is an elusive area of school management because it is basically concerned with the characteristics of the school as a social organization. It is about the feelings and vibrations given off by a school and the positive ways they can make learning more effective for the school's pupils. In looking at the characteristics of positive and negative ethos, the chapter moved towards identifying ways of changing the negative to the positive by means of people and structures. The headteacher's leadership style was seen as being extremely important, as was the involvement of governors and teachers in creating a workable plan that would not only identify the school's strengths but would recognize weaknesses and make plans to change them. The processes involved in the School Development Plan draw on all those aspects of team-building discussed in Chapter 1 but stress again the leadership qualities of the headteacher which will be examined in more detail in Chapter 3. One obvious conclusion, however, is that an effective school with a positive ethos will, by auditing its successes and failures, draw on a wide variety of sources and collect evidence from teachers, parents, governors and pupils while always bearing in mind its own broad and general aims.

FURTHER READING

DES (1991) *Development Planning: A Practical Guide. Advice to Governors, Headteachers and Teachers* (1991) London: HMSO.
This is an extremely useful step-by-step guide to School Development Planning.

Elton Report (1989) *Discipline in Schools: Report of the Committee of Enquiry Chaired by Lord Elton.* London: HMSO.
Despite having little to say about how to control and manage pupils, this report does present some useful evidence about the negative and positive influences schools have on pupils.

Mortimore, P., Sammons, P., Stoll, L., Lewis, D. and Ecob, R. (1988) *School Matters: The Junior Years.* London: Open Books.
Although this is a study of 7–11-year-old children, some of the implications can be transferred to secondary education.

Rutter, M., Maughan, B., Mortimore, P., Ouston, J. and Smith, A. (1979) *Fifteen Thousand Hours. Secondary Schools and Their Effects on Children.* London: Open Books.
In recognizing that school ethos does have an effect on pupil success this study presents some interesting and useful research.

Smith, R. (1992b) *The Heads and Deputies Handbook: Managing Schools in the 1990s.* Lancaster: Framework Press.
This book contains some interesting and useful practical activities that are designed to help teachers and governors construct a positive ethos.

CHAPTER 3

MANAGEMENT ROLES

CHAPTER OVERVIEW

There are many diverse events that take place in schools and in order to make them happen certain people have to complete certain tasks in a certain way. This chapter concentrates on the roles managers have to take on as well as the kinds of leadership styles that are the most successful and effective. In examining leadership, it is recognized that both the headteacher and other leaders such as curriculum co-ordinators have to manage and implement change. This is a difficult area and is here discussed in detail.

LEADERSHIP

In order to examine management roles we must look at leadership, which in turn involves examining the role of the headteacher. However, it has to be recognized that whatever an effective headteacher does can be applied in other situations and to other people in the school. As Bell (1989) suggests:

Opportunities for leadership may be presented to an individual by virtue of his or her position in the school, but holding a particular office provides no guarantee that leadership behaviour will be forthcoming from the incumbent although the expectation is that this will be the case.

(pp. 47–8)

Different aspects of what is or is not an effective school as examined by Rutter *et al.* (1979), Reid *et al.* (1987), Mortimore *et al.* (1988) and the Elton Report (1989) make it clear that the leader's role is essential if the school is to be successful in educating its pupils and efficient in using all its resources. This is really about the leader as the person who can influence group activity, determine what needs to be done, organize how it is done and know when it has been successful. Pondy (1978) explores this in greater depth and suggests that the success of a leader lies in their 'ability to make activity meaningful...not to change behaviour but to give others a sense of understanding of what they are doing' (p.94). It is worth repeating here that the headteacher has to have these abilities, but it is also true that many other teachers need these kinds of leadership skills.

When teachers begin their careers they usually concentrate on developing their classroom and subject skills, but if they are promoted to positions of responsibility they need to learn and develop those leadership skills that will help them to take on different managerial roles. This is certainly the case in schools in the 1990s, where change and new directions can no longer rely on leadership based on stability and historical acceptance but have to depend for their vigour and growth on individuals who are able to embrace change.

A further attempt to define leadership would have to relate to the school's needs. This would mean that as well as understanding these needs the leader would be able to adopt attitudes and behaviours that would meet them. They should, if they are effective, be able to recognize the needs of the tasks to be undertaken and how to achieve these tasks; be aware of the needs of the staff team as a whole and how to build and maintain these teams; and be able to recognize the needs of the individual within the staff team and know how to develop each individual potential.

When looking at what leaders actually do, Solity and Bull (1987) make it clear that the class teacher is in many ways a leader. Not only do such teachers demonstrate leadership by organizing and managing the learning environment but those who are most successful can model behaviour that is consistent with effective leadership in their relationships with their pupils. In accepting that 'good' leadership has invariably emerged as a characteristic of 'good' schools, Stogdil (1974) suggests further issues, many of which will be explored later. Traits which characterize effective leaders include: a sense of responsibility; concern for completing tasks; energy; persistence; risk-taking; originality; self-confidence; capacity to handle stress; capacity to influence; and capacity to co-ordinate the efforts of others. It is interesting and important to be able to recognize these traits, but in themselves they do little to suggest how they will effect the day-to-day activities of leaders. In order to be more useful they would have to help us define and understand what it is that leaders actually do.

WHAT LEADERS DO

By introducing the concepts of whole-staff and individual needs, the issue of leadership becomes one of what leaders actually do, rather than who they are. This fits neatly into the idea that although the headteacher has many responsibilities in terms of leadership, there are others who need similar skills. If leadership, rather like management itself, is judged more by results than intentions, then this places the emphasis on behaviour rather than on plans and policies, the processes rather than the content. Leadership in this case becomes a function of the staff team and not just the responsibility of a named individual. Day *et al.* (1990) suggest that many teams are successful because they have the capacity to allow the leadership to emerge in response to the need of the moment. When the team or group regards a single individual as 'the leader', successful team work can become inhibited and constrained. An example of this might occur in a small primary school, where the headteacher becomes a team member in a specific curriculum team that is led by the curriculum subject co-ordinator. Such a team needs to have delegated powers of leadership and should be responsible for taking decisions without constantly having to refer them to the headteacher. In order to achieve this kind of leadership there are various managerial roles to consider.

Management roles

Management roles in both primary and secondary schools can be divided into three broad areas which are discussed and extended in Nias (1979), Coulson (1986) and Southworth (1990). They are as follows:

- Roles relating to other people.
- Roles relating to the collection and passing on of information.
- Roles involving taking decisions.

Roles relating to other people

This is where leaders have to be competent in several areas of human relations. They have to act as a kind of figurehead who speaks at functions such as PTA meetings, speech-days, leaving ceremonies, etc. while at the same time being able to supervise, select, train, appraise and motivate the staff in the school. This is often achieved by liaising with different teams and departments including staff meetings, departmental meetings, governors' meetings, etc.

Roles relating to the collection and passing on of information

This role involves three basic processes. There is a need to monitor, fact-find and assess needs by collecting as much information as possible from individuals and teams as well as from meetings, documents and reports. It is also important to disseminate information and communicate it to whoever needs it. This can be achieved by written memos, reports and policy documents or in face-to-face meetings. The third aspect is a more public one and involves communicating the school's views to parents, advisers, governors, education officers, etc.

Roles involving taking decisions

A school cannot function without decisions being taken efficiently. As in the discussion in Chapter 1 of how groups work together, this is by no means an easy task and will often involve consultation and consensus. To do this, leaders have to find strategies within which to work, to initiate change and to see the changes through.

This will mean being pro-active in the sense of recognizing what aspects of the organization need changing, as well as responding to incidents as they arise. Many decisions which involve change and which affect people as well as budgeting scarce resources, will mean balancing the needs of individuals as well as departments. As it is such a difficult task, it is important to involve as many colleagues as possible and to be prepared to state quite clearly why certain decisions have been taken.

To function effectively as a leader within the parameters of these roles suggests quite clearly the complexity of the task because if decisions involve people – and they invariably do in schools – leaders have to contend with a variety of personalities, viewpoints and philosophical stances. There needs to be a commitment on the leader's part to try and make it clear that what has to be done has to be organized within the school's structures, aims and ethos by leaders who adopt a style which allows certain processes to take place. There thus has to be a 'style' of working that will both embrace conflicting views as well as be capable of bringing together diverse beliefs.

LEADERSHIP STYLES

In many ways, it is futile to search for the ideal 'style' of leadership. Such opposites as autocratic versus democratic (see Chapter 1) or directive versus permissive imply that one is 'good' and the other 'bad' (Landers and Myers, 1977).

It is not, of course, that simple. Autocratic leadership will obviously not achieve certain goals and with the movement towards collegiality, where the vision is shared and not exclusive to an individual headteacher or other leader, it becomes doubtful whether it would ever be the 'ideal style'. If decisions have to be made about health and safety and the administration of lists, birthdates and other minor order tasks then there is no reason why an instant autocratic decision should not be more appropriate than any other. What is important is that the style must fit the task or the process in hand and, where necessary, allow time for reflection and planning. There is an important distinction here between process and content, and it is certainly true that a leader's role has to reflect a concern for accomplishing tasks while at the same time having a concern for relationships between people in school. Hersey and Blanchard (1982) suggest that there is a continuum of 'leadership style' which is linked to the maturity of colleagues or what they call followers. In their proposed leadership styles there are four general types of behaviour, each of which is appropriate to a particular level of maturity. Beginning with immature colleagues and moving towards the more mature, they suggest that with this increasing maturity, the leader should move through styles designated as: *'telling'* (high on task/content, low on relationships/process); *'selling'* (high on task/content, high on relationship/process); *'participating'* (low on task/content, high on relationships/ process), and *delegating* (low on task/content, low on relationships/process). There are similarities between these suggested 'styles' and the results/relationship continuum proposed by Tannenbaum and Schmidt (1973), which is discussed in Chapter 1.

Whatever leadership style is developed, it must not encourage dependence on top-down decision-making; nor must it stifle creativity and innovation, and it must certainly not be afraid of change. What has to be seen as important to the school before this can happen is a sharing of views, an ethos where colleagues work together to solve problems and where decisions are taken and change managed by consensus and democracy rather than autocracy.

Everard (1986) notes that an industrialist would expect a manager who is a leader to be able to adopt the following roles:

- Cause events to happen and know what he or she wants to happen.
- Exercise responsible stewardship over resources and turn them to purposeful account.

- Promote effectiveness in work done, and search for continual improvement.
- Be accountable for the performance of the unit he [sic] is managing.
- Set a climate conducive to enabling people to do their best.

These criteria would seem to apply to all teachers in leadership roles; however, in recognizing two kinds of roles necessary for a leader's 'authority', one deriving from the office held and the other from personal abilities and experience, Fayol (1930) added to the debate by suggesting that if a leader is to be successful he or she needs to be able to: forecast what needs doing; plan how to do it; organize what needs to be done from the plans; nominate an individual or group to carry out whatever is necessary; and co-ordinate and control the exercise.

All these aspects of leadership management roles will depend for their success on an appropriate style and an effective approach to both organizing how the school functions and leading it forward. Such a concept not only involves reflecting on how a leader works and shares the tasks of leadership with colleagues but how this will affect forward movement and planning.

SHARED LEADERSHIP AND THE LINKS TO PLANNING

It was stressed in Chapter 2 that a positive ethos does not simply happen. The establishment of such an ethos involves leadership being shared in a structured way with teachers and governors. This is not devaluing the role of the individual leader but recognizing that schools are not fairy stories, and being able to change a toad into a princess with one kiss is highly unlikely. Similar, as implied by Georgiades and Phillimore (1972), is

> the idea that you can produce...a knight in shining armour who, loins girded with new technologies and beliefs, will assault his organizational fortress and institute changes both in himself and others at a stroke. Such a view is ingenuous. The fact of the matter is that organizations such as schools...will, like dragons, eat hero innovators for breakfast.
>
> (p.33)

If leadership is not always an individual acting alone but an individual who can only be as effective as the sum of all the people within his or her organizational sphere, then what are the attributes that will improve school management? Chapter 2 suggested some such attributes in connection with the School Development Plan. *Development Planning: A Practical Guide* (DES, 1991) also gives a list that can act as a summary because it includes many key issues. It implies that the headteacher or indeed any leader:

- has a mission (*aim*) for the school;
- inspires commitment to the school's mission (*aim*) and so gives direction and purpose to its work;
- co-ordinates the work of the school by allocating roles and delegating responsibilities within structures that support collaboration;
- is actively and visibly involved in planning and implementing change; but
- is ready to delegate and value the contribution of colleagues;
- is a skilled communicator, keeping everyone informed about important decisions and events;
- has the capacity to stand back from daily life in order to challenge what is taken for granted, to anticipate problems and to spot opportunities;
- is committed to the school, its members and its reputation; but
- objectively appraises strengths and weaknesses so as to build upon the best of current practice in remedying deficiencies;
- emphasizes the quality of teaching and learning, lesson by lesson and day by day;
- has high expectations of all staff and pupils;
- recognizes that support and encouragement are needed for everyone to give of their best.

While it is possible to agree that many, if not all, the attributes in this list apply to leaders in school, there has to be a link between an effective leader, who may possess many of them, and an effective school. If they exist as separate entities they will fail to complement each other in a way that will help ensure success.

LEADERSHIP AND THE EFFECTIVE SCHOOL

Finally, it is important to recognize that a consideration of effective leadership involves deciding what is an effective school. Both Rutter *et al.* (1979) and Mortimore *et al.* (1988) suggest that such schools have similar attributes. It is significant that in both these studies and in further HMI reports (see, for example, HMI, 1977) the most significant factor has been the effectiveness of the headteacher.

A further factor to consider is that other senior staff need to have leadership roles and that the ethos of the school should support a broad curriculum rather than a narrowly conceived one. Again, to achieve this aim, leadership must be seen to involve many individuals rather than one single omnipotent figure. The HMI study *Ten Good Schools* (HMI, 1977), which described ten successful and effective secondary schools, cited four characteristics shared by their headteachers:

- They communicated specific educational aims to staff, pupils and parents.
- They displayed sympathetic understanding of staff and pupils and were accessible.
- They showed good humour, a sense of proportion and dedication to the task.
- They were conscious of the corruption of power: power-sharing was a keynote of the schools.

In understanding staff, communicating aims to others, having a sense of proportion and being conscious of the corruption of power, it must be the case that the leadership style or indeed, the pattern of leadership, has to be one where concerns are shared, different views listened to and decisions taken, and change only considered and embarked on after listening to the views of colleagues.

THE MANAGEMENT OF CHANGE

Perhaps one of the major tests of effective leaders is how successful they are in taking on the role of managing change. By involving themselves in the change process they will inevitably have to take on a leadership role. To be successful they will have to recognize what motivates teachers and how this motivation can be harnessed to the whole organization in a way that makes it easier to achieve objectives. This cannot take place, however, without recognizing the wider demands from the LEA, local community and national legislation. Another factor is the ability to analyse the complex systems that are present in schools, including simplifying and processing material, setting appropriate goals, managing conflict and consulting all appropriate individuals in an attempt to achieve as much consensus as is possible.

This is a considerable list of attributes for a change manager or change agent to have. If we consider that it is often the headteacher who initiates change and sees it through there is considerable onus on one person to perform minor miracles on a regular basis. If we argue that change agents should be other teachers and colleagues, then the onus is on the school to be staffed with teachers who have many of the attributes already suggested, as well as their 'routine' classroom management skills. It is an important part of good management and certainly part of a school's positive ethos for change to come from sources other than the headteacher. There is the view that whatever is being changed and how the change works needs to be 'owned' by all those involved in the process. A head as leader imposing all change will fail for many reasons, one being that he or she will have a vested interest in the success of the change but no one else will really understand or care. Change may come from individuals or staff groups. It may result from the suggestion of someone outside the school, for example, an inspector. Parental complaints may also stimulate change. Havelock (1970) suggests that a change agent has to be *a catalyst, a solution-giver or a process-helper*. It might help if they could combine parts of all three.

Change agent as a catalyst

In adopting this style or taking on this role the headteacher or other leader will begin the process of change by putting pressure on the school or individuals and groups to make people start to think in a different way about things that had previously been accepted.

Change agent as a solution giver

Initiating change by using this method means not falling into the trap of having all the answers but helping people to do their own problem-solving and find their own answers. Being a good solution-giver means knowing when and how to offer suggestions.

Change agent as a process helper

This means showing colleagues how to recognize and define needs, how to diagnose problems and set objectives, how to acquire relevant resources and how to select the correct solution.

In many ways managing change is like solving problems. The problem has to be recognized and suggestions made as to why it exists and what is likely to resolve it. When considering a proposed change, those managing it and leading the process as change managers or change agents must consider factors that are likely to promote the change and those likely to restrain it. This kind of relatively simple analysis was first described by Kurt Lewin (1947) and is based on the assumption that a change situation is a balance between two sets of forces. Using Figure 3.1 consider a change that is needed, e.g. a completely new mathematics course. Write down a description of all those people and circumstances that might either resist such a change or contribute to creating a situation that will make such a change difficult. These are the restraining forces.

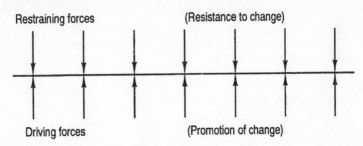

Figure 3.1 The change force-field

The next stage is to describe the people, reasons and circumstances under which the change could be promoted fairly easily. These will become the driving forces. Leadership and effective management will develop strategies to decrease the restraining forces and increase the driving forces. By doing this in a

Box 3.1 The process of managing change

Stage 1 Identify and describe in writing the problem or change that is needed. Don't just think about it.

Stage 2 Split the problem or change needed into:
(a) The current situation
(b) The desired situation.

Stage 3 List the driving and restraining forces (see Figure 3.1). These forces are anything that could hinder or help the change go through and could be people, events, money, time, etc. It is important to be specific.

Stage 4 Find some way to highlight those forces that are the most important.

Stage 5 Look at the restraining forces that have been highlighted; write them down and alongside them list all the actions that could reduce or eliminate them.

Stage 6 For all the driving forces that have been highlighted list actions that could increase the force.

Stage 7 Work out from the responses to stages 5 and 6 the most promising steps which could now be taken and identify the resources that are available.

Stage 8 Look closely at the most promising steps and place them in order of priority, using this as the final chance to omit any that will not work. It is useful at this stage to suggest when various stage will be completed.

thoughtful and structured way which involves colleagues, it should be possible to initiate change and see it through more easily to a successful conclusion.

As the management of change will be a continuous process in all schools, it is worth looking at what is involved in more detail. This applies to those with very different roles. The process of change involves everyone and cuts across their expectations and work patterns and will create different ways of working and new objectives to be achieved. The process illustrated in Figure 3.1 can be divided into eight basic steps (see Box 3.1).

If change in schools is inevitable and the change involves considerable leadership skills, it is not only important to be aware of the processes involved but to recognize the likely responses to particular types of change and the types of problems they will present to the change agent or change leader. It will be helpful to look at a change which can be identified in most schools and examine how stages 1 to 8 can be used to make the change easier and more beneficial. Short-term planning looms large in OFSTED's approach to teasing out high-quality teaching and learning. Most schools will have to make changes to their existing pattern of planning, so the example could be 'Making changes to the weekly short-term planning methods'. Individual schools obviously need to be more precise than this, but it is useful as a general example.

Stage 1 identifies the problem. This really means recognizing that there *is* a problem. In this example it could be that lesson plans and whatever else the short-term planning consists of is not sufficient to meet OFSTED's demands.

Stage 2 analyses exactly what is happening at the moment and what exactly should be happening. In other words, the school needs to know where it is going in terms of short-term planning. It should be obvious at this stage that the more people involved, the more ideas will develop.

Stage 3 lists both the driving and restraining forces. For our example the driving forces might include: OFSTED need to see clearer planning; this has to specify what is being taught, how and what the pupils are learning. It could also include built-in assessment opportunities, evaluation and where the pupils need to go next. Restraining forces will include arguments directly against those that are presented for the change. They will, however, go further and bring in personalities and human nature such as 'It's worked for a long time now so why change at this stage?' and 'I've been doing it my way all my career and I'm not having someone tell me how to plan lessons'. There will also be restraining forces related to time and energy. By highlighting the most important of those forces in Stage 4, it will be possible to remove those that are relatively irrelevant and reduce the number of points to be dealt with in stages 5 and 6, where the team or group considering the change should be able to begin to actually produce a plan of action that will move the change forward.

Stages 7 and 8 depend on a formalized plan because they involve selecting resources and prioritizing what the forward movements of the change process should be. In any school, there will be colleagues who resist change for all kinds of reasons. They can be historical in that they have always done things in a certain way or they can be threatening in that a teacher's bedrock of professionalism often depends on doing certain things in a certain way. There are, however, different types of change and different ways of responding to it. It is also useful to consider the different managerial roles that need to be adopted. Both Plant (1987) and Miles *et al.* (1988) suggest several interesting ways in which change can affect both the individual and the school.

TYPES OF CHANGE AND LIKELY RESPONSE

Organizational change

This is concerned with how the school is organized. It could be new departmental structures, separate facilities, or the imposed structural change of the National Curriculum when year groups assumed different names and numbers and groups of years became Key Stages. There will be concern among all those involved in the change and they may try to deny that it is happening, and certainly in the early stages they will lack commitment, feel incompetent and become stressed, until they become involved in the process and are reassured about the possible outcome.

Behavioural change

This concerns changes in attitude which can be necessary because of other changes, or desirable because of colleagues' or individuals' needs. An example might be when dealing with new initiatives in special needs, gender or race. Because changes in attitude involve personality and the self, there may be alienation, withdrawal and assertiveness in order to try to prevent the changes from occurring. On the other hand, if several colleagues are in agreement this could be an enriching managerial move which helps improve relationships.

Employment change

This is more about change affecting status. It could involve promotion, demotion or a withdrawn contract. In all these situations there is often a transition period where competence sags and individuals, and therefore teams, become less effective and less inclined to work hard.

Procedural change

This kind of change disrupts the individual's and the group's way of working. It could be a new way of timetabling, changing the time of the school day or changing the way class groups are allocated. Whatever it is, some people will try to ignore the changes and to avoid taking any decisions. Some may even counter the change and revert to the original status quo. In many ways these blocking tactics are understandable; after all, most of us prefer life as we know it rather than the unknown consequences of operating a programme of changes, whether they are small or large scale.

Part of a leader's management role has to be to deal with problems associated with change; that is, the negative responses to the proposed changes. Colleagues will experience frustration, worry, doubt, anxiety and uncertainty and relationships between colleagues may well alter because of change. The leader's role must be to respond to such negative responses, but Fullan (1985) suggests that in order for change to be implemented successfully there is a need for pressure on the individual and the group. What has to be avoided is too much pressure which will lead to stress or too little which will lead to no change at all.

NEGATIVE RESPONSES TO CHANGE

It is important that negative responses are kept to a minimum by making sure that those leading the change see their role as crucial to the process and who are reasonably skilful at managing it. Resistance to change is lowered when colleagues know why a change is being made and what the advantages are likely to be. Hand (1981) divided the teaching force into four categories:

- those who are frustrated in their ambitions;
- those who are happy to be in their final career posts;
- those likely to gain further promotion;
- those who are happy to be in their current post but who find it difficult to cope with the stresses caused by externally imposed innovation.

Not all schools contain, as Day *et al.* (1990) suggest, 'all these clear-cut categories of teachers' (p. 119), but leaders and managers need to recognize the 'complex web of role expectations, institutional constraints, professional experiences, teaching attitudes and approaches and personality factors that may influence the responses of teachers to any form of new idea' (p. 119).

One conclusion that can be drawn is that if leaders are trying to match individual and institutional needs during any process of change then there may be conflict created by the tensions between the two. If this is the case it will be increasingly important to involve all the participants so that they feel that they have some vested interest in the change and ownership of it. This can be achieved by avoiding mistrust, rumour and misunderstanding. Sharing information and allowing opportunities for discussion and, where necessary, complaint, will allow the change to be more successful. Retaining or withholding information will inhibit communication and lessen the chance of the change being successful. This kind of open communication with all the participants in the school can only improve the working relationships and should help teams filter the information and use it well. What needs to be avoided is the situation where the school or an internal team fails in the management of change. If this happens and confidence is lowered, it will be difficult to feel confident next time. There are certain inappropriate management techniques which should be avoided. These include the following:

- Not being specific about what needs changing; this usually means a broad and poorly defined area of change which is not specific enough to identify where to begin and the kind of change process that is needed. An example might be changing the curriculum planning. A more precise area might be changing the short-term planning in National Curriculum technology.
- Not being able to justify the need for change; this will occur if a particular change appears to be linked to an individual's or group's bandwagon, where they see the need for change but others do not.
- Failing to involve colleagues/the group/the team.
- Not communicating the intricacies of the change process and/or not sharing all the information available.
- Creating excessive work during change or giving the impression that more work will be necessary after the change.

It is in both the individual's and the institution's interest to make sure, as far as possible, that the negative responses are managed in such a way that they do not inhibit the change process to the extent that it either stops or slows down to such a pace that it becomes unmanageable. The onus is on heads, other leaders and often specific curriculum co-ordinators to make sure that agreed and accepted changes move forward as smoothly as possible.

LEADERSHIP AND THE CURRICULUM CO-ORDINATOR'S ROLE

Allowances over and above the main pay spine exist in all schools and if these roles are those of co-ordinators who are responsible for specific subjects, it becomes necessary for them to take on the mantle of leadership. This is perfectly in accord with the idea that the headteacher does not always have to mastermind change. Day *et al.* (1985) suggest that in leading change 'It is a prime management task to plan, support, and monitor the innovation process, but not necessarily to initiate it' (p. 109).

Both Bell (1989) and the National Union of Teachers (NUT, 1991) suggest, in quite different ways, the importance of adequate and accurate job descriptions which are communicated to all staff. The headteacher must endorse their position as co-ordinators and invest them with the power to do a specific job. Their role as manager, leader, change agent and, of course, co-ordinator will be enhanced if they are known to be all these things and are not just seen as toothless mouthpieces for some other leader. As it is, they have a complicated job and Dean (1987), writing about primary school allowance holders with extra responsibilities, suggests that their managerial duties and roles include the following:

- supporting colleagues in their particular area of the curriculum;
- overseeing the 'subject' content and the processes and teaching styles which are used in the classroom;
- preparing schemes of work;
- working with colleagues to select appropriate resources;
- inducting new colleagues into the work of the school in their 'subject';
- ensuring that adequate records are kept;
- advising the head on the specialist needs of the subject area.

Most of these duties involve leadership of some kind and the need for a co-ordinator to lead is important. If the leadership of a particular subject area is delegated to a specific person, they need to have the power and authority to lead. In other words, they must be allowed to do so. It will be very ineffective if a head-teacher only delegates part of the role or interferes in the co-ordinator's job in such a way that their leadership is not recognized by themselves or their colleagues. Rather than creating less work for the headteacher and senior managers, delegation without power will create more.

As it was written in 1987, Dean's list of attributes – which incidentally applies equally to secondary schools – would not enable a co-ordinator to do all that was required within the demands of the Education Reform Act and the National Curriculum. Times have changed very rapidly and all teachers have had to move forward with these changes and to be part of them. There are gaps in Dean's general summary which include National Curriculum assessment, curriculum planning and incorporating subject needs into the School Development Plan. It will be useful in this final section to briefly address the management roles and leadership skills that an effective change manager or change agent should possess. These will include the following:

- enthusiasm about the specialist area;
- being able to use specialist knowledge and experience to help colleagues plan their work;
- attending INSET and feeding back the knowledge to colleagues;
- keeping up to date with the specialist area by reading National Curriculum updates, journals, etc. and sharing the information with colleagues;
- making sure that governors and parents are familiar with what the 'subject' is about;
- skill in working alongside colleagues in their classrooms and helping them with their teaching skills;
- budgeting and purchasing resources for the benefit of the 'subject' and of the pupils;
- adopting appropriate procedures for assessment in their subject areas;
- using the assessments diagnostically and making sure that colleagues are able to do the same;
- knowing what year groups and Key Stages are doing in particular subjects.

Above all, one of the key managerial roles for any leader is that of implementation. Change needs implementing. Decisions need to be implemented. Once schools have begun to make certain things happen then those leading this particular area need to be persistent and have a sense of direction. Playfoot *et al.* (1989) suggest that 'The person leading the change needs to be *visible*, working with their "sleeves rolled up", touring, talking, making practical adjustments, listening and leading on the job reports' (p.73). Implementation and all management roles, especially those involving leadership and change, need energy, time and the commitment and ability to work with other people.

CHAPTER SUMMARY

There is a relationship between the quality of leadership and the success of those with specific managerial roles, and the effectiveness of the school. This has been recognized in many studies. In examining what a leader is able to do within a certain number of identifiable roles, however, it has been suggested that other teachers have to take on roles associated with leadership because schools can only function successfully if the work-load is shared through some delegation of what the leader has to do. The styles of leadership and the roles leaders have to perform are linked quite closely to the management of change and the processes involved. Change is ongoing and the ability to make it work effectively has to depend on high-quality leadership from the head but also from colleagues such as those with incentive allowances who take on the role of co-ordinating certain subjects. The idea of shared responsibility is important and the quality of leadership within specified management roles, especially that of managing change, is not one person's responsibility. The headteacher's role is vitally important but it needs support and assistance from colleagues who, according to Elliott and Kemp (1983) and Rogers (1980), have the following characteristics:

- *Self-awareness*: being aware of our own attitudes and values and how they affect other people.
- *Will to achieve*: seeking new challenges.
- *Optimism*: feeling positive about the future and the part to be played in it.
- *Positive regard*: responding to others with warmth and respect.

- *Trust*: the extent to which we are prepared to place trust in those we work with.
- *Congruence*: the security to be ourselves with colleagues.
- *Empathy*: understanding others' points of view.
- *Courage*: taking risks to find more effective ways of working with colleagues.

FURTHER READING

Havelock, R.G. (1973) *The Change Agent's Guide to Innovation*. Englewood Cliffs, N.J.: Educational Technology Publications.

Georgiades, N. and Phillimore, L. (1972) *The Myth of the Hero Innovator and Alternative Strategies for Organizational Change*. London: Department of Occupational Psychology, Birkbeck College.

These authors suggest possibilities in terms of what leaders can and cannot hope to achieve.

Mortimore, P., Sammons, P., Stoll, L., Lewis, D. and Ecob, R. (1988) *School Matters: The Junior Years*. London: Open Books.

Reid K., Hopkins, D. and Holly, P. (1987) *Towards the Effective School*. Oxford: Basil Blackwell.

Although based on different standpoints, both these books discuss many of the key issues associated with management roles and their link with effectiveness.

Nias, J. (1979) Leadership style and job satisfaction in primary schools. In Bush, T., Glatter, R., Goodey, J. and Riches, C. et al. (eds) (1980) *Approaches to School Management*. London: Harper & Row.

This is a detailed and interesting analysis which covers in more detail many of the subjects raised in this chapter.

Southworth, G. (1990) Leadership, headship and effective primary schools. *School Organization*, **10** (1).

A broad, sweeping analysis which presents arguments that will be useful and interesting to both primary and secondary schools.

CHAPTER 4

MANAGING THE CURRICULUM AND THE CLASSROOM

CHAPTER OVERVIEW

It is not easy to define what the curriculum is, although it is certainly not just the National Curriculum. *A Curriculum for All* (NCC, 1989b) opens with the sentence: 'All pupils share the right to a broad and balanced curriculum including the National Curriculum' (p. 1). Elton (DES, 1989) states: 'On the curriculum there are issues at three levels. First the National Curriculum. Second the curricula offered by individual schools. Third the curricula pursued by individual pupils' (p. 103). In *The Curriculum from 5–16* (HMI, 1985) there is the suggestion that 'all pupils should have access to a curriculum of similar breadth and balance irrespective of their level of ability, the school they attend or their social circumstances' (pp. 3–4). This chapter examines many of these issues including broad curriculum aims, equal access for all pupils, differentiation, and match, and briefly looks at some of the issues, relating to effective teaching, the National Curriculum and assessment and planning the curriculum.

CHARACTERISTICS OF THE CURRICULUM

When a school makes a statement about the curriculum, it is usually expressed in terms of its content or what the school intends its pupils to learn. Of equal importance, however, are the processes which help pupils to learn. They include how the curriculum is taught, what teaching styles are used and how classrooms are managed. Processes and teaching methods are an important part of the curriculum and one definition could be the suggestion that the curriculum will include everything that happens in a school, whether intended or unintended, which promotes some form of learning. This, however, raises the issue of unpredictability. Educational management must be able to concentrate and focus on what can be anticipated and this can refer to the coherence of a school's curriculum which is the extent to which the various parts of a planned curriculum relate meaningfully. Pollard and Tann (1993) argue that the opposite of coherence is fragmentation and if we accept the suggestion made by Bruner and Haste (1987) that learning could be thought of as a process of being able to make sense of the whole of what is being taught, then clearly fragmentation is to be avoided. This must not mean, however, that we need to adopt the constricting view of the curriculum being the 'syllabus', or the curriculum being what is stated in the National Curriculum. It is not sensible just to limit curriculum management to what is taught to whom and by whom. There are the written policy documents, the schemes of work and of course the decreed parameters of the National Curriculum, but there are also the 'hidden' extras which, while not being the intended outcomes, are still taken away from school by the pupils. These hidden extras are what has come to be known as the hidden curriculum. Hargreaves (1984) writes that this is represented by the values and attitudes that are conveyed by the way the school operates and the way that teachers behave. A careful and wise curriculum manager obviously focuses on the curriculum which manifests itself as the public face of the school, i.e. its subjects, its classroom styles, its syllabuses and its treatment of the National Curriculum. At the same time it is important to bear in mind that there is this hidden and more private curriculum of processes, of how pupils are treated and the importance of teachers as models for the values they wish to communicate to their pupils within the broad brushstrokes of the School Development Plan and the school ethos.

COMMON CURRICULUM CHARACTERISTICS

In all schools, whether primary or secondary, and at least until a pupil is 16, there are some common curriculum characteristics. *The Curriculum from 5–16* (HMI, 1985) describes five.

Breadth

The Education Reform Act (1988) suggests that the curriculum should be broad and balanced, and HMI (DES, 1986; DES, 1987) make it clear that in schools where the curriculum does have breadth, with a wide range of subjects including the National Curriculum and extra-curricular activities, there seems to be higher achievement in basic skills. Even in secondary schools it would seem that a wide-ranging curriculum offers pupils the opportunity to practise 'basic skills' in a context where they see a purpose in what they are doing. There should also be breadth within and across areas of the curriculum.

Balance

Different aspects of the curriculum need to be given an appropriate weight of time. In the primary school this might mean one teacher organizing each 'subject's' work so that over an agreed period a significant amount of time has been spent on each subject. In a secondary school this 'appropriateness' of time will depend on the skill of the person responsible for the timetable. What was recognized in *Curriculum Organisation and Classroom Practice in Primary Schools; a Follow up Report* (DFE, 1993c) was that 'If schools were overstretched to provide the National Curriculum, depth was likely to be sacrificed in pursuit of breadth. The aim should be to strike a better balance than currently existed which meant attempting less but doing it more thoroughly' (pp.15–16). Perhaps, while recognizing the constraints and pressures of examination schedules, this sentiment applies equally to secondary schools.

Relevance

What is learned in school needs to be recognized by pupils as having some relevance. This could be laying foundations for the future as well as being directly applicable to their lives. All pupils need to be told why they are learning certain things as well as it being in a context that they recognize.

Differentiation

Different pupils bring different experiences, interests and abilities to their learning. The curriculum has to be 'matched' to the whole group needs as well as to the individual. Differentiation implies that there is an awareness that pupils need to be challenged at the most suitable level and that the work that is set in the classroom is differentiated in such a way that the teacher is able to match tasks to pupils as effectively as possible. Pollard and Tann (1993) see differentiation at either a general or a specific level. The general level relates to the appropriateness of the curriculum for pupils with specific needs, e.g. young children who are learning to read are significantly different from those pupils writing essays in GCSE courses. It is also true that matching tasks to ability in relation to pupils with special educational needs is equally important to doing the same for exceptionally gifted pupils. As Hurst (1992) suggests, the curriculum must be planned with this broad span of differentiation in mind.

On the other hand, at the specific level differentiation is concerned with the appropriateness or otherwise of particular classroom tasks. There needs to be a match between pupil and learning task in such a way that pupils learn effectively. This will mean that there is little boredom because tasks are too easy and no frustration because tasks are too hard.

Progression and continuity

The curriculum which a pupil experiences throughout primary and secondary school should be seen as a whole. This means that not only should teachers have an idea of what happens at all stages in their own school but they should also know something of other stages of education. The National Curriculum has ensured that this is beginning to happen by prescribing the content, and to some extent the level at which that content should be pitched at certain ages. What needs to happen, however, is that by making progress in their learning all pupils should build on and integrate their knowledge, understanding and skills.

BROAD CURRICULUM AIMS

As suggested in Chapter 3, the school's aims are the beginnings of the process that will not only define in a more precise way what the school ethos will be, but will play a significant part in suggesting the breadth and development of the curriculum. For example, if the aims set by the governing body and the head-teacher were to produce pupils who believed in traditional values and followed the instructions of their superiors without question,

Box 4.1 Broad curriculum aims *(Example 1)*

As a school, we expect all pupils to experience achievement and to reach their full potential in the following areas:

Academic attainment. Pupils must express themselves in written form, retain knowledge, give appropriate responses without reference to sources of information and have the capacity to memorize and organize material.

The capacity to apply knowledge. This deals with the practical rather than the theoretical, the oral rather than the written. Problem-solving and investigational skills are very important.

Personal and social skills. The capacity to communicate with others in face-to-face relationships, the ability to co-operate with others in the interests of the group as well as of the individual. Importance is placed on initiatives, self-reliance and the ability to work alone without close supervision, and the skills of leadership.

Motivation and commitment. The readiness to persevere, to learn in spite of the difficulties of the task, to be willing to try to be committed to all aspects of school life.

---

the ethos would be unlikely to be one of personal freedom, joint decision-making, etc. The broad curriculum aims of the school, which must be defined in consultation with the governing body, will set the stage for what is taught and, more importantly, now that the National Curriculum defines much of the content, how it is taught. Boxes 4.1 and 4.2 show two real-life examples of broad curriculum aims.

Box 4.2 Broad curriculum aims *(Example 2)*

The school governors would like to emphasize certain areas which are being developed within this particular school:

Decision-making and independent learning. All pupils in the school will be encouraged to exercise choice, take decisions and express fluently their own points of view. The aim will be to foster independent rather than teacher-controlled learning.

Equal opportunities. Everything which happens in the school will take place under an umbrella of commitment to equal opportunities for all children.

The curriculum will reflect a positive attitude to our multi-racial society and pupils will learn to appreciate other people's right to be different and the value of different cultures.

The school aims to take a positive action towards breaking down stereotype attitudes.

The governors welcome the view that children with special needs are entitled to full access to the curriculum and they wish to see a policy of total integration in the school with appropriate support.

The pupils' role in the community. The school will promote links with the local community and develop altruistic and responsible attitudes in pupils to prepare them to play an active role in society.

The wider world. The school aims to increase pupils' awareness of the need to care for the environment locally and on a world scale. It also aims to develop pupils' understanding of their place in world issues.

Health and Fitness. Pupils will be encouraged to take responsibility for their own well-being by eating healthily and acting to ensure their general physical fitness.

By suggesting that curriculum and learning processes rather than content will allow schools to develop a certain ethos and attitude towards what is taught, both examples lead the management of the school foward in quite broad areas. They stress independent learning and equal opportunities and recognize that learning extends beyond the school and the purely academic. They also suggest that personal and social skills and motivation and commitment will be values that will help schools attempt to meet the needs of a wide range of pupils as well as developing a curriculum that will be relevant to all pupils.

A CURRICULUM FOR ALL

It should be possible to see obvious links between the broad curriculum aims of the school and the aims statement which 'fronts' the School Development Plan. They should both link to form the umbrella under which the school organization operates and is structured. The curriculum is of course about what happens in the classroom, about pupils' needs and how those needs can best be met. Two vital ingredients which have been raised but not developed are that the curriculum, both in process and content, should offer equal opportunities and, in order to achieve this, there should be differentiation in how the content is presented to pupils.

If pupils begin failing in school, then whatever curriculum is devised there will be difficulties in meeting their learning needs. Even at an early age those who begin to fail will find that their failures are cumulative and will continue beyond the primary school into the secondary school. There are many pupils who will have experienced difficulties at home which have not encouraged them to succeed, and will, in some cases, have led pupils to expect failure before they reach the reception classes of primary schools. If this pattern of failure and low self-esteem continues, life for these pupils, their peers and their teachers will be difficult. Whatever curriculum is planned will depend on a teacher adopting a style of classroom management that is able to cope with a variety of learning styles and pupils' strengths and weaknesses.

Schools and the teachers who work in them have to devise curricula and teaching strategies which will enhance each pupil's self-esteem. This applies to the National Curriculum within the broad and balanced whole curriculum. Purkey (1970) suggests a number of essential factors that will help teachers do this when they are managing their classrooms. They include bringing the pupil to the point where the chances of success are good and then issuing the kind of challenge that means 'This is hard but I think you can do it'. Allowing the pupils to retain a sense of worth and at the same time having the freedom to make real decisions is also very important. This must take place within conditions of safety with lots of support from the teacher as well as firm, reasonable and fair limits where success rather than failure is the norm. Despite the problem of too much prescription on subject detail and too little guidance on how the demands of all its components fit together, the National Curriculum should still, after the modifications in 1995, allow individual teachers the freedom to make sure that every child is able to benefit from it.

THE NATIONAL CURRICULUM

Since 1987, when the Secretary of State for Education and Science published a consultation document on the National Curriculum (DES, 1989) there have been statutory requirements to teach and assess certain curriculum areas. In other words, part of a school's curriculum has been imposed from an external source. The statutory requirements and the assessment processes have changed almost annually and will no doubt continue to do so. Schools must have a flexible management structure that not only allows these changes to be absorbed but reacts positively to continuous new initiatives and changes.

The intention of the National Curriculum was and is to ensure that all pupils aged between 5 and 14, i.e. before examination courses begin, study a broad and balanced range of subjects throughout their school career. Progress through teacher assessments during each year and by standard assessment tasks (SATs) at 7,11 and 14 will be checked and reported to parents, LEAs and the DFE. The structure of much of the curriculum, through the National Curriculum together with 'standard' assessments, was designed to enable schools to be more accountable to parents, governors and their own teachers. Judgements may be able to be made of how individuals, classes and schools compare to the national SATs results. Theoretically, parents will be able to take decisions about schools by examining each school's record of achievement within the National Curriculum. Assessing pupils, despite being a legal obligation, has been implemented, changed, reviewed and changed again. The purpose of the assessment has in fact changed. Gipps and Stobart (1993) suggest that what began as a formative approach to provide feedback about an individual's progress and which could have been part of their record of achievement, has become a summative means of evaluating school and LEA performance by means of aggregated data. Extra subjects have come on line and the SATs have changed each year since the pilot tests in 1990. The paperwork to be read, implemented and assessed has proved to be difficult. The ideals have proved delicate to manage even in the most effective schools, and teacher, headteacher, governor and parent anger has resulted in changes being made that will reduce the teacher assessments and the number of SATs being used.

It is difficult to write about the National Curriculum without being instantly out of date. The Dearing Report (1994) is hopefully the last in a long line of changes. It was commissioned by the government to examine the whole of the National Curriculum and assessment after complaints and test boycotts by teachers. The report suggested that the National Curriculum should be streamlined to release one day a week for teachers and schools to use at their discretion, provided that the reduction was not taken from the time used for the core subjects. A further recommendation was that the ten-level assessment scale would be simpler and would stop at the end of Key Stage 3. In assessing pupils, teachers would no longer have to use tick sheets and other complex methods. According to the report, this meant that teachers' work-load would be cut, releasing time to do other things.

Dearing also recognized that continuous change was not appropriate and suggested, much to most teachers' relief, that while the National Curriculum would be reviewed it would only be examined once more and by the end of 1995 would be finished. From then on there would be no further changes for five years.

WHAT IS THE NATIONAL CURRICULUM?

There are ten core and foundation subjects. They include:

Core subjects

Mathematics
English
Science

Foundation subjects

Technology
History
Geography
Art
Music
Physical education
Modern languages (from the beginning of Key Stage 3)

Religious education needs to be added to this list, as do wider curriculum areas such as personal and social education, education and industry, etc. All these areas have been the subject of advice from the National Curriculum Council.

The main aspects of each subject are defined in Attainment Targets (ATs) and Programmes of Study (PoS), which are listed within each Key Stage in the National Curriculum documents. Attainment Targets are defined from the Programmes of Study and set more specific targets for the knowledge, skills and understanding which pupils are expected to master as they progress through the school. Brighouse and Moon (1990) suggest that the ATs provide the basis for national and school-based assessments at 7, 11 and 14. The Programmes of Study, however, set out the essential knowledge, skills and processes which need to be covered by pupils in each subject at each stage of schooling. Pollard and Tann (1993) argue that all PoS are intended to be used by schools in constructing their own specific schemes of work.

At the end of each Key Stage there are statements against which pupils are assessed. These are called Statements of Attainment (SoA) and they provide an even more precise detailing of Attainment Targets. They attempt to describe what is expected at each of the ten levels of attainment and they provide the specifications against which tests, assessments, judgements and decisions are made about individual pupils. Although there are slight variations within subjects, the content of each National Curriculum subject is laid down in a similar way. Planning and teaching most of the subjects involves thinking about the Attainment Targets and the Programmes of Study simultaneously, because pupils can only usually meet the ATs by acquiring the content prescribed by the PoS. As they progress through the levels of attainment (Box 4.3), pupils are able to demonstrate a wider and deeper knowledge of the content of each subject. There are slight variations of this, especially in art and PE, and of course there are no guarantees that there will not be other changes while this book is being written and read.

Box 4.3 Key stages and levels of attainment

Key Stage 1 ages 5–7	Levels 1–3	Average level 2
Key Stage 2 ages 7–11	Levels 2–5	Average level 4
Key Stage 3 ages 11–14	Levels 3–7	Average level 6
Key Stage 4 ages 14–16	Levels 7–10	Difficult because of GCSE

Despite the fact that there are 'average' levels of attainment, e.g. Level 2 at KS1 (age 7), and that theoretically teachers can recognize what programmes of study might be relevant to their pupils, the Key Stages and ten levels present problems. The most important is that at age 11 the span of levels in a class may be from Level 3 to Level 7 and at age 14 this could be 3 to 8 (DES, 1988). If this is seen in terms of ten subjects across all the levels it is easy to see the difficulties involved in planning, teaching and assessment. The managerial implications are vast. Campbell *et al.* (1987) suggest that there are several key management issues associated with attainment levels and assessment which need to be addressed.

Entitlement

There is an assumption within the National Curriculum that pupils are entitled to a broad and balanced curriculum that draws on their individual talents. The major concern to head-teachers and curriculum leaders will be to avoid planning just to meet the needs of the prescribed PoS within the ten subject areas.

Consensus

There has to be consensus that the levels of attainment within the subject actually work and do assess individual pupils at specific ages, as well as consensus that individual classrooms and whole schools will have the resources, finance and teacher skills available to teach and assess what is statutorily laid down.

National Curriculum content and attainment targets

The National Curriculum exists to contain separate subjects and because of this separation it is not always easy to reconcile it with the thematic approach of the primary school. At the same time it can be perceived that, by having Attainment Targets at all ages, these targets might not be met by individual pupils at a specific age and this may well create a sense of early failure. This is especially true if individuals stay at a certain attainment level for a considerable period of time.

Professionalism

Professional control over the content of the curriculum has to a large extent been taken away from teachers. Motivating staff to maintain their professional grip on the processes of teaching and to a certain degree on choosing aspects of each subject is an important part of the management of schools.

Responsiveness

Effective teachers usually recognize that the curriculum needs to start from the pupil's own knowledge and ability as far as is possible within the constraints of examinations at 16 and 18. By prescribing the content of what is to be taught and learned in specific Key Stages, The National Curriculum to some extent moves these decisions away from the teacher and the school to the DFE and SCAA. The Dearing Report (1994) should, if it is accepted and acted upon, present a modified curriculum and assessment structure which might mean that it has to be managed in a slightly simpler way, although by theoretically releasing one day each week the report does stress that the 'work' done during this time is part of a rigorous process of accountability to both governors and inspectors. It is also apparent that teacher assessments will play more of a role in Key Stage SATs. In order to make this effective schools have to moderate their assessments more carefully and produce key portfolios of this moderated work, especially in the core subjects. Certainly the suggested reduction in SATs helps teachers, because it means reducing the amount of time spent on them. What schools have to beware of, however, is reducing the curriculum to match the reduced assessments.

DIFFERENTIATION AND MATCH

It is difficult to be totally effective in ensuring pace, rigour and challenge for able pupils while at the same time making sure that low achievers complete work with understanding and enjoyment. Harlen (1979) and Bennett *et al.* (1984), together with most HMI reports since the mid-1970s, have recognized that differentiation and matching the level of work to pupils' needs has always been a problem in both primary and secondary classrooms.

The HMI report (DES, 1990) suggested rather vaguely that at Key Stage 1 nearly all the work in the core subjects was pitched at levels 1 and 2 and that there needed to be more attention paid to improving tasks at more than one ability level in classes and groups. While Dearing (1994) has suggested some reductions, teachers are still expected to be familiar with a huge number of Attainment Targets and hundreds of statements of attainment. This is more of a problem for the generalist primary class teacher than for those working within the boundaries of one, or at the most two subjects in a secondary school. Many schools have embarked on various methods of assessment which, together with the research activities developed by the consortiums designing the SATs, have revealed the continuing problem of match and how teachers may not always be able to correctly assess the ability levels of their pupils. For example, the NFER/Bishop Grosseteste consortium revealed that 34 per cent of children fared better in the SAT reading scores than in the teacher assessment, 8 per cent did worse and 58 per cent did as expected. Nearly half of the children fared better in speaking and listening, and in Science 74 per cent did better than expected. Writing was the only area where the teacher assessments of these 7-year-old pupils were higher than the SAT scores. In general terms the SAT scores were higher in 21 per cent of cases, lower in 16 per cent and the same in 63 per cent (*Times Educational Supplement*, 16 November 1990). There are many arguments to suggest that the SATs were and are very flawed assessment instruments and the fact that the SATs and teacher assessments were 'right' 63 per cent of the time suggests a successful record by teachers. In one sense this can be considered a good correlation when the number of assessments that teachers have to make is balanced in the primary school against the number of 'subjects' and the number of children in each class. However, match and differentiation remain key issues which, despite all the real and imagined obstacles, must be cause for concern.

INDIVIDUAL TEACHERS AND MATCH

The observation and recording of what pupils are actually doing lies at the heart of matching classroom work to an individual's ability. This is the fundamental starting-point and schools must manage assessment processes and the recording of assessments in such a way that teachers can understand what their own assessments tell them and identify strengths and weaknesses in their pupils from the assessments of their colleagues. It takes time, skill and patience to manage this as a whole-school issue but it needs to dominate long-term, short-term and medium-term planning. In trying to itemize what general issues are important, the following are suggested:

- we need information on the stages pupils pass through in their development;
- we need to develop methods to find out where pupils are now;
- we need to know about the kinds of activities and approaches which are likely to help pupils take the next step and make progress;
- we need to make sure that short-term aims are met before we continue and that when we do move forward through the curriculum we plan for continuity of purpose from week to week and, in the longer term, between all classes, year groups and Key Stages.

In order to achieve this there has to be a structure within the school, within year groups and within classrooms which ensures a smooth flow of events and helps to achieve continuity. This requires whole-staff discussion and whole-staff agreement in terms of adopting the planning structures that the school designs. Match and differentiation within the classroom and after the basic planning structure has been agreed is where it will succeed or fail. This process requires a lot of teacher–pupil contact and will involve year team and department or Key Stage meetings to negotiate and debate *what the pupils are doing; what they are learning; what use it is;* and *what pupils need to do next.* There needs to be a balance between pupil choice and teacher direction within a framework where the teacher has a clear knowledge of the stages they want children to reach. Time must be made available for curiosity, co-operation, perseverence, responsibility, independence, originality, open-mindedness and self-evaluation in the classroom.

Montgomery (1989) suggests three ways of modifying teaching technique to achieve some degree of differentiation: she calls the first *differentiation by giving more time* and by using this method she suggests that if the teaching is aimed towards the middle range of ability, the slower learners and lower attainers will experience difficulties and lose motivation. Most teachers try to give these pupils more time. This is the least efficient method of dealing with the problem because the rest of the group or class receive less time and the able pupils who finish quickly have time to become disruptive.

The second method that she advocates is known as *differentiation by content level* and this is merely a form of streaming by ability within the same class. It is a widely used method because it limits the problems pupils have with the material and allows the teacher to spread attention fairly between all pupils. However, the pupils will know who is being given lower-level work and may regard this as of lower status, so making this form of differentiation potentially socially divisive. Its success or failure depends on the attitude of the teacher and to some extent the attitude of the school towards individual pupils' needs.

The third suggestion is *differentiation by personal contribution*. This is where pupils are set the same task but the manner in which it is set and the strategies for its completion, together with the acceptance of different outcomes, mean that individuals work at their own level. This work relies on individual and group strategies and a co-operative approach. It can avoid social divisions and overcome attention-seeking and disruption and all pupils should feel some kind of ownership of both the content of the curriculum and the processes they are going through.

PROBLEMS WITH MATCH

Bennett *et al.* (1984) suggest that busy teachers sometimes assume that if a pupil is getting on with his or her work quietly and peacefully then match has been achieved. This is not necessarily true. Many pupils accept what is given to them and give no obvious signals that their task is too easy, too difficult or repetitive. It is also difficult to differentiate and achieve match if there is too much reliance on a single published scheme. Such resources are often more concerned with mechanical progress, procedure and content than with allowing for individual differences and rates of understanding. At the very least, there must be many published resources if the needs of a wide range of abilities are to be met and if teachers are to avoid a narrow range of skills, fragmented experiences and low expectations. Match is often difficult to achieve when there has to be a concentration on closed areas of knowledge. This is difficult to overcome as a pupil becomes older and there are more demands centring around examinations. The National Curriculum itself is governed by 'areas of knowledge' in the subject divisions and the Programmes of Study within each subject. The processes of teaching, however, should allow for open-ended study with some responsibility for their own learning placed in the hands of pupils. It is difficult to overcome problems such as these as well as recognizing ways forward. The considerable anxiety about the pace of change can result in teachers feeling de-skilled and undervalued. To be successful and effective in teaching the curriculum to every child, there have to be initiatives within and outside the school which improve staff development and promote the view that curriculum planning can both include the National Curriculum and move beyond it to meet the needs of all pupils.

PLANNING THE CURRICULUM

The National Curriculum provides the detailed content of most areas of the curriculum. The school's actual curriculum has to be wider than the statutory National Curriculum and will include such 'subjects' as personal and social education. Of course, the increased numbers of subjects to be taught within a finite time span will mean that both the method of teaching and the time allocated to different curriculum areas will have to be decided after sensitive and careful debate.

A useful way of doing this is to look at the planning in terms of long term, i.e across a year group or a Key Stage; medium term, i.e. over a period of a half or whole term; and short term, i.e. a day or week. It is useful to suggest how this might happen and who will be involved. It is impossible to suggest all the ways in which individual schools can do their detailed long- and short-term plans but we must try to suggest what has to be included if the curriculum is to be managed effectively.

Curriculum planning in the long term

It is appropriate to plan either across a year or even a Key Stage in order to give pupils in a year group common experiences. The planning should involve as broad a spectrum of informed colleagues as possible, including all those who are actually teaching the classes. The kind of informed discussion that should take place means that continuity, progression and broad learning objectives are all considered and that the purposes of planning in the long term ensure: coverage of all National Curriculum subjects across the year or Key Stage; progression; balance; appropriate allocations of time; appropriate links between subjects, and continuity between years and Key Stages.

Long-term planning has to reflect the overall philosophy of the school and, as Pollard and Tann (1993) suggest, it should tie in with the aims statement, the School Development Plan (see Chapter 2, this volume) and be fully discussed with school governors who have legal responsibility for the school curriculum. This is the broad swathe of curriculum planning. Medium- and short-term planning is more precise and represents 'the statements of purpose and framework for action' (Pollard and Tann, 1993, p.158).

Curriculum planning in the medium term

Here, the time span should be over one month, a half term or term and, as with long-term planning, all teachers who are involved in the teaching should be part of the planning team. The main aim is to define the long-term plans in terms of coherent blocks of time as well as to suggest the sequence of the content and the links between subjects and specific subject planning. The outcomes of the planning discussions must make sure that: specific learning objectives will be identified; priority and depth will be established; resource requirements will be known; assessment opportunities and criteria will be established; and strategies for differentiation will have been discussed.

Curriculum planning in the short term

Here the individual teacher has to create lesson plans on a daily and weekly basis. The purpose of this more detailed planning should identify specific learning activities which will meet the objectives identified in medium-term planning, suggest evidence of attainment and inform future planning. It should certainly make sure that there will be: a balance of activities/lessons throughout the week; differentiation; opportunities for feedback from pupils; time for assessment and monitoring; evaluation; and modifications to medium-term plans.

In looking at planning in this way, it is possible to see many of the management threads discussed in earlier chapters. For example, it is important to plan together and to work in teams within a whole school plan which has recognized aims and objectives. As well as parents, the governors are involved in formulating the original aims and Development Plan. The links between such meticulous planning and other areas of management, such as accountability and communicating to parents what the school is actually doing, are discussed in later chapters. One area that is certainly very much a part of the public debate on education is that of assessing what is taught and learned.

TEACHER ASSESSMENTS

The Dearing report (1994) has changed some of the structures and processes of the National Curriculum. It recognizes the administrative load which teachers have seen as part of assessments. The suggested planning structure in this chapter has differentiation and planning for assessment as part of the processes teachers need to attach importance to. Dearing (1994) implies that in the future management of assessment there should be a reduction in the work-load in certain areas where teachers had kept too detailed records in the past. There are, the report suggests, no requirements to tick off every Statement of Attaiment associated with a particular level. Judgement of whether a pupil is working at a particular level will depend on the teacher's assessment of which level best corresponds to the pupil's performance as a whole, using the statements of attainment as a guide. How this reduction in the amount of assessment and recording is managed is a matter for each school, and demands considerable skill for individual teachers when they are managing their own classrooms. They must be able to track pupils' progress satisfactorily, so that all concerned are able to tell, at important moments in their school career, what level of attainment they have reached. Records of achievement, profiles, record sheets, everyday marking and samples of pupils' work all have a part to play in this process.

MANAGING THE CLASSROOM

Assessment should not be separate from teaching and learning but part of the long-, medium- and short-term planning. It needs to have a purpose other than to tell us how an individual has performed. The present system has been partly recognized by Dearing as being unwieldy. Gipps and Stobart (1993) go even further and suggest that it is judgemental, summative, fragmenting and instruction driving. They suggest that the whole process of assessment should move towards a system where competence would be established through continuous assessment based on exemplar materials that are provided for them. Unfortunately, it is not yet possible to state with any clarity what the future methods of assessments will be. It seems, however, that teachers and schools will have a larger part to play.

This means that there will need to be whole-school structures and systems in place as well as those which apply to individual teachers managing their classrooms. It is essential that the management of assessments is seen to be effective. What has to be remembered is that they are no longer the sole property of the school. Many assessment results are public property and are seen by those outside the school who will probably have a vested interest in what they believe the 'scores' on such assessments say about the school's success or failure. The School Examinations and Assessment Council (DES, 1989) suggests that when creating structures and systems for managing assessments the results of any assessments should be made available to the following people, who have a legitimate interest in the outcomes of the assessment of individuals and groups:

- The pupil as evidence of progress.
- Parents so that they can work in partnership with the school.
- The pupil's next teacher to know what has been done and how far each individual has progressed and to ensure continuity.
- The headteacher so that there can be central monitoring of progress throughout the school.
- Prospective parents need an indication of what the school sets out to achieve and how well their child's needs may be met.
- The LEA will need certain assessment results in sufficient detail to recognize curriculum needs in order to plan INSET programmes.

The kind of information available has to begin in the classroom, and demands that teachers are not only skilful in assessing pupils against the SATs but that they are skilled in the processes of teaching. Classroom management techniques and skills associated with effective teaching are discussed in both chapters 9 and 12, but certain general issues have to be raised because they demand whole-school agreement. Many of these issues are discussed by OFSTED (1993) where they divide those factors that are associated with effective and successful classroom practice into the following two areas: organization in the classroom, and teaching techniques.

ORGANIZATION IN THE CLASSROOM

How pupils are grouped so that teaching and learning can take place largely depends on what the aims, objectives and outcomes of the lesson are intended to be. How the class is managed should also be partly governed by the need to plan teaching so that there is time to give instructions, to teach the whole class, and to teach individuals and groups in such a way that it is possible to move between activities to instruct, question, explain and assess. There should also be a recognition by the teacher that pupils' time needs to be planned carefully so that realistic deadlines are set and routines within the classroom are well established and easily understood.

TEACHING TECHNIQUES

It would be futile and certainly unhelpful to try and cover all those aspects of 'how teachers teach' that are currently available. What is well understood is the difficulty of categorizing teaching styles by using such labels as progressive, traditional and formal. Boydell (1980) suggested that, depending upon circumstances, class teaching, group work and individual approaches can all be equally successful. Some of the techniques that are appropriate include:

- Good oral instructions to set the scene and explain tasks to the whole class or group.
- Opportunities provided for pupils to raise questions about tasks or activities and for teachers to listen to pupils.
- Skilful questioning to encourage children to think and use the knowledge they already have.
- Observation of pupils' work to help with assessment and the regular monitoring of pupil progress.
- Teacher interaction and purposeful intervention in pupils' work.
- The use of good work by pupils as a model to stimulate other pupils.
- Targeting the teaching to specific individuals or groups.
- Appropriate use of praise and encouragement.
- Feedback to pupils during lessons.
- Continuous assessment as an aid to the learning process.
- Criteria for assessing work is made explicit to the pupils.

It is important to emphasize that although it is possible to suggest certain effective teaching techniques and certain ways of organizing the classroom, there is no simple 'right' technology of teaching. Teachers have to be sufficiently flexible to adapt methods and styles to circumstances that are generated by the interaction between pupils, curriculum content and the teaching and learning processes. It should be possible, however, to suggest to those who manage schools that there are certain skills, styles and techniques that need to be encouraged and developed because they are effective and successful.

WHAT MAKES A GOOD TEACHER

If high-quality learning experiences are part of an effective school, it is important to know what needs to be managed when the quality of the actual teaching is considered. Smith (1988) takes the factors summarized from OFSTED (1993) a stage further by pointing out that the organization of a classroom and the techniques involved rely heavily on the teaching 'style'. While some of these issues appear in later chapters on appraisal and inspection, it is worth considering them at the end of this section. The first of Smith's lists tries to define what happens in an effective classroom when the teacher's action is related to the content and processes of the curriculum. Smith looks at what should happen in an ideal classroom by attempting to identify 'good' and 'bad' teaching styles. The assumptions behind this view are simply that the better the teacher and the more effective the classroom the higher the quality of the teaching and learning process.

An effective classroom

This is primarily concerned with the management of pupils and resources within the finite space of a classroom and is concerned with the following:

- Pupils should be involved in the work they are doing and 'own' part of it because they have been involved in the planning process.
- What the pupil brings to the task has been noted and taken into account, thus helping to match the task to the pupil.
- There are opportunities for framing and solving problems.
- Each pupil is helped to make sense of the world they live in.
- Pupils are encouraged to work co-operatively in groups. When the short-term curriculum planning is organized, targets and outcomes are built into the programme together with the flexibility necessary for pupils' individual needs.
- One of the teaching styles used is that of facilitator, so that pupils do not rely on adult help all the time.
- Record-keeping is thorough and realistic.
- The curriculum has breadth and balance.

Of course, how a teacher behaves and the kinds of styles he or she adopts also have a significant influence on the quality of the teaching and learning process.

A good teacher

Smith's (1988) 'good' teacher is able to raise pupils' self-esteem, develop a positive work ethos without resorting to a punitive regime, praise rather than criticize and use pupils' enthusiasms and interests in a creative and positive way.

There are obvious management implications raised by such a list. If 'good' teaching and 'good' curriculum management does rely on the effectiveness of teachers who can demonstrate their commitment to such positive styles and techniques, then schools must work towards a whole-school agreement that certain things must happen to the curriculum in the classroom. To reach this agreement there has to be a commitment to change, leadership that promotes change, and team work that means working positively together to take decisions that will promote such change. The classroom will no longer be able to be 'closed' to the outside world. There is an overt suggestion that parents know what is happening and may well be able to help, certainly in primary schools. There is also an attitude towards the learners where individuality, creativity and enthusiasm are valued. The leadership of schools and the creation of a Development Plan within the bounds of an ethos that values such attributes must move alongside what is required in the classroom. It must be a whole-school issue that accepts that what is important in the classroom also has whole-school implications.

THE TEACHERS' WIDER ROLE

Unfortunately, the Education Reform Act means that looking at what happens inside classrooms involves identifying a wider definition of teaching. Busher and Saran (1990) suggest that teachers should no longer be seen purely in terms of the classroom and of being responsible for pupil performance. Their other specified duties which have widened their role include:

essential administration to maintain the organization of the school; attendance at parents', curriculum development and in-service meetings; and more detailed preparation, marking and assessment. What in the past have been recognized as the teachers' classroom responsibilities have widened and developed to include administrative and managerial duties. Campbell *et al.* (1991), when studying Key Stage 1 teachers, recognized that there was a common perception among teachers that work-loads were unreasonable and unmanageable and that a consider-able amount of time was being spent on relatively low-level administration such as registers, collecting money, moving pupils round the school, etc. Campbell *et al.* conclude that if the curriculum is to be managed successfully within the class-room there are management implications for headteachers to consider such as limiting the amount of superfluous informa-tion teachers receive, limiting the number of twilight sessions, not making teachers feel that they have a time management problem because of the extra workloads and improving the pupil–teacher ratio.

With these suggestions in mind, perhaps it is useful to refer back to the main purpose of managing the curriculum and the recent continuous curriculum reform. It must set out to improve the quality of teaching and learning and, of course, the achievements of pupils. It must also be concerned with the abil-ity of teachers to relate all aspects of the curriculum, its content and the teaching and learning processes, into a coherent whole. This is extremely important. Schools and those who manage them must be able to use the energies and expertise of the whole staff to create and adopt strategies for a whole curriculum that meets the needs of their pupils. This will mean meeting changing curriculum needs as well as the statutory require-ments of the National Curriculum. Teachers meeting these challenges still need to be able to operate effectively in their classrooms. It is difficult for those trying to establish what suc-cessful teaching is to identify the skills needed for 'delivering' a broad and balanced curriculum. Schön (1983) raises an interest-ing point on which to end this chapter by describing the skilled actions of a teacher as 'knowledge in action'. This, it is suggest-ed, can be demonstrated in action but is extremely difficult to verbalize. In other words, 'good' teachers can teach well, i.e.

they can demonstrate their classroom management skills and all the other wider roles, but have difficulty in actually stating what it is that makes them effective practitioners.

CHAPTER SUMMARY

There are several key elements when considering the management of the curriculum. There needs to be breadth and balance in terms of the content of what is taught and the time allocated to each subject. The curriculum needs to be relevant to all pupils and this is achieved through creating teaching styles and methods of classroom management that allow differentiation to take place. What is taught in particular year groups cannot be seen as existing alone. It needs to be part of the school's overall plan where progression and continuity are managed through the processes of long-, medium- and short-term planning. The curriculum content is largely, but not totally contained within the elements of the National Curriculum. The content, however, must be 'delivered' to learners using effective processes which include not only the academic but also the capacity to apply what is learned and the ability to persevere and know how to learn more. Teachers need to have the necessary skills to assess the curriculum in terms of where individual pupils are, where they need to go next and what steps need to be taken to ensure this process. Curriculum management needs to recognize that certain methods of teaching, that is, the delivery of the curriculum, are more effective than others and that while there will be variations in content and process from school to school, such differences should not lead to the sacrifice of any part of the breadth and balance necessary for pupil success.

FURTHER READING

Dearing Report (1994) *Implications for Teacher Assessments*. London: SEAC/NCC.

OFSTED (1993) *Curriculum Organization and Classroom Practice: A Follow-up Report*. London: OFSTED.
Both reports are important for the impact they have had on how teachers and schools examine the taught curriculum.

Gipps, G. and Stobart, G. (1993) *Assessment: A Teachers' Guide to the Issues*. London: Hodder & Stoughton.
A useful and thorough examination of the development, functions and uses of assessment and its impact on pupils, teachers and the curriculum.

Harlen, W. (1979) 'Making the match', *Primary Education Review*, Spring, No. 6.
This article is an early examination of differentiation and match. Many of the issues raised are relevant in the 1990s.

Montgomery, D. (1989) *Managing Behaviour Problems*. London: Hodder & Stoughton.
A very useful book which, despite some lapses into stereotyping, deals practically with many aspects of teaching styles and classroom management.

Moon, B. and Shelton-Mayes, A. (eds) (1994) *Teaching and Learning in the Secondary School*. London: Routledge/Open University.
A useful compilation of articles on many aspects of the school curriculum.

Smith, R. (1990b) *The Effective School Vol. 2: Classroom Techniques and Management*. Lancaster: Framework Press.
This pack of materials suggests many practical activities that individuals and teams can use to develop their planning techniques and teaching styles.

CHAPTER 5

FINANCE AND RESOURCES

CHAPTER OVERVIEW

The local management of schools (LMS), which delegates
financial responsibility of a fixed budget to individual
schools, has given both headteachers and governing bodies
greater managerial functions. The aims of LMS were to make
schools accountable to parents and the community regarding
how they spend their delegated budgets and to give governors
of all county and voluntary secondary schools and of larger
primary schools the freedom to take expenditure decisions
which matched their own priorities. This chapter examines
the basic principles of LMS and some of the contradictions.
It also deals with the governors' responsibilities, the effect
LMS and budgeting has on the management of schools, how
the budget is divided between schools and within individual
institutions and how spending the money that is available
can be delegated.

THE AIMS OF LMS AND GOVERNORS' RESPONSIBILITIES

It is reasonably clear that local management of schools is a movement that was designed to remove much of the control of education from locally elected representatives and transfer it to teachers, headteachers and school governors. In many ways this has been part of a government policy which, on the one hand, has fragmented education by giving individual schools more control of how they manage their 'affairs' and on the other has removed local education authority (LEA) support and replaced it with much of the control of the 'fragments' coming from central government.

Individual schools are now increasingly able to set their own aims and objectives because of the new educational changes, and it is important for them to have the financial control to meet their objectives. Gilbert (1990) adds a further dimension by suggesting that LMS was introduced to allow schools to decide for themselves how best to spend money to meet their pupils' needs. If this was the case, and there is probably some truth in this assumption, the concern would not so much be the idea of self-management as concern that the budget would be so small that the school would be unable to manage itself effectively.

The Financial Delegation to Schools offers the suggestion that: 'Governors would be free to spend the delegated budget at their discretion, provided that their own and the LEA's statutory duties were met' (DES, 1987, p.3). Headteachers have always controlled certain items of finance including school funds that are raised by the school and funds allocated by the LEA (in the past called capitation) for consumables, materials and equipment. It would have been a foolish head who did not acquaint the school's governing body with the sum of this money and how it was spent.

Local management of schools, however, has given schools responsibilities for much larger amounts of money. In taking much of the responsibility away from LEA officers who were 'experts' in financial management and who were paid to manage educational budgets and giving it to unpaid governors and headteachers who may or may not have the skills, interest and enthusiasm to do the job properly and effectively, it has created new managerial tasks. It has already been emphasized that LMS represents a fundamental shift of responsibilities between LEAs, the community and individual schools. It is however important to recognize that it does not stand alone in this shift but has to be seen alongside other factors such as open enrolment, City Technology Colleges and grant-maintained schools. Open enrolment occurred when the Education Reform Act gave more freedom to parents in their choice of schools and radically changed the concept of an individual school's catchment area which had traditionally been the area where most of the school's pupils came from. Grant-maintained schools were given the opportunity to 'opt out' of LEA control and for their administrative needs and budgets to be met by central rather than local government. The creation of City Technology Colleges meant that certain secondary schools would be classified as centres of excellence in some way, e.g. for their teaching of information technology, and once again would be funded differently and more favourably from both national and industrial sources. Many of these 'innovations' have been introduced because it is believed by some influential pressure groups, for example, the Adam Smith Institute (1984), that educational standards need to be raised and that one of the most appropriate ways to do this is to provide more educational choice.

LOCAL MANAGEMENT OF SCHOOLS AND CHOICE

Some of the key issues raised by these radical methods of funding schools seem to be contradictory and difficult to reconcile with how schools can be managed effectively. The basic idea seems to be to secure maximum delegation of finance and choices to governing bodies, schools and parents. Open enrolment is about choice of schools. Because of the legislation of the late 1980s and early 1990s which is related to National Curriculum testing at ages 7, 11 and 14, parents are expected to have more information on which to base their choice of schools because they will have access to more information about individual schools. Hughes *et al.* (1990), however, reported that proximity of the local school was the most important factor in influencing parental choice of a primary school. While it seems reasonably obvious that choice of a secondary school is bound to be linked to successful examination results, there is no reason to suppose that Hughes *et al.*'s first ten issues influencing parental choice cannot be linked to schools serving the whole age range. Rather than reflect the effective management of finances or high test scores the first ten factors in order of priority which parents looked for were: relationships between parents, teachers and children; the staff; the atmosphere; the ethos of the school; good discipline; wide-ranging education offered; the headteacher; development of the whole child; academic results; and good resources. It is useful to recognize that academic results are in ninth place and yet part of the package of reforms which includes LMS relies on the assumption that test results will increase accountability, increase competition between schools and assist parents in choosing a school for their child.

Much of this information, especially the SAT results, will be difficult to understand and almost impossible to use in comparing one school with another. There are many reasons for this. Gipps and Stobart (1993, p. 97) certainly envisage difficulties when they suggest that comparing the performance between individuals and schools is very problematic:

> Girls are differentially allocated to lower status maths exams; ethnic minority students are underestimated by their teachers; girls have had to do better than boys on the eleven plus in order to get a grammar school place; girls perform better than boys in public exams yet few go on to higher education. And so on. Reducing bias in assessment is only part of the task.

Once again, this questions the assumption that the information flow from schools and governing bodies will help parents to make a more informed decision when choosing schools.

There will have to be ways whereby heads and governors can 'market' what they have to offer in managing schools. They have to make sure that they attract parents and their children because a significant part of their budget allocation depends on how many childen are on a school's roll. This area of funding moves with the pupil. If a school loses pupils for any reason, or fails to attract them, they receive less money. If a school gains pupils, either at the beginning of the year or part of the way through, they receive a higher allocation of funds. There is of course a limit to how many pupils a school can take. There will therefore be a time when the school is full and cannot take any further pupils. This will to some extent be helped by the concept of 'standard number', where schools are allocated the number of pupils that should be in each of their year groups. Popular schools that are 'full' and have reached their 'standard number' will not be of much help to those parents who are exercising their right to choose. By being oversubscribed, popular schools will receive a relatively high income from the number of pupils on roll and schools that are undersubscribed and probably less popular will, over the period of years that they are less popular, receive reduced funds and, by implication, this will increase the likelihood that there will be a continuing downward spiral that can only increase the difficulty of turning a 'poor' school into a 'popular' one.

LOCAL MANAGEMENT OF SCHOOLS AND THE MARKET ECONOMY

It has already been suggested that there is something flawed about the assumption that parents will make choices based on large amounts of information that are provided by schools such as SAT results and subsequent league tables. Dennison (1990), like Hughes *et al.* (1990), suggests that it is more likely that parents will consider a few, or even one factor when choosing a school. The largest numbers of parents choose the nearest school but, as Dennison makes clear, a decision may be triggered by some rather mundane unplanned event such as a pupil misbehaving outside the school or a report of a sporting triumph in the local press. In trying to make schools and education part of a market economy there is the possibility of creating a two-tier system. Schools that are less popular will lose money and even with the most enlightened management will find it difficult to improve what they have to offer parents. Rather than a system of state education, where schools share the responsibilities and develop strategies of working together, this kind of unfair competition will, despite the fact that the National Curriculum is designed to provide equality of opportunity, only divide schools into the 'haves' and the 'have less'.

Those who are managing schools in such divisive circumstances may well see that the creation of grant-maintained schools and City Technology Colleges is removing the icing on a rapidly shrinking cake and overtly changing the powers of LEAs and those local government officials who have been elected to take decisions on educational matters. When heads and teachers see their own budgets decline in proportion to those received by grant-maintained schools it might lead them to view the equality of opportunity provided by the National Curriculum with some cynicism. Grant-maintained status is achieved by parental choice and is funded from central government. Governors of such schools have far wider powers than those schools remaining within the 'control' of LEAs. It is reasonable to expect deep divisions to occur between grant-maintained and LEA schools, especially where, because of wider powers, GM schools have begun to operate selection systems which differ widely from those of local LEA schools. This could be seen as the real danger of not only the financial side of LMS, but the whole concept of removing LEAs in favour of schools becoming much more autonomous. Gilbert (1990) suggests that LMS will encourage schools to go down individual and isolationist paths which will slowly but inevitably break down the local systems of education and the co-operation between schools that has enabled LEAs to provide an excellent education which will not be achieved by each school going its own way. It is in this wider context that the main aims of LMS need to be seen. They have been stated as giving greater flexibility in the expenditure of the school's budget and allowing the school to respond more readily to the changing needs of its pupils and the local community. Of course the flaw here is that to do this, and to meet 'customer' expectations, the budget has to be adequate to meet the school's needs within the whole wider context of LMS.

The wider context of LMS

The financial side of LMS is fundamental but it has much wider implications than the allocation of resources. Three areas of particular concern are: appointments of teaching and ancillary staff; dismissals; disciplinary procedures; and marketing. The first two areas are now firmly in the hands of governors.

Because most schools and their governors lack the expertise necessary to manage such areas, it is essential that they take and follow, wherever practicable, the advice offered by LEA officers. Marketing is concerned with 'selling' the school's strengths to the local and wider community and whereas traditionally this has not been a major part of a school's management function, it now takes on a much more important role.

The shared responsibility of managing LMS lies with the governors who have the difficult task of working with and through the headteacher. Their increased responsibilities include the following:

- Teaching and other staff, i.e. salary, incentive allowances.
- Day-to-day premises maintenance, e.g. decorating, repairs, health and safety. This is mainly internal and does not always include the outside fabric of the building.
- All energy costs, i.e. electricity, gas, oil and water.
- Capitation purchases of books, furniture, etc.
- Rates, telephone, postage, etc.
- Insurance, supply cover, service contracts.
- Local bought-in services, e.g. peripatetic music staff, library services, etc.
- Bursar services and other administrative assistance formerly provided by the LEA.

These areas of responsibility may be viewed with either optimism or trepidation. Whatever, they have to be carried out and managed effectively so that the school's main function of educating its pupils can take place successfully. It is important for managers to find ways of effectively handling a budget, while at the same time recognizing the adverse effects it might have on the roles that headteachers and senior managers have to play. There are certain responsibilities laid firmly at the feet of governors and there is a need for headteachers to make sure that certain functions are carried out so that they can be released to perform other roles within the school. Governors need to take on managerial duties and they will need help and training to do this, as well as an acceptance by the school that there is a need for a strong partnership between headteacher, teachers, governors and parents. Deem (1992) makes the point quite clearly when suggesting that governors need to be seen as central to schools as organizations rather than as bit-part actors. This is very much the case when dealing with the complex issue of budgeting.

THE SCHOOLS BUDGET

Most LEAs are close to meeting all the government's statutory requirements relating to LMS and have delegated to schools approximately 90 per cent of the total education budget. It is impossible to indicate which position each LEA has reached in this delegation process but there are common positions that they are all rapidly moving towards.

The LEAs' educational budgeting is called the General Schools Budget. It is the amount of money available to be divided between all aspects of 'education'. It is set aside to meet direct and indirect total costs associated with LMS. In most LEAs it is separated into three budget headings.

Mandatory excepted items

These are items of expenditure not delegated to schools and are prescribed by the Secretary of State for Education. They include:

- Central administration
- Inspectors/advisers
- Capital expenditure
- Grants such as education support, travellers' children, LEA training, Section 11
- Home–school transport
- EEC grants.

Discretionary excepted items

These are either held centrally at the discretion of the LEA or are delegated to schools. There will be differences between individual LEAs but this area of the General Schools Budget can only be 10 per cent of the total.

It might or will include:

- LEA initiatives
- Governors' insurance
- School meals
- Structural repairs
- Educational psychologists (they are mandatory in many LEAs)
- Educational social workers
- Premises insurance
- Peripatetic teachers, e.g. music
- Pupil support
- Special staff costs, e.g. cover for long- or short-term illness
- Library, museum services

The aggregated schools budget

This is the amount of the General Schools Budget that is left after deducting mandatory and discretionary items and is the total amount available to be delegated to and managed by schools. It has to be made clear that rapid changes to LMS nationally and to the levels of delegation reached by different LEAs means that some of this information will have changed. This is especially true with special needs budgets, where statemented pupils take specific sums into schools for the purchase of educational psychologists' time, classroom assistants' time, etc.

MANAGING THE AGGREGATED SCHOOLS BUDGET

The Aggregated Schools Budget is important for the management of schools. It is the share of the budget that schools actually receive in any financial year. The delegated budget is the share over which an individual school's governing body is given control. How different LEAs calculate the amount that each school receives varies, but as Playfoot *et al.* (1989) argue, this amount (at least 75 per cent) is usually determined by the number of pupils on a school's roll weighted by age. In other words, older pupils are worth more money than younger ones, thus raising an issue about the value placed on primary education. It will include other factors affecting the needs of individual schools such as split sites, social needs, the number of children with special educational needs, etc. It is immediately obvious that keeping the school's pupil numbers high is extremely important. The more pupils in the school, the more money that is available.

What is less obvious, but is a key assumption in the local management of schools, is that the deployment of resources at the school level should lead to more effective learning. In order to achieve this, *Further Consultation on LMS Related Matters* (Warwickshire County Council, 1989) recognizes that it is important that the evaluation and monitoring of educational processes and outcomes are compatible with financial monitoring. In other words, the budget received by a school – that is, its delegated budget – and how it is split into component parts should contribute to an understanding of the educational direction and achievements of the school.

THE SCHOOL'S DELEGATED BUDGET

It is important to recognize that when the management implications of LMS are considered there are both positive and negative views about its effectiveness. This can affect how teachers, headteachers and governors react to the demands made on them and what some of the management priorities might be. If the positive implications of LMS, such as more financial independence, wider and greater choice and more freedom from bureaucracy, were accepted as a key management issue then some headteachers and governing bodies may well see this as almost a separate management structure and one that will dominate the school's management in a way that is detrimental to other areas such as staff development, planning and the actual delivery of the curriculum. On the other hand, the negative implications such as, for example, additional management tasks and responsibilities and the diversion of teacher time from the curriculum can take on absurd proportions and de-motivate headteachers, governors and teachers. A middle ground must be struck where finance and dividing the budget do not control the management but are tools to be used to improve teaching and learning.

DIVIDING THE BUDGET

It is important that the school knows what its budget is and how it is to be divided. To make the most of the freedom of choice provided by managing a budget and to cushion the negative points the total resources need to be managed effectively. Decisions have to be taken on basic set expenditure costs, estimated expenditure costs and what could be unpredictable contingency costs. To help reach these decisions various areas of the budget have to be costed out and linked to the School Development Plan and any new resource requirements. Gilbert (1990) goes so far as to suggest that by doing this, heads and governors will to some extent be able to limit some of the work involved in budget preparation and division, because, by basing it on the priorities identified in the School Development Plan, many of the decisions about areas of spending will be easy to make and the amounts of money to be spent will already be known.

What is really important is that LMS income in terms of the budget allocation must match expenditure. While there are opportunities to carry over funds from one year to the next or to carry through an overspend, it is not possible to plan to overspend.

The budget or income as discussed earlier is largely made up of money allocated because of pupil numbers. Schools can also charge for lettings to the community and make a slight income in this way, but the bulk of the 'income' or budget for the coming financial year is normally known in February and it is at this stage that heads, senior managers and governors need to create a financial plan that will work effectively for the needs of the school. This will mean concentrating on how to develop a few basic budget headings. While it cannot be a definitive list, most schools will have similar headings which include:

Basic set expenditure

- Salary costs including long-term supply insurance
- Contents insurance
- Bought-in contracts for repairs to equipment
- Bought-in library and museum services

- If special needs is part of the school budget then the cost of educational psychologists may be quite closely linked to the number of statements
- Rates, i.e buildings and water.

Estimated expenditure

- Energy costs
- Premise repairs and refurbishment
- Caretaking materials
- Furniture
- Teaching consumables, e.g. paper, exercise books, etc.
- Teaching resources, e.g. texts, computer hardware
- Externals, e.g. window cleaning
- Administrative costs, e.g. photocopiers, telephones.

Unpredictable contingency costs

- Unexpected repairs or health and safety issues
- Unforeseen curriculum needs, i.e. caused by new external demands
- Inaccurate costings of estimated expenditure
- Staff changes resulting in more expensive staffing costs for the financial year.

It will be obvious that there are responsibilities and management tasks needed to allocate and divide the funds available. Those schools which are able to manage their budgets effectively will have accepted the difficulties involved and will be aware that despite the additional management tasks, there is to some degree greater flexibility and more positive opportunities. An instance of this flexibility is the transfer of money from one budget heading to another, for example, if money has not been spent on staffing it can be used for redecoration. Hargreaves and Hopkins (1991) argue strongly for the empowering nature of LMS and how, if it is used well, it will help make schools better and more effective places for all pupils and teachers. Whether such independence, choice, flexibility and opportunity outweigh the additional tasks and responsibilities is perhaps a matter for debate. What is clear is that all the areas of expenditure have to be managed in such a way that the education of all pupils bene-fits. There has to be a reason for schools managing their finances successfully. The divisions of expenditure are convenient in that they split the spending up into more manageable and understandable sections, but they are not as absolute and clear-cut as is suggested. It is interesting and important to examine the overlaps and to try and link the three sections to each other and to the other aspects of school management.

Basic set expenditure

This is, as has been implied, largely fixed and less controllable than other sections. It is not totally static, however, and there are some significant choices to be made. Contracts, insurance and bought-in services are fixed for a year and it is known in advance whether the school changes them or they change because of increased costs from outside. Once fixed into a year's budget these costs usually come out of the budget automatically throughout the year.

Special educational needs

This has to have a short separate section because of its complex-ity and the fact that different authorities fund this area in differ-ent ways. To a certain extent it is part of the basic set expenditure because all schools receive special needs funding through whatever formula the LEA use to allocate budgets to schools. This may be determined by the number of free school meals the school is entitled to or, because of the lack of sophistication of such a measure, funds may be allocated after a thorough audit of the school's needs. These funds can be built in to the budgetary planning because they remain fixed and can be used to provide support staff, both teaching and non-teaching, teaching resources and support from outside agencies, such as behaviour support units, etc. There are certain funds, however, which are not part of the basic set expenditure. These are related to pupils who have a statement of special educational needs. If extra funds are necessary for such pupils they will 'follow' the pupil from school to school. While many schools know in advance who their statemented pupils are likely to be it might be the case that, due to the system of parental choice, pupils with statements might suddenly 'arrive' at a particular school bringing with them certain funds which have to be managed specifically for that pupil. This may well prove to be not only a sensitive but a difficult area of the budget to manage. It implies 'good' whole-school management and a well-structured special needs department which is good at meeting the needs of individual pupils and which can react swiftly to changing circumstances.

Salary costs

The largest proportion of any school's budget is salary costs. Eighty per cent and upwards of a typical budget goes on fixed salaries. Most of these costs are for teachers, although administrative and ancillary staff such as secretaries and bursars, caretakers, cleaners and lunch-time supervisors are all included. The numbers of teachers will be determined by the numbers of children on the school roll and the number of teaching groups that have to be formed. Similarly, more administrative staff, cleaners, etc. will be needed in larger schools than in smaller ones. Governors and managers will have to take decisions about how many of each category of employees they will need. While they are part of basic expenditure, they can also be flexible in many ways. Obviously, if fewer cleaners are employed than necessary, this may well result in issues that might involve health and safety; fewer lunch-time supervisors may create problems as to whether lunch-times in school are as safe as they might be. Employing fewer non-teaching staff such as classroom assistants will release funds to spend elsewhere and may or may not be an effective way forward.

Teaching costs

Because much of a school's budget is allocated in direct proportion to the number of pupils, a certain number of pupils have to represent one teacher. Again, governors and headteachers have to reach decisions as to what this proportion is. Their decisions not only affect the quality of education provided to pupils but may well have repercussions when parents are choosing schools for their children. Basic class sizes, tutor groups, etc. are important indicators for parental choice. A second basic factor involved when considering teachers as employees is that the older the teachers the more expensive they are. There should be, within the personnel policies decided by the governing body, some indication as to how this dilemma will be resolved when employing new staff. Has the best person been chosen for the job that is advertised, or will a new appointment depend on how much a teacher costs? The School Development Plan identifies curriculum needs over a three-year period. There are incentive allowances and some existing teachers are on higher points on the teachers' pay spine. It may well be that new curriculum initiatives as identified by the School Development Plan can move forward by adjusting the responsibilities of specific teachers. If this is not the case then to make the School Development Plan work it is important to take decisions about increasing a teacher's salary so that he or she can take on this extra responsibility. Once again, this is dependent on other decisions that are taken in other areas of the budget. It is important to recognize that the movement of large sums of money is possible in the area of salaries, but this must only be seen to work within the context of 'the best person for the job'. Cheapening the role of teachers by suggesting that lower pay improves the effectiveness of the school will not help develop and raise the morale of teachers. Reducing the teaching staff, or to a lesser extent other staff, releases money, and increasing staff involves finding large sums of money from the delegated budget. The fluctuation of pupil numbers from one year to another may make this possible, but hardly helps employment stability.

Estimated expenditure

This does not mean guessing what costs fall under which expenditure headings but assumes that it should be possible to base current costs on the expenditure of previous years. This is the most flexible section of the budget in terms of rapid changes in expenditure. However, in managing such areas as energy use, telephones, photocopying, etc., governors, heads and other senior managers should be aware that large amounts of time can be spent adjusting and readjusting these sections of the budget without making much difference to the total school budget because the amounts involved are so small. In other words, the question has to be asked: is it worth saving or moving a few hundred pounds around when the financial needs of the school actually involve thousands?

Energy savings are possible and schools do need to monitor energy use and adopt a workable energy policy through the expertise of the caretaker. It can result in money saved that can be used elsewhere in the budget. Repairing and refurbishing the school buildings is largely the responsibility of the school. External repairs, external decoration and other aspects of the heating plant, etc. usually remain the responsibility of the LEA although this varies between authorities. Advice is needed and can be bought in from the LEA or other sources. There needs to be a baseline agreement of what needs to be done to maintain health and safety standards and also a future plan to make sure that the inside of the school reflects pupil and teacher needs as well as meeting the needs of parents in terms of its looks and general maintenance. Schools periodically have to find funds from their budgets for redecorating, rebuilding, etc. If the money is not available then only very basic repairs will be completed.

Perhaps the budget area that can most easily lose money in lean years and benefit in years of plenty is the one related to furnishings, consumables, teaching materials, etc. Once again this should be School Development Plan- and curriculum-driven. There are obvious consumables which rely on a fixed budget with some kind of agreed annual increase but the management of change and new initiatives in curriculum innovation often requires increased funds. The sums of money that are being allocated in this way can be large. Certainly over a period of years they must have some effect on the success of the school and its pupils. Day *et al.* (1990) recognize the importance of planning but take this a step further by linking it to evaluation, where it is important to determine how well a decision has worked in practice.

EVALUATING THE BUDGET

Most schools have a central administrative team including governors who are responsible for monitoring spending of the budget. This does not mean that departments and individuals are not accountable for their particular part of the spending process. In a primary or secondary school it is relatively easy to evaluate whether an actual amount had been spent on, for example, maths textbooks. Indeed, Downes (1990) suggests that an accurate understanding of the costs of any curriculum spending and development should be available to all involved; otherwise a great deal of time can be wasted and the frustration level increased. This is certainly true if different departments are competing for funds from the budget when neither department knows what is available, what their share of the money might be and whether other departments might also need funding.

It is, however, more difficult, although more time-consuming (but equally important) to evaluate whether pupils are learning more, teachers are teaching more effectively, and whether the quality of assessments has improved by spending such an amount. There are all kinds of areas within financial budgeting where individuals and groups need to evaluate how money has been spent. It is important to do this on a regular basis, because unpredictable contingency costs such as a major unforeseen repair can create large deficits in any planned budget.

It is obvious that in order to evaluate the budget effectively there have to be decision-making processes already in place. Planning the budget carefully and thoroughly is essential. Levacic (1992) sees this planning process as three interlinked stages. First, there needs to be a decision-making structure which co-ordinates what the school expects the budget to actually provide. Second, everyone needs to know what choices are available and what will happen if certain choices are accepted and others rejected. Third, and this takes us from evaluation toward accountability, there needs to be an annual cycle of review, planning and implementation which brings together all the relevant parts of the budgeting process. If this is done thoroughly, if governors play their part, and if individuals who are responsible for that part of the budget that has been delegated to them monitor and evaluate their own spending carefully, there should be few problems. Most LEAs provide their schools with sophisticated finance packages for their computers and it is usually possible to use the expertise of finance officers whose job it is to meet headteachers and governors to help them to not only set an accurate budget but also monitor and evaluate spending on a regular basis. Schools have been delegated public money and therefore need to be able to account for how they spend it.

RESPONSIBILITY, ACCOUNTABILITY AND DELEGATION

Local Management of Schools has radically changed how finances are dealt with at school level although when staffing costs, which can take up to 85 per cent of the total budget are removed, what money is actually available for serious planning remains a fraction of the total budget. It must be accepted that in large secondary schools there are times when staff changes result in the need for large-scale financial decisions but in smaller schools much of the budget as described in earlier sections is fairly tightly targeted. The amounts available, however, are public funds and those who manage this money not only have to satisfy criteria laid down by financial auditors but they need to recognize that the responsibility for determining, managing and being accountable is at the heart of LMS (Maychell, 1994).

There are of course other 'spending' accounts held by schools: for example, journeys or general school funds, which can, together with Parent–Teacher Association (PTA) funds, result in a considerable income. There is no reason why these funds cannot be SDP- and curriculum-driven but it is important when dealing with PTA money – and indeed with all funds – to make sure that parents and teachers are involved in any decision-making that involves the spending of such money. There are, however, problems with this approach, and Maychell (1994) suggests that the degree of openness and discussion in the process of allocating funding for the curriculum was found to be most positive where there were sufficient funds to meet perceived needs. In those schools where the curriculum budget was very restricted, discussions were felt by some to be demoralizing and counter-productive (p.135).

The governors have the responsibility of managing the

school's finances, yet much of that responsibility is passed on to the headteacher who in turn delegates where and when necessary. There are fairly common ways in which governors might allocate the spending of money. They can form subcommittees to oversee all financial areas and allocate the funds themselves. It is more usual, however, for the governors to delegate day-to-day decisions to the headteacher and after the initial setting of the budget either work in consultation with them, or keep a watching brief by receiving regular budget reports. Whatever method is adopted It is important that there is frequent contact between governors and the school. In fact delegation, responsibility and accountability are at the centre of the original decision to introduce LMS. The DES Circular 7/88 (Section B, paragraph 9) suggests that:

> Effective schemes of local management will enable governing bodies and head teachers to plan the use of their resources, including their most valuable resource, their staff – to maximum effect in accordance with their own needs and priorities, and to make schools more responsive to their clients – parents, pupils, the local community and employers.

Without labouring a point that has been already made, it would seem that LMS will function best where all those responsible and accountable for the school's success work together in order to achieve its effectiveness and that they do so within the boundaries of a sound and workable School Development Plan which propels the budget forward rather than allowing it to be driven by its vagaries and shortfalls.

CHAPTER SUMMARY

Local management of schools has changed how schools are managed. It has, together with issues such as grant-maintained schools and City Technology Colleges, transferred a considerable amount of control from central government and LEAs to schools. The idea behind this shift is to give control to those who know the needs of the school best, namely parents and governors. In fact, LMS and governors having more say in what happens in schools goes hand in hand. Schools have to build management structures that allow this to happen and there are certainly both positive and negative opinions about how much autonomy particular schools have through LMS. The allocation of budgets based largely on the number of pupils on roll has made schools part of a market economy which moves them towards isolated competitiveness rather than involving them in sharing scarce resources. Individual schools manage their own budgets through structures where teachers, heads and governors work together to divide the finances available into manageable chunks. The management structures must allow the budget allocations to be driven by the curriculum and the School Development Plan so that everything possible can be done to raise the level of teaching and learning by using scarce resources effectively.

FURTHER READING

In order to actually manage a school budget it is more appropriate to use whatever material is provided by the LEA to help schools to become more effective. The following texts make interesting general points rather than give specific examples of how to allocate and divide a budget.

DES (1987) *Financial Delegation to Schools: A Consultation Paper*. London: HMSO.
   This provides a useful broad sweep of budgetary issues.
Warwickshire County Council (1989) *Further Consultation on LMS Related Matters*. Coventry: Warwickshire County Council.
   This is a useful example of an LEA booklet. There are no doubt other examples from other LEAs.
Gilbert C. (1990) Local management of schools: an introductory summary. In C. Gilbert (ed.), *Local Management of Schools: A Guide for Governors and Teachers*. London: Kogan Page.
   This provides a competent summary of many of the important budgetary issues including the planning and control of spending.
Levacic, R. (1992) Coupling financial and curriculum decision making in schools. In M. Preedy (ed.), *Managing the Effective School*. London: Paul Chapman.
   The budget has to improve the effectiveness of the teaching and learning that takes place in the school. Levacic has many interesting points to make about the links between the budget and the curriculum.

CHAPTER 6

APPOINTMENTS AND STAFF DEVELOPMENT

CHAPTER OVERVIEW

In dealing with financial management, Chapter 5 suggested that within the whole range of a school's resources it is people who are the most expensive. This means that selecting the best and maintaining their motivation is extremely important if the ethos of a school and the quality and effectiveness of its teaching and learning are to be preserved. This chapter attempts to summarize the recruitment and selection process by beginning with the school's needs and moving through the interviews to the mentoring of new colleagues. It also recognizes that there is a need to motivate all teachers, from the newly appointed to the most experienced, if they are going to continue to be effective and it presents a scenario for student teachers to be aware of when they are thinking about applying for jobs.

SELECTING THE RIGHT STAFF

Everard and Morris (1985) suggest that:

> In many ways we should treat people as any other resource, selecting the best for the purpose we wish to accomplish, and

maintaining, improving and adapting the resource as we would a building or piece of equipment to ensure that it meets our needs. However, there is one important difference: people are thinking resources, who, whether we like it or not, will decide jointly with their superiors and colleagues on how their time, energy, knowledge and skill will be used.

(p.66)

In the reality of the market economy which is being imposed on schools, teachers and ancillary staff are expensive, but this bleak scenario of human beings as abstract resources should not conceal the fact that effective school management is not about individuals working in isolation, but about groups and teams working together with a common purpose in mind. The appointment process, however, is only the first crucial step in recruiting individuals and building teams. In teaching it is difficult, time-consuming and destructive to invoke sanctions against any 'incompetent', unreasonable or divisive staff. Schools are thus very dependent on good selection processes and an effective and continuing programme of staff development that will motivate and progress the relationships and teams that are necessary for the organization to be effective. These structures and strategies are certainly important when staff vacancies arise because a teacher leaves or when there are other opportunities for recruiting new teachers.

Staff vacancies

The educational reforms of the late 1980s, together with local management of schools (LMS), shifted powers of recruitment from those operated by LEAs to those carried out at school level by heads and governors. As Gilbert (1990) points out, however, the LEA remains the employer of staff and needs to be consulted on all the finer points of employment law and on fair procedures for appointment, discipline, grievance and dismissal. While governors take on key roles in the decision-making process, it is the headteacher and any appropriate management teams who usually manage the procedures associated with recruitment. The existence of these teams is important. Campbell (1993), in commenting on the curriculum pressures created by the National Curriculum in primary schools, suggests that it will become increasingly difficult to conceive of any one person being capable of doing justice to the whole curriculum, the implication being that teacher 'expertise' in different and varied areas of the curriculum will be essential when recruiting new staff. Even so, and despite what are probably fully realized difficulties, most schools need knowledgeable governor subcommittees who will, if they are effective, take all the advice they need from the LEA, be aware of all the issues involved that might affect personnel and who, when a vacancy exists, have agreed procedures which meet the school's needs and satisfy such external legislation as equal opportunities and sex discrimination.

A staff vacancy and the need to appoint someone to fill the vacancy is a major management opportunity for the headteacher and the school. A valued colleague with specific expertise may have left and filling the vacancy could thus be difficult to envisage, but it is an opportunity to rethink roles rather than to automatically adopt the job description of the teacher who has left. In the preliminary discussions about filling a vacancy it is often all too easy to attempt to satisfy all the school's needs in one fell swoop and to use a new appointment to accelerate change in an unrealistic way which not only harms the management processes already in existence but also the potential for success of the newly recruited member of staff.

This is particularly important for those who are being recruited: for example, the demands made of newly qualified teachers should be realistic. If they are not and if recruitment patterns demand the impossible, then inexperienced teachers will begin their careers with falling morale. There needs to be a structured process in place that deals with all aspects of recruitment, including the initial step of establishing that a vacancy really does exist through to the interview and selection process. The steps outlined in Box 6.1 are there to be initiated and followed by both managers of schools and those who are applying for vacant jobs. Most of the steps will be discussed in separate sections of this chapter.

Box 6.1 Steps in the recruitment process

- Does a vacancy exist and who is going to be involved in the selection process?
- Assess the school's needs.
- Provide a job description and person profile for candidates.
- Advertise the job.
- Prepare application forms.
- Shortlist candidates for interview.
- Apply for references.
- Arrange for interview candidates to visit the school.
- Prepare interview questions.
- Interview candidates.
- Debrief unsuccessful candidates.
- Induct the new member of staff.

Does a vacancy exist?

This is a question that needs to be asked as soon as a teacher resigns, retires or accepts a job elsewhere and before any other action is taken. It may be that the loss of a colleague means no replacement will be found because the number on roll has fallen or because the budget is such that substantial savings need to be made and the only way of making savings is by not filling a vacancy. The decision will be an important one because a school that has operated with a certain number of staff will always, even if numbers of pupils have fallen, find it difficult to operate without that number. It is not a decision for the headteacher and senior managers alone. It has to include governors. It might be the case that the whole governing body has to be involved in the initial discussions about the vacancy and how it relates to the needs of the school that are reflected in the School Development Plan. This will be an important discussion because there are several factors which might influence and shape the decision-making process. For example, it will have to be accepted that spending money from the budget on a teacher will in turn improve the quality of teaching and learning. Perhaps the easy answer is that if an appointment is not made there will be thirty pupils in the school without a teacher. However, the thousands of pounds needed to pay for a teacher could improve the quality of learning in other ways such as by being spent on books, science equipment, classroom assistants, etc.

After these early decisions have been taken it is usual for a number of governors to form a 'team' which takes part in the whole selection process and sees it through until the vacancy has been filled. Adopting this kind of structured process helps safeguard both the school and those who will apply for the vacancy.

Assess the school's needs

When a vacancy exists and is to be filled it is important to involve as many people as possible in reviewing the school's needs. The ethos of many schools is designed so that the staff as a whole are active participants in their management. Day *et al.* (1990) suggest that it is necessary during this time to be reminded of the work currently in progress and of the plans due to be implemented in the future. What better way of doing this than to consult working teams and the School Development Plan. By involving staff in the process it is more likely that they will have a vested interest in making sure that the new appointment is a success.

There is the danger, however, that separate departments and even individuals will concentrate on their own particular needs and philosophies rather than on the wider requirements of the school. If, after consultations, a suitable way forward is accepted, then the recruitment of new members who will affect how the teams within the school operate must also be a shared experience with as many staff as possible participating. One way of doing this as part of an assessment of the school's needs is to follow an agreed sequence of steps which, as Day *et al.* recognize, would monitor the present situation by examining the SDP in terms of:

- where the school is hoping to go;
- where the school has come from;
- where the school is at the present moment;
- what the school is currently engaged in;
- what the school needs to do next.

In assessing needs, however, it is important to make sure that the discussions held are structured in such a way that they are chaired and led meetings rather than being small-scale casual and informal gatherings. This is important, because such meetings will inform any final decisions that need to be taken. By assessing past, present and future developments and examining the School Development Plan, it should be possible to begin to recognize the type of person needed who will be able to make a positive and effective contribution to the school. An example might be that if a school is redesigning its science resources it may need a teacher who is an able resource manager and can meticulously organize the purchase, storage and distribution of new equipment. Day *et al.* (1990) suggest that in assessing needs, attention has to be paid to what they call 'professional qualities'. They provide a checklist of categories (see Box 6.2) which can help to isolate the types of skills and qualities the school needs in a new appointment. The idea is to involve as many interested parties as possible in ticking the appropriate categories and then reaching some kind of consensus as to the professional qualities that will be looked for in applicants.

Box 6.2 Checklist of professional qualities

Categories	*Knowledge*	*Skills*	*[Qualities]*
Teaching			
Planning			
Creating			
Communicating			
Motivating			
Organizing			
Evaluating			
Leading			

If any specific skills are required, it would also be useful to be more detailed in those areas that are important. For example, if the school needs to update its use of a wide range of teaching styles then more details are needed in the teaching section. If short-term planning is lax or non-existent then the school might wish to recruit someone with expertise in this area.

Having asked for opinions and perceptions from a wide range of people, it is useful to consider the type of personality likely to match the needs that have been identified. In most schools, heads, teachers and governors will be anxious to appoint someone who is likely to 'fit in'. This notion of the right fit is usually associated with enhancing the social cohesion of the staff. No staff, however, is fully cohesive and there are always conflicts of some kind in any social group. What the recruitment process should avoid is employing someone who is destructive and who will create more problems than are solved. There are several ways of doing this but whatever is decided it must include strengths and weaknesses of the school and its teachers.

In schools where continuous self-appraisal is the norm, this process should not take too long but it is still important to identify those qualities that the school needs from applicants.

The person you need

There are several issues involved in deciding the match between personal qualities and the job that is available. However, it could very well be argued that many if not all of them will apply to most teaching jobs. Appointment panels need to consider whether any specific skills and experience are necessary. For example, do candidates need to have taught a certain age range, do they need a knowledge of certain subjects or do they need to have higher qualifications than is usual. It will also be useful to study any special abilities which may be necessary. It could be the case that the person appointed will need initiative and certain aptitudes and interests such as good sporting skills, being able to play a musical instrument or the ability to run a library. In many schools it would be very useful for new teachers to have certain attitudes which would help them relate to their colleagues. These might include being ambitious, or indeed, not being ambitious, being able to 'get on' with other teachers and being a useful and trustworthy team member. Trying to find out whether an applicant is the kind of person you need is far from easy. Playfoot *et al.* (1989) make it clear that they view the selection process as

> a matter of making a prediction and only when the person is actually in the post, settled in, and doing the full range of tasks described in the job details can you really say whether they are the right person for the post or not.

(p.112)

This may be close to the truth, but what schools cannot afford is a series of disastrous appointments that will undermine the confidence of other teachers and certainly not improve the quality of teaching and learning. It is always useful to look at the existing staffing structure and see if there are any internal adjustments that can or need to be made. Once needs are identified it might be possible to meet those needs by using existing staff. When considering new initiatives, any changes that are necessary and any restructuring that might need to be done, it is important to consider internal candidates first because there may be untapped talents which can either be used instead of making an external appointment, or which can be used in such a way that the new job becomes vacant in a completely different area. The departure of one member of a teaching staff can often motivate colleagues to take on new challenges. Members of the appointment panel should spend some time considering what they know about the ability of colleagues who are already working in the school. One of the most interesting ways of doing this is to look through the school's job descriptions.

Job descriptions and personal profiles

Bell (1989) suggests that 'a crucial element in the deployment and development of staff . . . is the job description since this provides each teacher with a reference point for her own work in the school' (p. 70). The National Union of Teachers (NUT, 1991) implies that a model job description will include the salary grade, a brief description of the job, to whom the person is accountable, the purpose of the job, the specific responsibilities and the key tasks (p. 18). Whatever job description is written for the appointment process it should be what the school wants after it has assessed its needs. It should also be open for

121

revisions after appointment, as a candidate may emerge with talents needed from the job description but also with unforeseen expertise which can be used by the school. This means that both the school and the applicant will be trying to make and achieve a quality appointment and that those who apply for jobs in schools should read the job description for the job they are applying for very carefully.

The second key document that each candidate needs to have is the person specification. The team of governors and teachers should, once again, know what this will contain through their assessment of the school's needs. It should include the knowledge skills and experience required for the job and should specify particularly the professional competencies expected in the specialist areas of the job, e.g. curriculum co-ordination, or team leadership. Minimum criteria should be established, below which an appointment would be undesirable (Day *et al.* 1990, p. 64). Everard and Morris (1985, p. 69) suggest that certain characteristics will be 'essential' within a person specification, in that it will be impossible to do the job without them, and others will be 'desirable' in that the school would not cease to function effectively without them but would certainly be enhanced if staff were recruited with such characteristics. The school itself will have to take decisions about what are 'essential' and what are 'desirable'. The list includes:

- personal characteristics and physical factors, e.g. age, speech, dress;
- achievements and experience, e.g. general education, degrees, etc.; jobs, special projects, awards;
- abilities: basic abilities, aptitudes, effective application;
- motivation: ambition, social, intellectual, level of 'drive';
- personality: leadership, relationships, emotional stability.

There are obvious overlaps between those 'formal' methods of assessing needs and the criteria for an effective job description and person specification. The same ground may be covered, hopefully in a slightly different way in both processes. It is important for governors to approve a selection process which is fair to all candidates whether internal or external and which is founded on a sound, stable and manageable structure. The end products of the process so far are job descriptions and person specification documents that are sent, usually with a job application form, to every applicant and are understood by everyone who is involved in the selection process.

The job advertisement, application form and references

Advertisements are based on the job description and person specification. It is placed depending on where you wish to recruit and how much money is available in the school budget. The immediate LEA and near neighbours will have a wealth of talent if the post entails mainly class teaching. The governors may decide, however, to advertise nationally for a senior post.

The application form is usually a standard LEA format designed to bring out all the factual information needed and also to elicit data which may give the selection panel a clue to past behaviour patterns. As Bell (1989) recognizes,

> the application form is more valuable than is generally realised. If carefully designed and interpreted, it can provide a wealth of information about a candidate, for example: previous jobs, courses attended, educational background, personal interests etc. Conversely, it will prove to be a blunt instrument if these conditions are not fulfilled.

(p.97)

A successful application form will be able to be read so that significant issues can be raised immediately. An unexplained break between teaching jobs needs to be investigated. Many short-term jobs in different schools may also have some significance as to the candidates' commitment to individual schools or to their need to move schools because of ambition. But interviewers need to recognize that there are unpredictable career paths and they must balance their expectations so as not to exclude a candidate who has taken time out to do other interesting activities that could make a valid contribution to the job. When taking a decision on which candidates to shortlist a note should be made to ask specific questions about certain 'facts' on the application form and any shortlisting process must involve reading the application forms by comparing them with the 'essential' and 'desirable' criteria in the job description and person specification.

Another document to be taken into account and measured

against these criteria is the candidate's references. A reference is not always an easy document to read. By being confidential and yet deemed a professional gesture, and available to the person who is being written about, it often does not refer to a candidate's shortcomings. During the shortlisting process the selection panel must ask: what is missing? Do I really have a positive statement about those criteria that are important? Finally it is extremely important that candidates see the school. They need this opportunity so that they know as exactly as possible what the job entails and if they dislike what they see they will be able to exercise their own negative preference.

Candidates visiting the school

Broad and general details should be given about the school either as part of the information pack sent to applicants with the application form or to candidates who have been selected for interview. Many of these details will be available in the school prospectus or brochure but there might be other issues pertinent to one particular job. If candidates are given as much information as possible it should be easier for them to make an informed choice about applying for a specific job. This will be increased once it is the norm for all applicants to visit the school. This is not always possible in practice because of such factors as distance from the school but there have to be opportunities to visit for those shortlisted for interview. The school should make time available for these visits which ideally need to include seeing the building, visiting classrooms and meeting as many staff as possible on an informal basis. This kind of school tour should be kept reasonably short so that the candidate has time during the visit to move around the school on their own and balance their own feelings with those of the pupils and staff they meet. Many selection panels reciprocate this type of visit by the head-teacher visiting the candidate in their school and classroom. When this happens it is important for all parties to be meticulous about their professionalism and to recognize that a satisfactory assessment is difficult to achieve after only a very short visit. What is important is that both the candidate and the school have gained as much pre-interview information as possible before the actual interview takes place.

Interviewers and the interview

Bell (1989) sees the interview as the final stage in a process that is designed to find the most appropriate candidate for the post based on all the available evidence. The main reason for holding interviews, therefore, is to find out which of the shortlisted candidates best fits the school's needs. It is an opportunity to find out about those essential and desirable characteristics that are not apparent from the application form and letter of application. The formal selection interview is a well-established, traditional part of any selection process and because of its formality it is usually a nerve-racking experience. In many ways it is such a rare occurrence for even the most job-hungry interviewees that it demands a rather artificial and unnatural way of behaving and, unless great care is taken, it is possible for the interview to be unreliable.

As far as the interviewers are concerned this unreliability usually takes the form of: making hasty and subjective judgements; failing to ask appropriate questions; taking small pieces of evidence and expanding them to create negative impressions of a candidate; spending too long thinking about the next question and failing to listen to the answer to the present one; and not studying the documentation on each candidate in depth. As there are faults in the system the interview has to be managed in such a way that most if not all the problems are eliminated. This means careful planning by the selection panel or whoever is going to be an interviewer, each of whom must have access to all the documentation on each candidate and to have read it thoroughly. It is this information that will provide the areas of questioning. Before the interview there has to be a list of questions that are both relevant to the job and designed to elicit enough information from the candidates for the panel to make as sound a judgement as possible. Goodworth (1984) argues that because the interview should not be an interrogation, those asking the questions need to think carefully about the type of questions they wish to ask so they can make sure that they are open-ended and require candidates to give explanatory answers. The onus is on the interviewers to be well prepared and to acknowledge both their own difficulties and those that are likely to affect the interviewees. This is an important point

125

because, as Rowland and Birkett (1992) suggest: 'When you meet someone in an interview situation, you are, instinctively, hoping for behaviour which corresponds with the acceptable norm in your school...however, quite often an interview...is far removed from everyday experience' (pp. 119–20). The tension and difficulties need to be negated as far as is possible. One way of doing this is to be aware that decisions must be taken as to who will ask what question, how the candidate will be welcomed, who will lead the panel, and how long the interview will last. While the same questions should be put to all candidates there must be the opportunity for individual interviewers to phrase the question to suit their interviewing 'style', there must be opportunities for follow-up questions, and for questions that will be unique to particular candidates because they will be based on the application forms and letters of application.

Questioning is important. Some useful do's and don'ts to bear in mind suggested by, but abbreviated from, Everard and Morris (1985), include the following:

Do not:

- Start with intimate, personal or argumentative questions.
- Use closed questions which will lead to a yes or no answer unless there is a need to establish a clear and specific fact.
- Use loaded questions, trick questions or jargon.
- Lead (the interviewee); for example, 'I suppose you...', 'No doubt you enjoy good relations with...'.
- Indicate disapproval or show that you are shocked.
- Worry about silences.

Do:

- Use open-ended questions which allow the candidates to express themselves and to demonstrate knowledge.
- Probe tactfully using 'why?', 'what?', 'how?' questions or:
  'Tell me about . . . '
  'What did you enjoy most about . . . ?'
  'What was your role in . . . ?'
- Reassure a nervous candidate by smiling and making relaxing small talk.

- Listen for at least two-thirds of the time.
- Guide the candidate tactfully into the areas you wish to explore.
- Close down one area and open up another with remarks such as: 'OK. I think we have covered that; now could you tell me about...?'
- Come back to areas a candidate tries to avoid.
- Get his or her views on the job and invite views on the school.
- Observe behaviour such as nervousness, aggression, signs of stress, etc.
- When the candidate has had time to settle down, look for clues of 'difficult adjustments' at previous schools. (The inability to relate well to other people is the most frequent cause of disaffection with staff members of all kinds.)
- Beware of your prejudices, e.g. accent, dress, men with beards, women with ear-rings, etc.
- Give the candidate a chance to ask about the job and check whether there are any reservations.
- Make sure that the candidate knows the next steps in the selection process, e.g. what happens after the interview.
- Finish the interview when both you and the candidate have gathered enough information.
- Recall your overall impressions before you meet the next candidate. (pp. 73–4)

Effective questioning should allow the interviewers to listen to the answers and closely observe the candidate. The ability to listen is not only about hearing what is said, although this is vitally important, but about distinguishing between factual answers, those that describe skills and qualities and those that reveal the candidate's attitudes and values. Note-taking is a vital part of the listening process because what is said can be used and recalled during the decision-making process. At the same time that questions are being asked and the candidate's answers are being listened to the interviewers must observe what is happening. The candidate – this can be either an experienced teacher applying for a senior position or a newly-qualified colleague – is presenting an image, and the non-verbal behaviour can give important clues as to suitability. Day *et al.* (1990) suggest that facial expressions, eye contact, body movement, tone of voice and gesture are all important. Not only should they be noted down alongside what is said in answer to questions, but the interviewing panel should be trained in what to look for and what interpretation to put on both verbal and non-verbal communication. Certainly if an interviewee sits in a particularly strange position, uses inappropriate hand and facial gestures or fidgets to such an extent that the movements detract from what is being said, they need to be told during their voluntary debriefing why their body language is unhelpful and inappropriate. Most job applications involve an interview as part of the selection process. Many candidates underperform in what is a very false situation. Unless the selection panel is properly prepared, the interview will be even less reliable than it already is. Some candidates will obviously be unsuccessful but equally, for others, the interview may well have been a two-way process where he or she was able to determine whether they wanted to work in the school.

Debriefing for unsuccessful candidates

This needs to be managed sensitively and swiftly. It is usually done by the headteacher or other senior manager and the selection panel should decide what to tell the unsuccessful candidates before they disband. There should be enough information from the interview notes to help in the debriefing session. If appropriate, these notes can be written out as a debriefing sheet, or used in a face-to-face meeting or during a telephone conversation. Not every candidate will request to be debriefed but it is important that if internal candidates from the school are interviewed, feedback is provided in all cases. What is said should be based on how the candidate responded in the interview when these responses are related to the job description and person specification. It should be useful and designed to help the candidates improve their performance in future job applications and interviews. Of course, as Bell (1989) recognizes, the appointment process does not end when the successful candidate has accepted the post. 'The appointment is, in fact, the start of another process, that of induction' (p. 121).

Induction of a new member of staff

A new member of staff, whether a newly qualified teacher or someone appointed after several years' teaching somewhere else, will find a new school daunting. Any new place of work will have different routines, structures and means of organization.

Brand (1993) gives some indication of the sense of newness when she writes of her new appointment:

> You have survived a tour of the school with everyone staring at you. You have had the interview and answered questions which ranged from the innocent enquiry to the poisoned chalice. You've met your colleagues – you can't remember their names but you've met them – the dapper, the trendy, the prim, the positive and if you are unlucky the one who has a special seat in the staffroom.
>
> (p.58)

New colleagues need a mentor who will be able to give professional support during the first weeks, months and even year. They should be chosen carefully and matched to the needs of the recently appointed colleague. A newly qualified teacher will have different needs from a new colleague with an incentive allowance. One of the keys to the success of the mentor system is not to choose someone because of their hierarchical position. This can often cut across the notion of confidentiality which is important in the mentor system. It is also useful to fit the mentor to the new colleague rather than expect the newly appointed teacher to fit in with the school's permanently designated mentor.

At least in the first few weeks, time must be allowed for meetings to take place where the mentor can discuss important structures of the school and the new colleague can talk, ask questions and generally use the mentor as a counsellor. There should also be written documentation and a list of issues that the mentor can raise during these meetings. Different schools will want to raise different issues and a newly qualified teacher will have different needs, but there must be documentation of various rules, routines and management structures. Schools which are well documented with written policies, parents' brochures, staff handbooks, newsletters, etc. can be confusing if they are all issued at once. There is a need for planned induction over a period of time involving certain key areas which will include many, if not all of the following:

- Map of the school
- School brochure for parents
- The most up-to-date governors' report to parents
- List of staff, departments, etc.
- LEA organization
- Channels of communication in the school
- Health and safety routines
- How to get access to resources
- School aims and the School Development Plan
- Policies for the subjects taught and schemes of work
- Long-, medium- and short-term planning methods
- Classroom management and teaching styles
- Job description and explanation of the appraisal process
- Methods of assessment and record-keeping

Even the most experienced teacher would find such a mass of material daunting. For many teachers and especially those who are newly qualified there are other methods of induction that could be added. Brand (1993) suggests some of these and at the same time raises the important and final point in this section which is that the induction process should not be one of indoctrination. Schools do have managed routines and obviously, if they are going to function effectively, they have to maintain these structures, processes and routines, but within them are teachers with individual strengths and beliefs. Brand (1993) goes on to suggest:

> I felt strong enough not to let myself slip into established ways just because they were there. I refused to abandon what I knew were good methods and to teach in a manner which went against all the reasons that I had entered the profession. Throughout the year I was supported by colleagues in many ways. I visited other schools, colleagues' classrooms and the deputy head taught in mine. I watched, listened, learned and I hope taught colleagues something new occasionally.
>
> (p.59)

Brand is identifying her own sense of individuality as a teacher while at the same time recognizing that the school was supporting her within its own parameters, using its own structures and processes. The sum of all these parts of an induction process is wittily and pertinently summed up by Peters and Waterman (1982) when they link induction and making colleagues feel good about their jobs with motivation and suggest that management's principal job is to get the herd heading roughly west. It has already been suggested that selecting the right applicant for the job needs to be followed by a period of induction. Similarly, there is a continuing need to satisfy colleagues' needs and motivate them so that they continue to be effective teachers. This applies both to newly appointed teachers and those who are already working in the school.

Motivating colleagues

It is obvious that whatever the skills, enthusiasm and expertise of the headteacher and senior managers and however successful the selection strategies are when recruiting new staff, no school can survive effectively without well-motivated teachers. If, however, the selection process has been effective, a 'new' teacher should begin working in the school in a highly motivated frame of mind. They will know what their role is, the job they have to do and will, through the interview questions and documentation, know enough about the school to feel confident. There is no doubt that motivation is difficult. Different people react in different ways to the situations in which they find themselves. It is possible to suggest some basic common needs that, if met, should help motivate all of us. For example, it is important that all staff, whether old or new colleagues, should feel that they are members of the school community. At the same time they should have a sense of progressing achievement, of 'getting somewhere', of not 'standing still'. If these criteria are met, most colleagues will know that what they do is appreciated and that through their efforts they can exert some influence over what is happening within the school.

The school ethos and how colleagues are expected to relate to each other will have implications for motivation because, although the senior staff and the headteacher have the hierarchical power to initiate change to the management structures and the organization which may or may not help to motivate individuals, it is also true to say that motivation should come from working together as part of an effective team.

131

Smith (1992a) elaborates on this theme when he suggests that in managing motivation we need to be aware that teachers who are recruited to a school need to have a job that is satisfying and which offers them the kinds of rewards and encouragement that will continue to motivate them. This can frequently mean that they need to be told that they are effective teachers and are doing a 'good' job. As Smith goes on to suggest, this should increase their self-esteem and ensure that they are able to work towards their objectives, make their own decisions and select their own goals.

Smith's criteria go further and dip into the realms of scarce resources such as financial rewards and motivating colleagues by increasing their salaries through promotion. This can only add to the problems managers have when making sure that their 'team' is motivated. Well-motivated colleagues can not only enhance their own individual careers but they should, through their own enthusiasms, increase the enjoyment and hopefully the productivity of the group or team they are working with. They will be higher achievers than those who adopt a less positive role and are less well motivated. Smith (1993a) suggests management strategies which could help motivate colleagues. In introducing them he makes sure that they will need to apply to teachers, headteachers, deputies and heads of department and that they involve working together to increase self-esteem and effectiveness. He recognizes that everyone needs to know what is going on; thus keeping staff informed is important but at the same time senior staff need to be seen to ask for advice and feedback in a co-operative, friendly and professional way. Discussing problems and new developments is very important and all senior managers need to develop listening skills that are recognized by all colleagues as part of the school's sharing of skills.

Obviously these strategies and the techniques that are used to motivate colleagues should prove to be useful managerial tools. What still remains difficult, however, and will continue to remain so, is motivating colleagues who feel financially undervalued and those who have felt de-skilled in the light of too many changes and too much negative media coverage of the supposed ineffectiveness of teachers generally. This could be summarized by the suggestion made by Campbell *et al.* (1991)

that the pressure which teachers were put under within the school day was creating a sense of working hard but achieving little. Many of the techniques depend upon effective management structures which support an ethos where praise is given, where all teachers have a share in the decision-making processes and where the communication of ideas is open and successful. If staff are not motivated and have low morale there may be indicators such as arguments between colleagues, deadlines not being met, unexplained absences, lack of interest at meetings, etc. It may also be the case that the work being done, at the same time as not satisfying the needs of the organization, is also not meeting the needs of the individual teacher.

It may be that the school is neither satisfying an individual's basic needs nor their motivational needs. It may be possible to manage the situation so that both sets of needs are met; or in the case of basic needs there may be problems outside the scope of the management of the school. Basic needs are usually quite simply expressed as being able to maintain a reasonable standard of living with a sense of stability and reassurance for the future, and being able to provide housing of some kind together with food, warmth and clothing. If colleagues' basic needs are not being met they will probably talk frequently about their earnings, seek reassurance about job security, follow instructions but never show initiative, frequently express concern about working conditions, and show little interest or enthusiasm for the job in hand. There has to be a management structure that can, by clear forward planning, offer hope and advice to many teachers who are trapped in positions within the pay structure that do not reflect their true potential.

The demands made on teachers by the school are often immense but they must be balanced by accepting that domestic arrangements might be complicated and sometimes affect what needs to be done at work. As far as possible, those who work need reassurance about promotion prospects and security of employment. Receiving a salary is an important basic need and goes hand-in-hand with tolerable working conditions and instructions about roles, duties and objectives. Like pupils, teaching staff have a sense of what is fair. High motivation and morale cannot exist if there is no system for handling promotions and job changes so that everyone has the feeling that they are needed. If schools can move towards satisfying basic needs then they will be helping to motivate their human resources. Teachers, however, have motivational needs centring around achievement, friendship and power. Indicators of these kinds of needs might include such things as: a highly competitive spirit; pride in certain skills; an enthusiasm for working alone; a need to set goals and deadlines; a need to be liked but also a need to persuade and influence people; an ability to take charge in times of crisis; and an eagerness to take on greater responsibilities. These needs must be met or at the very least it must seem to colleagues that the school is moving some way to meeting such needs. Motivating such people, however, can mean quite radical changes in the structure and organization of schools but it will be necessary if success and effectiveness are to be a priority of school management. As a closing statement to this chapter, it should be possible to allocate jobs to allow colleagues to make full use of their abilities, make sure that resources available are adequate to the job in hand, give colleagues plenty of responsibility, allow them to plan and organize their own work, involve them in team work and team planning, give lots of praise and encouragement and involve them in as many aspects of the school as possible. This is obviously a very difficult task for managers to do effectively.

CHAPTER SUMMARY

It is vital that the management of the school's human resources recognizes their potential, builds on their strengths and, as far as possible, meets their motivational needs. One part of this is in the appointment of new staff who, it has been argued, probably cost in excess of 80 per cent of the school's budget. The right people can enormously influence the effectiveness of the teaching and learning that take place and, this being the case, there has to be a structure in place which allows appointments to be made successfully. Governors who work alongside the headteacher and as many teachers as possible can be utilized to make sure that the appointments process will move logically forward from the first assessment of the school's needs, usually after a colleague has left or there is a vacancy for other reasons, through the creation of job descriptions and person specification to the interview and appointment. Of course the process does not end there. In most schools there will be an induction period to help any new colleagues settle into the school as well as a continuing policy of raising morale and improving motivation. Having an effective recruitment policy and strategies for induction will only be of benefit to the school in the short term if motivation is low. This needs to be seen and recognized as a vital management strategy if all colleagues, whether new or already established, are to fulfil their expectations and work together to improve the teaching and learning that takes place.

FURTHER READING

Day, C., Whitaker, P. and Johnston, D. (1990) *Managing Primary Schools in the 1990s: A Professional Development Approach*. London: Paul Chapman.
This is interesting both from a secondary and primary standpoint and it has a useful section on motivation.
Everard, K.B. and Morris, G. (1985) *Effective School Management*. London: Harper & Row.
A very practical, useful and yet thoughtful book with an interesting section on job descriptions.
Handy, C. (1976) *Understanding Organizations*. London: Penguin.
Both this and *Effective School Management* use an industrial perspective which is very useful when related to schools. This is especially true when examining motivation.
Bell, L. (1989) *Management Skills in Primary Schools*. London: Routledge.
Many aspects of this book are equally applicable in secondary schools. There is a concise chapter on the appointment of staff.

CHAPTER 7

COMMUNICATION

CHAPTER OVERVIEW

Communication is about the sharing of information, attitudes and beliefs and within schools this can cover both internal and external events involving speaking, listening, meeting, writing, discussing and reading. This chapter highlights the importance of communication, the kinds of barriers preventing successful communication and different types of communication, including what should happen within schools and the external communication that should take place between schools, parents and governors. Since the Cambridge Accountability Project (1981) when teacher–parent communication, pupil reports and parent–teacher meetings were examined, there has been inadequate research in this field and the chapter content is based on the general theories and opinions of others rather than useful and current research.

THE IMPORTANCE OF COMMUNICATION

Rowland and Birkett (1992) take the idea of communication being about sharing information, attitudes and beliefs a stage further and include the sharing of feelings and the passing on of knowledge. Bennis and Nanus (1985) suggest that the mastery of communication is inseparable from effective leadership. By widening our view of communication, they are stressing the importance of establishing processes and structures which make communicating in schools effective because it is the attitudes, feelings and complex issues of leadership which contribute to bringing individuals into conflict with each other. These conflicts are more likely to arise where channels of communication are blocked or where individuals do not have the opportunities to share ideas and debate educational issues. Rowland and Birkett go on to suggest that some of the main reasons why this complex process is vital include: gaining or passing on knowledge; getting or giving help; learning or teaching; changing ideas; and persuading and negotiating.

However, being an effective communicator is no help at all if no one is receiving the message. Communication in school has to be managed carefully so that information is provided on all aspects of the school for everyone who needs to be involved, including staff, pupils, parents, governors, LEA and the community. Dean (1987) recognizes that for communication to be effective, 'it must be appropriate to its purpose, the situation in which it is taking place and the audience and readership for whom it is intended' (p.148). This of course means effective communication systems where the information that is presented to colleagues moves upwards, sideways and downwards and where there is feedback to check that information has been received and that communication has been successful.

WHY IS COMMUNICATION NECESSARY?

Another interpretation of communication is that it has to happen so that jobs get done. This is simplistic but true, and it begins to reinforce the importance of making sure that the right messages reach the right people at the right time. By doing this effectively colleagues should receive information which they can act on. The kind of information that schools deal with can be separated into three types: long-term, medium-term and short-term communication.

Long-term communication consists mainly of policies and documents that are the umbrella under which the school works as well as being the linchpin of the School Development Plan and the aims and ethos of the school. If they are not communicated to teachers and other adults, then individuals would be working alone with their own agendas and the school would be fragmented without any coherent policies or any continuity of styles, beliefs and ways of working.

Medium-term communications are those which refine the long-term issues into something more immediate. For example, in a primary school which works through a cross-curricular approach there will be policy statements which communicate this to teachers, parents and governors. In the medium term there will be documents relating cross-curricular issues to half-termly or termly planning of cross-curricular themes. In translating long-term issues into action plans, medium-term communication involves communicating what is expected to be achieved to teams and is essential for continuity and for the school's common goals.

Short-term communication is about the day-to-day messages that have to be given to individuals and groups because without them the structure of each day and week would be chaotic. Informing colleagues that someone is ill and cover is necessary, or that a meeting scheduled for 4.15 p.m. has been changed to the following day is obviously important for the smooth running of the school. However, as Bell (1989) suggests: 'All communication will be just that little bit more effective if all the staff of the school recognise that they have a responsibility to ensure that the system works' (p. 175). Beare *et al.* (1989) take this a step further by recognizing that gaining this consensus, whereby colleagues do recognize their responsibility, is an important part of the communication process that has to exist within a school. Unfortunately it is far from easy to set up systems and structures where this is possible.

STRUCTURES, ATTITUDES AND ORGANIZATIONS THAT PREVENT COMMUNICATION

While it would seem to be more positive to address factors which facilitate communication, it is absolutely essential to state what prevents good communication because unfortunately there are many barriers which prevent it from happening. Greenfield (1990) suggests that some of these barriers are the fault of the school system, some the fault of the headteacher and some the fault of the staff. It is important to look at why communication can be unsuccessful and why there is frustration because messages do not reach those who need them.

Any effective manager will, if the information is important, have set up routes to pass the information on to those who need to receive it. These systems, networks and structures need examining in terms of their successes and failures but it has to be recognized that the personalities within an organization and their relationships with each other can affect communication. An awareness of some of the ways colleagues can misinterpret or block messages and information is important because if they are allowed to continue unchecked they will not only block or alter the kinds of messages that are part of the daily and weekly network of information in schools but they will begin to be an entrenched part of the school's culture and will subsequently prevent long-term change and progress. Methods of preventing communication, or erecting barriers to slow down, alter and divert messages and information include: censoring what has been communicated by only recognizing what is welcome and discarding what is not; having an emotional interest in the information and allowing this to get in the way of the real message; distrusting the information by not believing information that is received from certain colleagues; distorting the message by passing on information that is only a partial reflection of the original; being confused by too much information and not knowing what to do with it; being in conflict with colleagues and subsequently withholding information; keeping information secret. Thus, because of an inferior–superior status, or vice versa, it becomes difficult if not impossible to communicate in any depth or breadth.

Handy (1976) states, fairly obviously, that the most effective way to improve communication is to remove the negative factors because 'good' communications within an institution imply a well-designed and healthy organization. Bearing Handy's simple point in mind and with so many pitfalls, it is not unreasonable to suggest that it is important to manage internal communication within a structured plan. This can be informal in the sense that messages are sent and received *ad hoc* as they are felt necessary and in a relatively random way. However, this is probably how grapevines begin and rumours abound. Neither can be totally prevented and will exist in all schools, but it is vital that important information should not be misinterpreted in any way or allowed to be passed on in this fashion.

There is often a system in operation where communication is inferred. Colleagues and visitors will make inferences from each other's dress, manner, tone of voice, etc. Different people infer different things. An example could be that a headteacher might assume that because of his or her open door policy of not hiding behind a desk in an office, colleagues find it easy to talk and discuss relevant issues. Teachers, however, might disagree with this assumption that it is easy to discuss issues in this way and yet the head may be unaware of these difficulties. This may be equally true of the physical environment. Certain messages are sent to visitors and colleagues in the form of closed doors, formal seating arrangements, and even such notices as no entry, do not knock, etc.

There has to be a formal system of communication within the school which, through meetings, papers, documents and policies, can communicate accurately and thoroughly everything that needs to be known. Another great strength of many schools is that, apart from what is obviously confidential, everyone knows everything. Greenfield (1990) makes the point that if this kind of open management is recognized and accepted, more people will become more willing to share information among themselves and to discuss relevant issues with each other. This kind of open debate can only strengthen the effectiveness of a school's communication system. One way of recognizing its strengths and weaknesses, however, is to know what needs communicating and why, who needs the information, when they need it and how it can be most effectively communicated.

WHAT NEEDS COMMUNICATING WITHIN THE SCHOOL

The range of material that needs to be communicated is vast, and without careful planning the amount can be overwhelming. One way of breaking it down is to think in terms of long-term, medium-term and short-term information but in trying to list what exactly fits into each category it quickly becomes apparent that there is no definitive list and that there is considerable overlap. Long-term communication, for example, includes such items as: the school's aims; development plans; rules; behaviour policies; subject policy documents; schemes of work; staff development policies; the school handbook; resource storage; health and safety documents; pay policies; cleaning schedules; letting arrangements, etc.

In the more immediate future there will be such medium-term communication items as: the evaluation of all long-term communication; lesson planning; National Curriculum and assessment changes; team membership; the present year's teaching teams; current work within the School Development Plan; recent change, i.e. alteration of a recently implemented policy document, etc.

Short-term communication covers the immediate day-to-day communication that is either a response to current information or how the school begins to take decisions that will affect both long- and medium-term communication. It includes: all urgent daily messages; meeting times and places; daily and weekly happenings; reminders to pupils about behaviour and events; changes to routines because of sudden problems; times and places for working subcommittees, etc.

WHO NEEDS THE INFORMATION AND WHEN

Communication in the long term involves groups who function for quite long periods of time. It may be that these groups, for example, the team responsible for the School Development Plan, meet regularly and that a system of minutes or notes has been clearly established, whereas another group or working party, for example, one that looks at how ancillary assistants are used in the classroom, may be a one-off policy-making team who, when they have reached decisions, have then to communicate these decisions to other colleagues and monitor the action that is taken on a regular basis.

These situations also largely apply to medium-term communications with the proviso that some of the decisions taken on, for example, lesson planning, may have to be evaluated and modified on a regular basis and these modifications communicated quickly to colleagues. The immediate day-to-day messages in short-term communication are usually fast and in many cases need immediate responses. Once it has been established that certain people need to know certain things at certain times and that specific times are set aside for communication to take place then the way that information is shared should be relatively effective.

HOW COMMUNICATION TAKES PLACE

The obvious way of making sure that communications get through is to see that they are sent by the simplest and most direct method. This is not easy, because some long-term issues may involve meetings over a period of time whereas others will be no more than a short conversation in a corridor. Obviously the larger the school, the more complex the structure and the more difficult it is to monitor communication. The small school, however, where everyone works closely together, often has problems when everyone assumes, sometimes wrongly, that all teachers know about everything that is going on. Whatever the size of the organization, however, it is useful to recognize that if change is to be handled effectively and if collegiality is to be an accepted way of working it is necessary to accept Southworth's (1990) suggestion of the importance of interaction, communication and in-school dialogue concerning, say, teaching and learning styles or curriculum content. It is also important to decide on whether the school should have a closed system of communication where no one is told anything that they don't need to know or whether a system should operate where everyone is told everything that is not private or confidential. Obviously the second system is more appropriate in a school which believes in sharing knowledge and operating in a collegial way. It will also reduce suspicion and enable staff to be more willing to develop a communication network where everyone shares information.

Whatever internal system is set up, much of the long- and medium-term planning should (and I state this at the risk of repeating myself) involve groups of colleagues working in teams to solve problems and manage change. Not only must they communicate with each other but they will have to translate their conclusions, findings and policy statements to everyone else. This will involve meetings and more meetings and, while Chapter 1 examined some of these areas many of the criteria suggested in the following section should apply.

EFFECTIVE MEETINGS

Everard and Morris (1985) argue that: 'Meetings are of critical importance in co-ordinating effort and effecting change, and a very important part of the managers' role is to ensure that they are vehicles for communication and action rather than for confusion and frustration' (p.51). Certainly some of the criteria for judging a meeting's effectiveness must include such aspects as:

- everyone must understand the reason for holding the meeting;
- everyone taking part should have a vested interest in being there;
- the purpose of the meeting should be reflected in the agenda which is circulated in advance;
- the meeting should be held in an appropriate place: informal meetings need a different atmosphere from formal ones;
- choose a starting time which everyone can accommodate and stick to an agreed finishing time;
- make sure the meeting has an outcome and is reflected in the agenda for the next meeting: this will help with continuity.

Whatever form the meeting takes, there should be written conclusions, such as formal minutes which not only reflect what

143

the meeting was about but suggest what jobs need to be done and who is responsible for completing them. By doing this it is possible for all those who were at the meeting to see what actions need to be taken as a result.

Face-to-face communication

This is part of the short-term communication network in that all teachers talk to each other at some time in the school day and often these hurried conversations are about school matters that have some importance. Stenhouse (1975) sees this as one of the keys to successful change. He argues that this kind of collaboration between teachers, where they discuss and disseminate the 'community knowledge' of the school, is a way of removing barriers and constraints and of opening up the internal debates which will help to change and improve the school's shared community.

Headteachers talk to teachers both informally and formally and in the medium- and long-term there are meetings and more meetings where face-to-face interaction is how ideas are communicated. The main characteristic of this type of communication is the ability to listen. In fact, this is the golden rule in all areas of oral communication. Listening well is a real skill. Those colleagues who are bad listeners, as Rowland and Birkett (1992) suggest, cannot concentrate, often lack patience and are frequently too busy thinking about the next question to listen to the answer to the one they have just asked. Perhaps a reasonably obvious conclusion to draw would be that those who are least likely to listen are more likely to mishear or not hear at all and consequently to make mistakes. Day *et al.* (1990) recognize that a developed skill of active listening will be of great help in communicating effectively with other people. This kind of listening occurs when the listener understands and appreciates what the speaker is saying before beginning to interpret and analyse the information they have received. In order to do this, some of the rules for better active listening are as follows:

- Allow the person who is talking to finish speaking and avoid completing sentences or making it obvious that you are burning to say something.

- Try not to think about the next point or you will miss what is being said.
- Use your memory to recognize key points. It is often an aid to everyone's memory if you begin your reply by restating the key points that have been made.
- Be objective rather than subjective and try not to let your interpretation of what is being said be distorted by any adverse feelings you have about the speaker's clothes, appearance or manner.

In assessing feelings and reactions during the face-to-face sharing of information it is useful to be able to recognize four basic behaviour patterns which may, initially, appear to be over-simplistic but which are part of any method of meaningful communication. The more you know about your listener and their reactions the less difficult it will be to decide how you are going to use your voice and body and how you are going to phrase what you say. Similarly if you are the listener, the behaviour of whoever is communicating with you will suggest how you should behave. The more aware you are of this, the less conflict there is likely to be.

First, there is the colleague who is friendly and responsive. He or she will probably smile, nod, use open-handed gestures, have a relaxed posture with lots of eye contact and use a relaxed tone of voice.

Second, there are those who will want to control and dominate. They might point at others, lean forward when speaking, or indeed listening, they may interrupt, ignore responses, use loud, rapid speech and try to establish a controlling tone of voice.

Third, some of your colleagues will be, during some or, if you are really unlucky, all areas of face-to-face communication, both unresponsive and aggressive. They will greet any exchange of views and ideas with a set mouth and face, they will stare, have abrupt movement or speech, keep an inappropriate distance, and look beyond you while speaking in a harsh tone of voice.

Fourth and finally, there will be the timid and submissive. They will make nervous hand movements, avoid eye contact, allow colleagues to interrupt them constantly, and speak hesitantly in a soft tone of voice.

Recognizing these interactive styles may improve the

effectiveness of all face-to-face communications and could well improve the method of sharing information with those outside the school such as parents and governors.

METHODS OF COMMUNICATION BETWEEN THE SCHOOL, PARENTS AND GOVERNORS

Macbeth (1989) suggests that there has to be effective communication between home and school and that it has to be actively promoted. Inactivity, he believes, is to the disadvantage of both pupils and parents. He also recognizes the reality of teacher–parent communication when he suggests that it is easier for teachers not to enter into a partnership with parents that involves much communication. Similarly, it is easier for parents to 'leave it to the specialists' and limit their communication with the school. Failing to build up a strong partnership, however, is to the disadvantage of pupils and also, whether they realize this or not, to the disadvantage of both teachers and parents.

Similarly, there needs to be active communication between the school, parents and its governing body if there is to be the shared partnership that is necessary to achieve success and meet the needs of LMS. Brehony (1992) uses the phrase 'active citizenship' to describe part of the governors' role. It is suggested that the relationship between schools and governors should be one of democracy and accountability, and both concepts need clear communication if they are to be effective. It is important to examine some of the issues involved and to identify some of the communication routes that exist. Schools need to include regular written newsletters to parents and to have available such documents as a school brochure, discipline and bullying policies, and any other curriculum documents that will be of interest. They need to arrange informal and formal visits to school, including open evenings so that parents can look at what the school is like during a working day and talk to their child's teachers. On a more specific level each child has to have an annual written report. There should also be meetings arranged by the school and PTA together with social events such as dances, quizzes and wine-tasting evenings.

There is also a need for governors to communicate with parents, both as part of their statutory duties and to increase the effectiveness of home–school liaison. They must ensure that they communicate what they are doing through newsletters to parents; these are usually written by parent governors. There is also an annual meeting with parents in which governors report the school's achievements during the previous year. This meeting is meant to be part of a school's accountability to its parents. Unfortunately, at many schools very few parents attend such meetings, making them largely unnecessary and probably not wanted by the majority of parents. If a school has had an OFSTED inspection, a copy of the report has to be made available to any parent who asks to see it. This is also true of the follow-up action plan which the governors have to write as a result of an inspection.

There is other information which parents have to know, such as the official complaints procedure, but a sensible school will make sure that as many of its documents as possible are available to parents. This is certainly important if a school considers that education is a partnership between all the participants and that to achieve a level of collegiality and team work that supports this partnership everyone – parents, pupils, teachers, staff and governors – needs as much information as possible.

In many ways communication between the school and parents and governors is, as was suggested at the beginning of this section, about *accountability*. Many of the methods of communication with parents and governors will be similar to those occurring within the school and will demand the familiar skills related to meetings, face-to-face communication and written documents. What does need to be borne in mind, however, is that these skills need to be geared to the specific audience that is being addressed. Written newsletters to parents can and should represent long-term information with regard to the calendar year but should also have short-term messages relating to urgent decisions and the current week's news. The long-term documents are the ones relating to policy and should include all interested parties in their preparation through subgroups and working teams. While many of the methods of communication are dependent on what individual schools actually want to do and are prepared to do, several areas are subject to legislation.

Open evenings or parent evenings, while not being dependent on legislation for what parents are told, do have to be held to discuss pupil reports which, like the governors' annual report to parents and the school brochure, all have to include certain pre-scribed information.

OPEN EVENINGS/PARENTS EVENINGS

In most schools, meeting with parents is a pleasant and useful sharing of ideas as well as an opportunity to discuss pupil progress, future needs and to offer any advice on matters of concern. It is also a part of the school's process of accountability. Mortimore *et al.* (1988) see parental involvement in the life of the school to be a positive influence on pupils' progress and development and recognize the importance of their attendance at meetings to discuss children's progress.

There will be informal meetings with some parents, perhaps more so in primary schools, throughout the year, but at set times there will be pre-arranged open evenings with individual appointments for parents. These meetings represent the main opportunity to discuss progress and share concerns. For teachers they are a golden opportunity to 'sell' the school's and their own professional skills by conveying to parents a strong sense of personal interest in each pupil. Well-prepared teachers will meet each parent with all the necessary facts at their fingertips. They will have the right body language and tone of voice and will meet visiting parents in an appropriate place.

Most parents meet professionalism with professionalism but there will be occasions when someone will not behave within the bounds of normal convention. As Rowland and Birkett (1992) suggest: 'Due to some sense of stress they may shout, bluster, threaten, profane, cry, retreat into silence, become inarticulate, make false accusations, become hysterical or act in some other unusual way' (p. 96).

Rowland and Birkett (1992) also describe how it is possible to handle emotional outbursts and personal attacks in such a way that there will not be a complete breakdown in communication between teacher and parent. They also try and explain how it is possible to be successful in most meetings with parents. In accepting that it is extremely important that there is successful parent liaison, it is useful to recognize that for it to be effective, most of the following attributes need to be appreciated when meeting and dealing with parents:

- Do not try too hard to be liked. Attempting to be more than normally pleasant often comes across as strained or defensive.
- Always be a good listener. This is invaluable.
- As well as listening intently, observe closely. Try hard to develop a sensitivity to other people's motivations and wants.
- Try to be open-minded in the face of complaint or criticism; on the other hand, retain a little personal scepticism when faced with emotion.
- Never threaten someone, even in an implied way.
- Try not to feel uncomfortable when facing conflict. Analyse what signal you are receiving and deal with the reasons behind it.
- It is particularly important to try to think clearly under pressure. If you are unable to do this, slow the interview down or defer the topic until you are better prepared.
- Commit yourself to trying to give reasonable satisfaction.

GOVERNORS' ANNUAL REPORT TO PARENTS

Once again, the governors' annual report to parents is directly related to accountability. This time the governors' accountability is to the parents. Macbeth (1989) suggests that the report should be the governing body's main task; this task, however, is hampered by the notoriously low turn-out at the annual meeting with parents, where governors report on the business of the preceding year. This meeting, even though it may be seen by many parents and teachers as a means of communication they wish to avoid, is a statutory obligation.

The DFE consider this form of accountability, this forum where parents and governors can share ideas and report what has been happening, as a crucial method of communication.

Circular 5/93 (18 June 1993) states a further piece of information to be added to the governor's reporting to parents:

> Under separate regulations to be made shortly, governing bodies will be required to publish in their annual reports to parents from the 1993/4 school year onwards, in the same form as in prospectuses, information about National Curriculum test results and rates of unauthorised absences.
>
> (Paragraph 37)

Further additions have been made that now include details of the school's provision for pupils with special educational needs (SEN). This is in line with further LMS delegation where mainstream schools, after an audit of pupils with special educational needs, are allocated part of their budget for various levels of SEN including those pupils having statements of special educational need.

It is the view of many of those who work in schools that performance indicators, such as test results and rates of what is in effect truancy, do not, when presented as lists of figures and percentages, reflect the true worth and the true popularity and effectiveness of an individual school. By raising them as separate legislative issues, and by specifically insisting that they be reported to parents, both areas have been awarded increased status which will give parents a false sense of the importance of such figures in recognizing school effectiveness.

SCHOOL PROSPECTUSES/SCHOOL BROCHURES

The school brochure or prospectus has to be available to all parents, prospective parents and any other interested parties. The school's LEA will need one, as will all local libraries. Stott and Parr (1991) recognize that: 'The school prospectus is an example of publicity material which must reflect the quality of service which the school wishes to convey' (p.98). The quality and design of this major publicity document needs to be carefully thought out, well-written, professionally printed and translated into other languages where necessary and illustrated in such a way that it 'sells' the school's image. Its general contents need to reflect a corporate image in the sense that teachers, governors and parents should be involved in its production. Different schools will want to communicate different information but there are huge areas of the brochure where legislation dictates what should be written. As well as prescribing large areas of the content, there is also legislation for the processes of distribution, e.g. in primary schools it must be published six weeks before the final date by which parents must apply for admission. It must be available in all schools without charge and freely accessible as reference material. Circular 5.93 (18 June 1993), however, lists what must be the content of each prospectus. This has changed frequently and there is no reason why this form of communication will not be the subject of change in the future. A summary of the content in 1994 is as follows:

- Admission arrangements.
- Aggregate results of assessments.
- The number of applications received for places in the previous year and the number of places available.
- Routes taken by pupils over the age of 16.
- Practical details, e.g. school name, address, telephone number, type of school, name of head, name of chair of governors, etc.
- Dates of school holidays, times of school sessions.
- Summary of charges and remissions policy.
- Information on school performance in GCSE, A and AS, local and national averages.
- Rates of unauthorized absences.
- Details of arrangements made for special needs pupils and those with statements of special educational needs.
- Complaints policy.
- Summary of content and organization of sex education policy.
- Details of career guidance and work experience.
- Details of RE and collective worship.
- Statements on the curriculum organization and teaching methods.
- Statement on the ethos and values of the school.
- The time spent on teaching, including RE but excluding assemblies, registration, lunch and other breaks.

In deciding what to include under the heading 'School ethos and values', governors might like to consider such areas as school discipline, arrangements for pastoral care, main extra curricular activities, the school's uniform policy, etc.

Using the school prospectus as a public document to communicate the school's ethos, structures, aims and organization to parents has to be seen as a further part of the process of accountability. Schools also have to be willing to take a proactive stance and to attempt to make an impact so that the support of parents continues and is prolonged and extended. The danger is that this kind of communication becomes a form of competition between schools and moves away from the idea of engaging in a partnership with parents towards open conflict between schools where there is increased competition to attract and influence parents' choice of school for their children.

THE PUPIL'S ANNUAL REPORT

This is the main form of written communication to parents about an individual pupil. It should ideally be about positive progress and expectations for the future. According to Pollard and Tann (1993), there are two contradictory expectations: (1) the parent as a partner where parent–teacher discussions are likely to be wide-ranging and to cover many topics including the progress of the pupil; and (2) the parent as a consumer, where the school reports outcomes through which the school can be held accountable such as test and examination results. Hughes *et al.* (1990) (this has been discussed in other chapters) reported that parents, in choosing a primary school, suggested the following positive criteria in order of frequency: relationships between parents, teachers and children; the staff; the atmosphere, the ethos of the school, discipline, and the wide-ranging education offered; the headteacher; development of the whole child; academic results; and resources.

For secondary schools academic results may well be higher than ninth on a similar list but it does illustrate that in reporting to parents schools recognize that the report either becomes part of a wider record of achievement or the reporting process and the report itself is only part of a large number of messages that parents receive. There are, however, certain details that have to be included in an annual report to parents. It becomes obvious that many of the social and personal details that parents of primary pupils want are missing from the legislation. Schools will therefore have to balance the requirements of their own parents and pupils with what is required because of various Education Acts. This list closes this chapter and is a summary of details included in Circular 14/92, *Reports on Individual Pupils' Achievements*.

Before reading the report it is important to set it within the context of its compulsory nature and the statutory necessity of discussing its contents with parents and in many circumstances with the pupil. The areas that have to be written into the report to parents include:

- Comments on all National Curriculum subjects covered.
- Comments on general progress in all subjects and activities not mentioned elsewhere including subjects such as economics, cross-curricular work and health and activities such as work experience or mini-enterprise.
- Succinct comments should cover a pupil's progress and include strengths, weaknesses, achievements, vocational credits or qualifications.
- Public examination results if applicable.
- Attendance record.
- Comparative information about attainments of all pupils of the same age in the school (Years 2, 6, 9, 11).
- Comparative information about attainments of pupils of the same age nationally (Years 2, 6, 9, 11).
- National Curriculum results at the end of key stages including a brief explanation so that parents can understand the information. (There are further details in Circular 14/92 on each National Curriculum subject and whether the results apply to subjects or each attainment target within the subjects.)

CHAPTER SUMMARY

This chapter has been at pains to stress that communication does not just happen. It has to be managed and structures set up within schools to make it effective. It should also not be seen as a one-way process. It is about sharing information by giving and receiving. While it may appear obvious, it has to be recognized that if information is to be understood, the written message has to be read and the speaker listened to. There are barriers to communication in any institution, and it is important to evaluate why they exist and what communication they are preventing. What needs to be communicated, why is it necessary, who needs to receive the information, and what form should it take, are vital questions to ask when organizing an effective communications network. In setting up channels of communication it is important to recognize that there is information to be shared within the school between professional colleagues and this includes long-, medium- and short-term communication. There is also, however, an external system which includes parents and governors. Both rely to a large extent on either the written message, ranging from a long policy statement to a short memo giving precise instructions, or the oral, which can include meetings or other face-to-face encounters. Whatever method is chosen, the information being shared needs to be useful, clear, to the point and will, by being understood, move the school forward.

FURTHER READING

Pollard, A. and Tann, S. (1993) *Reflective Teaching in the Primary School: A Handbook for the Classroom* (second edn.). London: Cassell.
  An excellent reissue of a useful text that covers many areas of communication and, it must be said, should be read in conjunction with many other areas of this book.
Rowland, V. and Birkett, K. (1992) *Personal Effectiveness for Teachers*. London: Simon & Schuster.
  Written mainly from a 'management training' point of view, this book contains interesting sections which discuss communication.
Stott, K. and Parr, H. (1991) *Marketing Your School*. London: Hodder & Stoughton.
  Here the authors emphasize the importance of communication in presenting an appropriate image which will reinforce the school's popularity.

CHAPTER 8

APPRAISAL

CHAPTER OVERVIEW

The question of whether teachers will be appraised has been superseded by how, because every teacher has to go through the appraisal process as part of a two-year cycle. This chapter discusses the process of appraisal by examining what it actually means, the prerequisites necessary to make it successful and what the benefits will be. In looking at these issues it recognizes the importance of self-appraisal, classroom observation and the appraisal interview.

WHAT IS APPRAISAL?

As early as 1985, Suffolk LEA (1985) suggested that

> the cornerstone of appraisal schemes is the belief that teachers wish to improve their performance in order to enhance the education of pupils. Following from this is the assumption that appraisal systems should have a positive orientation: that is, the purpose should be to develop teachers professionally rather than get at them. This development process should be characterised by negotiation and agreement about priorities and targets.
>
> (p.4)

155

Teachers have a right to be suspicious of appraisal because of its chequered history. Sir Keith Joseph expressed a wish to sack 'incompetent' teachers and was notorious as Secretary of State for Education for promoting the view that appraisal should be linked to accountability, promotion and higher, and perhaps even lower, pay.

Early methods of appraisal, such as those suggested by Trethowan (1987), were quite clearly linked to those schemes found in industry and commerce. While recognizing that appraisal should be closely linked to staff development, they seemed to have as one of their guiding principles the idea of appraisal being solely about performance and making judgements about merit and ability. In examining schemes used by industry and commerce, *Those Having Torches* (Suffolk LEA, 1985) found that line management, where 'superiors' appraised 'inferiors' was the norm, with little if any dialogue and discussion. They also found schemes which began to move away from the confusion that seemed to exist about what purpose appraisal served and, where it was recognized, that merit pay based on performance was not an issue that should concern appraisal. In the early days of discussion about appraisal however, most schemes appeared to follow what Peters and Waterman (1982) saw as the 'Ready, fire, aim!' method and largely failed to recognize that teacher appraisal needed to be constructive, honest, professional and unthreatening if it was to lead to an improvement in standards of classroom practice. Wragg (1994) suggests that words such as 'trust', 'honesty' and 'frankness' occur frequently in LEA training documents and that the four most common suggestions for both appraiser and appraisee were:

- be objective, not subjective;
- look at performance, not personality;
- be supportive, not judgemental;
- be sensitive.

Such statements take us into a complex process which is costly in terms of time, and of course money from a school's budget.

The ideas gleaned from industry are usually rigid line management models involving a top-down hierarchy, concentrating on what is easily measurable. To compare an educational process with a commercial or industrial model is neither particularly appropriate nor very worthwhile. As Smith (1989) suggests: 'Many of the learning and teaching outcomes tend to be blurred and indistinct, leaving what is to be measured not easily identifiable or acceptable' (pp. 18–19).

Appraisal should also involve the examination of a professional's performance by another professional and as Montgomery and Hadfield (1989) recognize it should involve the assessment of performance, appreciate achievement, value the contribution of both appraiser and appraisee, identify areas for improvement, assess potential and contribute to the appraisee's personal and professional growth.

In order to achieve this objective, the process of appraisal usually has to follow a pattern which includes: an initial interview to discuss and agree on the areas to be appraised; classroom observation or observation of specific areas of the job being done; an appraisal interview; a written appraisal document followed by a meeting to agree the appraisal document; and evaluation and review during the next year. Obviously appraisal cannot and must not exist as a separate, added-on part of the school's management. It is part of other wider issues of trust, support and motivation and it is important to consider factors such as: the climate or ethos of the school; who will appraise whom; and what should be appraised in the case of each individual teacher.

THE CLIMATE OF APPRAISAL

For appraisal to be managed effectively all staff need to be part of the process. It is interesting to reflect whether this is possible if schools have not already had a history of sharing knowledge and managing change in a non-threatening collegial way. Smith (1989) suggested that before appraisal became a statutory requirement schools could have initiated a system based on mutual support and colleague observation (MSCO). While this is time-consuming and impractical it does avoid the pitfalls surrounding appraisal within a hierarchy and the worrying concept of 'superior' appraising 'inferior'. What this system also suggests, and this is directly applicable in establishing an appropriate climate, is the idea of strong and productive team work with teachers working together to support and develop each other's talents. Smith (1989) develops the idea of the prerequisites schools need to have in place before appraisal can be effective in improving what happens in classrooms and in developing teachers' talents. They include various issues that have been discussed in other chapters such as: staff normally participating in planning decisions; collaborative teaching rather than working in isolation; regular discussions of educational and pedagogical matters; teachers recognizing that they can learn from colleagues, and needs assessed and problems identified on an ongoing basis.

The key issue that has been discussed so far is that appraisal cannot take place in a vacuum. The ethos of the school, its aims and its Development Plan will form parameters within which teaching and learning take place. Pollard and Tann (1993) suggest that 'Few teachers, however committed, can hope to fulfil all their aims if the context in which they work is not supportive . . . teachers must continually adapt: they must both know themselves and know the situations in which they work.' (p.58).

Establishing a clear set of values, aims and commitments as well as understanding the context of the school is vital for the success of appraisal. If schools have established their curriculum content, the most effective teaching style, how teaching groups are managed and the most effective use of resources, there will at least be an awareness of this context and some attempt at standardizing fundamental issues. It is extremely difficult to create an appraisal process that is not threatening because any process to develop staff potential which involves examining how individuals do their jobs and discussing performance before producing a written document (which is how teachers are appraised) is bound to appear threatening. There are many reasons for this, including such issues as individuals not admitting to deficiencies of any significance and nervousness of an interview that is unproductive. There is a fundamental need to create an ethos or climate that does not threaten the appraisee, which minimizes anxiety and is separate from any connection with disciplinary procedures or any negative

Box 8.1

---

1. The benefits of appraisal for the school

- The aims of the school and of individuals can be better co-ordinated.
- Many of the school's priorities will be clarified.
- Staff responsibilities will be made more specific.
- There will be a greater exchange of ideas.
- Communication should be improved.
- It will be easier to meet school needs through targeting certain areas.
- Individuals and teams should belong to a more supportive environment.

2. The benefits of appraisal for the individual teacher

- Greater job satisfaction.
- Improved feedback and recognition.
- A more regular review of INSET needs.
- A better awareness of career development and possible routes to follow.
- More support in school.
- A better understanding of the job being done.

---

overt criticism. Handy (1976) seems to support this view when he suggests that 'Criticism arouses defence mechanisms and does not improve performance . . . Praise is ineffective unless close in time to the behaviour. General commendation is discounted as politeness' (p.266). He goes on to argue that

Criticism only improves performance when:
a. it is given with *genuine liking for the other person*;
b. it is related to specific instances;
c. the subordinate *trusts and respects* the superior.
Improved performance results when:
a. *goal setting not criticism* is used. The goals are specific, *jointly set and reasonable*;
b. the manager is regarded as *helpful, facilitating, receptive to ideas and able to plan*;
c. evaluation of performance is *initiated by subordinates* and as a prelude to further goal setting not further appraisal.

(pp.267–8) (my italics)

Appraisal obviously needs to be part of a school's staff development programme and it needs to be managed within a structure where everyone sees the need to monitor and improve performance and is accountable for their work in the school. If the school has had open discussions about appraisal and all staff have had training as both appraisees and appraisers, it should be easier to develop an ethos where appraisal would be less threatening and viewed with less suspicion. Where possible, it would be useful to suggest to teachers the possible benefits of appraisal as indicated in Box 8.1. These are often discussed in appraisal courses and are generally put forward as being key issues in the appraisal process. I think that they raise important issues but it is difficult to find evidence that they represent both appraisers' and appraisees' views. Seeing appraisal as part of a broader and larger system of evaluating a school's strengths and weaknesses would perhaps place the suggested benefits in a more realistic context.

WHO SHOULD BE THE APPRAISER?

There has to be adequate training for both the appraiser and the appraisee for any appraisal process to succeed. No appraiser should be responsible for the appraisal of more than four colleagues because of both the work-load and time commitment involved and each appraisee must be given a choice of appraiser. The headteacher has to take decisions about who should be the school's appraisers. Obviously the bigger the school the more appraisers are needed. In very small primary schools the choice of appraisers will be very limited indeed and there could be unforeseen problems if a teacher did not want the head to appraise them.

Wragg (1994) has added a further dimension to the relationship between appraiser and appraisee and has raised further questions about the match between the two. He suggests that while most teachers were satisfied with the outcome of appraisal there was a significant gender effect. Men who had been appraised by a male appraiser reported higher satisfaction than did women appraised by a female. The National Union of Teachers (1991) also has some interesting information for teachers and headteachers who are going to be appraisers when they insist that there is a fundamental need to help support and guide the appraisee while at the same time respecting the confidentiality of the whole process and basing it on trust and mutual respect.

Obviously if your appraisee does not have confidence in you as an appraiser, the whole process will not be able to go very far. There is also the practical question of whether the necessary peace and quiet can be found for the appraisal interview as well as questions such as: who will type the confidential appraisal statement, where will it be stored, who will have access to it?

Obviously a sensitive ethos, collegiality (Wragg (1994) suggests that teachers value care and collegiality) and a historic background of previously existing good management should help all staff to gain from appraisal. Difficult relationships and an atmosphere of mistrust among professional colleagues on the other hand will render appraisal perfunctory and meaningless. Rogers (1980) recognizes the importance of working collaboratively with colleagues and suggests that such relationships not only give interesting insights into our own practice but also provide support. As well as colleagues working supportively together, each individual needs to take stock of his or her own progress. Rogers states quite clearly that 'individuals have within themselves vast resources for self understanding and for altering their self concepts, basic attitudes and self directed behaviour' (p115). Wragg (1994), however, seems to suggest that the whole idea of appraisal being beneficial and that a certain 'ethos' will promote more satisfactory appraisal is not as clear-cut as it might be. In his study only 3 per cent believed that the process would aid their career development and less than half the teachers questioned said that appraisal had affected their classroom practice. These findings raise questions about the value of a process which is a legal obligation and also involves a considerable time commitment. Many aspects of the total process, however, seem valuable in themselves, especially the idea of looking at one's own practice during a period of self-appraisal.

SELF-APPRAISAL

Pollard and Tann (1993) use the phrase 'reflective teaching' and in attempting to define what they mean draw on the ideas of Dewey when they suggest that being a reflective teacher 'involves a willingness to engage in constant self-appraisal and development. Among other things it implies flexibility, rigorous analysis and social awareness' (p.9). What reflective teaching does not imply, however, is that it will lead to change or indicate how change will be achieved. Potentially, being reflective is merely self-indulgent if it does not lead to change.

The teacher who is effective in recognizing his or her own strengths and weaknesses and hopefully changing those weaknesses into strengths often has several well-developed characteristics. These might include: the ability to continuously monitor, evaluate and revise their own practice; approaching their job with an open mind; basing their judgement as teachers on insights gained from many educational disciplines; and enhancing the fulfilment they get from their job by collaboration and dialogue with colleagues.

Smith (1993a) suggests that the most effective teachers have learned from their successes and failures and have always been capable of identifying their own strengths and weaknesses. What is not addressed, however, is this further development of taking this concept of learning from experience a step further and translating what is found and discovered into successful action. This process of reflection and self-evaluation leading to action should be part of any teacher's professional development, especially now that teachers are becoming accountable to more people. Smith goes on to state that in many ways self-evaluation is a personal analysis that can be stimulating and invigorating, emphasizing effective skills and those that need developing:

> Knowing yourself in this way is essential if the appraisal dialogue is going to be meaningful. You will know what questions to ask, what help you might need and in what areas you don't necessarily need any help. Honest self evaluation should reduce the chances of any major surprises during appraisal.
>
> (Smith, 1993a, p.1)

Smith is not alone in suggesting the positive nature of individuals analysing their own strengths and weaknesses. The Advisory Council and Arbitration Service (ACAS) (1986) suggested that each appraisal should be preceded and informed by a self-appraisal: 'Pilot LEA's have emphasised to teachers the importance of self appraisal as a key part of the appraisal process. We do not consider that self appraisal can be compulsory: but all teachers should reflect on their own progress' (p.10).

It is a good idea for teachers to be self-aware and perceptive and those individual teachers who are looking at what they do in school should list all the job areas in which they are involved. One management tool for this is shown in Box 8.2. It is important to identify what is done under each heading because, while what happens in the classroom is a critical part of most teachers' jobs, there are often many other areas which are well worth considering when appraisal takes place. This method concentrates on these other areas rather than on classroom practice.

Box 8.2 Individual model of professional activities

- Work with parents and governors.
- In-service training.
- Work connected with a higher point on the teacher's pay spine.
- Contributions to team and department meetings.
- Non-teaching pastoral work.
- Extra-curricular activities.
- Research and study.
- Work with a wider community.
- Other whole-school meetings, e.g. School Development Planning, curriculum meetings, etc.

Teachers may also wish to consider the constraints placed on them by the school. Depending on the quality of a school's management such elements might include the failure to provide adequate training for curriculum development, lack of resources, or the poor quality of information within the school. Prompt lists could be drawn up as an aid to reflection. If such a lists were to cover classroom work it might include:

- What evidence do you have of pupil's progress?
- Do you differentiate and cater for the needs of all your pupils?
- How much time is spent preparing for your teaching?
- What indicators are there of learning failure?
- Is your teaching challenging for all pupils?

- Do you try to find new ways of teaching old topics?
- What new teaching techniques have you tried in the last half term?
- What have you learned from current research that has influenced your teaching recently?
- What new resources are you currently using?
- When did you last attend an in-service course that was designed to help you improve your teaching?

There are obviously many other headings which can help in self-evaluation, but whatever criteria or characteristics are used it is only a means to an end. The appraisee should take the opportunity to take stock. Appraisal is not about an appraiser making the rules and arranging what should be appraised and how. The appraisee needs to know what needs to be appraised, what the weaknesses are and what strengths an appraiser should recognize. These issues form the basis of the initial meeting. Without being part of the process and without having taken the opportunity to be self-critical, the initial discussion before the more traumatic area of classroom observation may well be less effective and perhaps weaken the whole appraisal process.

THE INITIAL MEETING

This does not have to occur after a period of self-appraisal and self-evaluation but needs to be recognized as the first part of the 'formal' process. Both the appraiser and the appraisee should be aware of the processes involved, have undergone the appropriate training and know what parts they have to play. It is essential that there should be effective training, preferably with both appraiser and appraisee learning about both roles. This is important because the appraisal process needs to be seen by everyone as open and fair. The initial meeting is the first part of appraisal that involves the appraisee and appraiser meeting together. Negative preference will have been part of the choice, where appraisees are allowed to take some confidential control over their choice of appraiser and the process is ready to start with this meeting where both parties begin to understand each other and agreements are reached on the best way to proceed. The ACAS (1989) pilot study suggested that this initial meeting should have a number of purposes including the following:

- Clarifying and confirming the purposes and context of the appraisal.
- Considering the teacher's job description and agreeing to its meaning and what emphasis should be attached to its various sections.
- Reaching agreement about the scope of the appraisal and identifying which areas of the job it is appropriate to focus on.
- Agreeing the arrangements for classroom observation including where it will be, when it will take place and what areas of teaching style and classroom management the observation will focus on.
- Agreeing on the method of collecting data for the appraisal other than by classroom observation, i.e. data about pastoral care, working with a team, etc.
- Agreeing on the timing of the appraisal in terms of dates and times for all the different sections.

In many ways this early preliminary discussion is not only about setting parameters and agreeing methods and timings; it also sets the tone in terms of a positive and hopefully an energetic start to the appraisal/appraisee partnership. It reflects the important management issue to which teachers are entitled, including consultation in the design, monitoring and evaluation of the whole process including participation in every aspect of the appraisal.

CLASSROOM OBSERVATION

There is obviously a need to observe teachers in the classroom doing what they are paid to do and what they spend most of their time doing. As Day et al. (1990) suggest: 'It is important to remember, however, that where classroom observation leads to change in classroom planning and teaching, this in itself will not necessarily result in "improved" learning by pupils. Research has demonstrated that there are simply too many variables to draw a direct cause and effect relationship' (p. 172). Observation, however, needs to be part of a wider process whereby teachers regularly evaluate their practice and any changes they make to see how they affect children's learning.

The initial interview will have resulted in an agreed time and place for classroom observation. It should also have recognized areas of teaching and learning that are going to form the basis of the observation. The appraisee must make sure that the appraiser is briefed in advance about the lesson the appraiser is going to observe, the context of that lesson, its aims and its purposes. During the observation it will have to be clarified what the lesson is about; otherwise the initial meeting will not have fulfilled its main purpose. The appraiser will have one or several specific areas of focus and, by being briefed by the teacher about the context of the lesson, should understand the teacher's intentions.

This information should make the gathering of evidence easier, but unfortunately it is extremely difficult to take decisions about the effectiveness of teaching and learning. There is no single method of teaching well. Many different styles will work successfully depending on the circumstances. There are probably hundreds of checklists in use for observing lessons. Many contain similar criteria for success but equally there are significant differences. The problems of classroom observation are further compounded by Wragg's (1994) findings that, given the sensitivity attached to the observation of teaching, surprisingly little time was devoted to classroom observation skills during appraisal training.

Smith (1990b, p.50) offers a broad approach of observing what both teacher and pupil are doing. He suggests the following checklist:

- Are books and artefacts displayed so that pupils find them stimulating and exciting?
- Is the class managed in such a way that pupils are encouraged to find and use appropriate resources without using up valuable teaching time?
- Is there evidence of appropriate teaching styles for different curriculum purposes, e.g. groups, individual, whole class, etc?
- Are there opportunities for pupils to discuss their work with the teacher and other pupils?
- Are the questions asked and the problems set open-ended when appropriate?

- Are there opportunities for responses other than writing?
- Is continuity achieved between different activities?
- Does the teacher's personal style, i.e. body language, frequency of shouting, position in the room, etc. influence the ethos of the classroom?
- Is the teacher able to tell you what the children are doing, what they are learning and of what use that learning is?
- Is the teacher able to tell you what he or she is aiming for in his or her teaching, what he or she is learning from it and how this experience will be used in future practice?

Wragg (1987, pp.33–4) adopts a more detailed and structured approach which, in summary, concentrates specifically on what the teacher is doing and includes sections on: lesson preparation; beginnings and endings of lessons; transitions between activities; how movement of pupils around the room is controlled; the kinds of relationships existing between teacher and pupils; whether the teacher is vigilant enough to know what is happening in the classroom; how they handle disruptive behaviour; the kinds of rules that are established; how involved the pupils are in the lesson; and how their progress is monitored. Whatever observation schedule is used it is important that the appraiser and appraisee agree on what is going to be observed. This needs to be quite specific and precise unless there is an agreement to use tape-recordings or videos. This, however, could be seen as moving away from appraisal towards the concept of checking, testing and inspecting.

Examples such as Smith's and Wragg's together with the results of discussions between appraiser and appraisee, should provide an effective and appropriate observation schedule. It is important to recognize that classroom observation is about being constructive and has to involve sharing information so that the appraisee is helped within the context of the school's development programme. As well as the skills necessary to be an effective observer, the appraiser also needs to be able to relate to the appraisee on a more personal level so that ideas can be discussed and shared within their professional relationship. This has to happen during the appraisal process because one of the major components is, of course, the appraisal interview.

THE APPRAISAL INTERVIEW

The appraisal interview brings together the previous steps (choice of appraiser, initial meeting, classroom observation, etc.) against a background of trust, mutual respect and agreed purpose. As with all meetings in school where professionals are working together, it has to be in the right place at the right time and conducted in the right spirit. It is absolutely crucial that the interview is interruption-free so that both parties are sufficiently at ease to approach the meeting in a positive frame of mind. Day *et al.* (1987) suggest what areas need further thought before the interview and what questions appraisees need to ask before the discussion starts. Although Day *et al.* concentrated on the primary sector there is no reason why the points they raise should not apply equally to the management of secondary schools, when they ask: what is the purpose of the interview; when and where will it be held; what form will the interview take; what questions will the appraiser and the appraisee ask; what other information, documentation, etc. might be required; what do both participants hope to gain from the experience; how long will the interview take and how will it be followed up?

In order to feel confident with the system, the appraisee also has to be protected and needs to recognize that they should be able to view the interview positively because it will be constructive, fair, confidential and positive. The discussion has to be managed in such a way that both appraiser and appraisee ask questions and listen to answers. This should form part of the training for appraisal because the interview must not just become a forum for the appraiser to run through his or her own agenda without recognizing the importance of the appraisee's views, opinions and feelings. The NUT booklet (1991) *Appraisal: Your Rights and Expectations*, suggests that the appraisee should speak for about 80 per cent of the time and the appraiser for 20 per cent.

It is important for both parties to reach some mutually agreeable decisions before closing the meeting. There should be a structured approach which involves identifying targets and objectives for the future. These targets should be achievable by a certain date and with specific resources that are able to be monitored. According to the NUT (1993), these targets should be:

- Specific so that they do not degenerate into general goals, e.g. I will take part in an LEA IT training course over the next six months, *not* I will learn more about computers.
- Attainable within a given period of time, e.g. a term or an academic year.
- Capable of being monitored or measured.
- Achievable.
- Relevant.
- Precise in relation to outcome but allow the appraisee to decide how each target will be attained.
- Phased to avoid the build-up of competing priorities and pressure.
- Set within the resources and support available.
- Designed to help, not hinder, the appraisee's professional performance.

It is important that both the appraisee and the appraiser take notes during the interview. As there will have to be a written record of what is agreed, it might be appropriate to stop the conversation at certain stages, summarize what has been agreed and write it down in such a way that it can be easily understood at a later stage. The main part of this 'later stage' is the written appraisal statement or record of appraisal.

RECORD OF APPRAISAL

In most if not all written appraisal statements both appraiser and appraisee have to agree that what is written is a true record of the appraisal and sign the document. The statement is extremely confidential and, as we have already seen, it must be written by an agreed person, which can have time implications if the appraiser rather than the school administrator is writing or typing the appraisal statement. Access must be limited to the appraiser, appraisee, headteacher and Chief Education Officer or a representative. A summary of the targets may be recorded separately and forwarded to those responsible for specific areas of the curriculum, e.g. English inspectors/advisers, etc. If the appraisal is going to be effective the written statement must be part of a wider staff development policy which actively encourages in-service training and makes systematic arrangements to guarantee that some kind of developmental training takes place. Most authorities have their own form of written statement. The example given in Box 8.3 fulfils most if not all the necessary requirements and could help schools to take decisions where the form of the written appraisal document is not prescribed. One of its benefits is that it is short and relatively easy to complete.

Box 8.3 Record of appraisal

Name of teacher....................................Date...................

Classroom management and teaching skills
- Preparation and planning
- Classroom management
- Communication skills
- Appropriateness of pupils' work
- Quality of pupils' work
- Control
- Tidiness and display

Evaluation and assessment

- Comments on pupils' work
- Statutory assessments for NC
- Record-keeping

Pastoral/relationships

- With staff
- With pupils
- With outside agencies
- With parents

Other professional contributions

- Attendance at and contributions to planning and departmental meetings

---

- Extra-curricular activities
- Work with PTA and governors

Appraiser's comments
- Teacher's strengths
- Aspects which need strengthening
- INSET needs
- Further recommendations

Appraisee's comments
- Comments from your self-appraisal
- Comments on the appraiser's remarks
- Your strengths
- What developmental support do you need from:
  1. within the school
  2. outside agencies
- What are your suggestions for improving the quality of your own teaching and for the wider aspects of the school organization, e.g. how the day is structured, school times, school rules or how the timetable is arranged?

Targets/objectives
What targets have been set for the coming year? (List no more than five.)
1.
2.
3.
4.
5.

Review
Intermediate reviews will take place on (not more than once per term):
1...............................2...............................3..................

This report has been read and agreed by both parties.
Date..........................
Signed......................(Appraiser)
Signed......................(Appraisee)

APPRAISAL FOLLOW-UP REVIEWS

In order to maximize the benefits of appraisal it is essential that there are follow-up meetings to review progress. Teacher appraisal works in a two-year cycle so it is appropriate to hold some kind of review at the end of the first year. Reviews are important in ensuring that progress is continuing, that the appraisee and appraiser are both interested enough to try and maintain progress and that any amendments are made which may relate to the agreed aims and objectives. In reviewing the agreed objectives it might be necessary to establish further targets, change some of those already agreed or even cancel those that are obviously wrong or unrealistic.

If there have already been informal but regular discussions throughout the year, the review meeting will be little more than a formality. However, as well as reviewing progress towards meeting agreed targets, it is also appropriate to check the usefulness of any training that has been taken and any future career moves that are likely. At the end of the review a written amendment to the original appraisal document must be made including any modifications to the original targets. At the beginning of the next appraisal sequence the review comments together with further discussion on the initial targets will obviously form the starting-point of any pre-appraisal meetings. Wragg's (1994) findings, however, raise questions about the viability of the whole of the two-year process where the follow-up review and any subsequent action is the end of one appraisal cycle and almost the beginning of another. Wragg *et al.* suggest that 'If appraisal is to be truly effective, rather than merely a soothing or irritating process, then in theory 100 per cent of teachers should have said they changed their classroom practice as a result of appraisal'. They found, as has been quoted already, that only 49 per cent said this was the case. This raises very important issues for both individual teachers, schools and the government. Decisions have to be taken about whether appraisal in its present form is a worthwhile use of time, energy, commitment and money.

CHAPTER SUMMARY

It is important to approach appraisal positively and schools which are most likely to use it as part of a successful staff development policy are those where there is an atmosphere of trust and open-mindedness and where the appraisee's self-image is important. If such schools have a management structure, where staff usually participate in planning decisions and collaborative teaching is a fairly normal occurrence, the benefits of appraisal should far outweigh the economics in terms of both time and training. For the individual teacher, each part of the process from self-evaluation through to the post-interview review should give them greater job satisfaction, a better understanding of the job being done and a clearer idea of possible future career routes. In order to achieve this, however, the whole process should be non-threatening and must work far better than Wragg (1994) suggests.

The aim of self-evaluation as a start to appraisal is to enable teachers to learn more about their own strengths and weaknesses. The next step of matching appraisee to appraiser has to allow some choice for the appraisee and this is usually achieved by allowing the appraisee to exercise a reasonable amount of negative preference. The period of classroom observation must be at a time and place comfortable to the appraisee and have agreed areas to look at in detail. The follow-up appraisal interview should be held in the right place and at the right time so that both participants feel at ease and can share their views in a supportive way within an atmosphere of trust. Thus any written statement will be known by all parties to be confidential and the targets or objectives which are to be reviewed during the year following the appraisal are clear and achievable. This is a daunting task for those who manage schools, especially when headteachers will have to appraise at least four of their colleagues and will themselves be appraised by a fellow head and, in most cases, an education officer from the LEA. This will place a series of competing demands on heads and senior managers but, despite the extra time and the increased work-load entailed in setting the right developmental and non-judgemental tone, it is essential if appraisal is to move the school towards improved liaison between colleagues, increased sharing of successes and a better climate for both teaching and learning.

FURTHER READING

ACAS (1986) *School Teacher Appraisal: A National Framework.* London: ACAS.
This was one of the earliest papers on teacher appraisal and it is useful to see how far appraisal has progressed.

Handy, C. (1985) *Understanding Organizations.* London: Penguin. Again, Handy has some important points to make.

NUT (1991) *Appraisal: Your Rights and Expectations.* London: National Union of Teachers.
This is a useful publication, especially from the appraisee's point of view.

Smith, R. (1993b) *Preparing for Appraisal: Self Evaluation for Teachers in Primary and Secondary Schools.* Lancaster: Framework Press. This provides a number of activities to help teachers reflect on their own practice before and during the appraisal process.

Wragg, E. (1987) *Teacher Appraisal: A Practical Guide.* London: Macmillan.
A wide-ranging and eminently sensible approach to appraisal.

Wragg, E. (1994) Under the microscope. *Times Educational Supplement*, London, 9 September 1994, summarized from the Leverhulme Teacher Appraisal Project.
This appears to be the latest attempt to find out how appraisal is affecting teachers and the way that they teach.

CHAPTER 9

DEVELOPING RELATIONSHIPS WITH COLLEAGUES

CHAPTER OVERVIEW

Self-evaluation, self-knowledge and the ability to constantly learn from experience are some of the keys to successful teaching and the effective management of schools. In order to plan for both the present and the future and to make appropriate choices, all those who work in schools should aim to understand themselves and know how to relate to colleagues in a way which enhances the professional development of everyone. This chapter explores these issues and suggests that in a sense some forms of behaviour are more appropriate than others within schools and an understanding of our own enthusiasms, drives and motivations should help us to see why others behave as they do and how it might be possible to change inappropriate behaviour and relationships into something more positive and fulfilling.

SELF-RECOGNITION

As early as 1927, in the *Handbook of Suggestions for the Consideration of Teachers and Others Concerned in the Work of the Public Elementary School*, HMI suggested that 'What every teacher teaches is himself. Whatever methods he (sic) may adopt, there is no doubt that his own character will be the most potent influence in determining the ideals of his pupils.' Carrington and Troyna (1988) further imply that 'Reflective teaching is applied in a cyclical or spiralling process in which teachers continually monitor, evaluate and revise their own practice...reflective teaching is based on teacher judgement, informed partly by self reflection and partly by insights from educational disciplines' (pp. 64–5). Collegiality, shared experiences and the idea that successful school management involves all teachers, governors, parents and, where possible pupils themselves, has so far featured strongly in this book. Certainly there were suggestions in Chapter 1 that change could be brought about by effective decision-making through groups and teams meeting together. Other chapters have also stressed the success of a more democratic style of leadership in terms of using the expertise of colleagues, for example, to reach conclusions about the most appropriate ethos and the format and content of the School Development Plan. The ability to control our own professional lives alongside the needs and aspirations of others, however, is not easy. Each of us has had particular cultural and material experiences which, according to Sikes *et al.* (1985), make up our individual 'biography'. It is difficult for us to be aware of how our personality and perspectives govern how we teach and relate to colleagues. Self-awareness will be helpful but it is notoriously difficult to achieve.

Pollard and Tann (1993) suggest we should bear in mind that in recognizing ourselves we need to be aware that early formative experiences are important and may influence how we behave and perform at work in such a way as to make it difficult to change such personal qualities as the capacity to empathize and the confidence to project and assert ourselves. Despite these difficulties it is important to try to work with and manage others in a confident and self-fulfilling way. There are several ways of examining oneself and one's relationships with colleagues. Using a self-recognition chart (see Box 9.1) will help to identify how you feel about yourself. If you wish to take it further you could ask a colleague to complete the chart for you and then compare any mismatches. There are problems with this approach because in choosing a colleague you will have to take decisions about such issues as: do they share my views about teaching; how well do they know me; are they too close to me on a personal level; do they work in a totally different way? You may like to live even more dangerously and try and pursue this task with the pupils you teach! If you choose this route and there are significant differences, it is important to decide how they might affect your attitude to the job you do and the colleagues you work with.

Box 9.1 Self-recognition chart

Read each pair and tick the place on the line between them where you feel you are, e.g. if you feel you are neither *quiet* nor *loud* when you are working, place a tick in the middle of line 1. If you feel you are *loud* when working place the tick nearer to *loud* on the line.

```
 1. Quiet————————————————— Loud
 2. Attractive——————————————— Unattractive
 3. Active———————————————— Passive
 4. Kind————————————————— Unkind
 5. Happy———————————————— Sad
 6. Fair————————————————— Unfair
 7. Modest——————————————— Boastful
 8. Intelligent—————————————— Unintelligent
 9. Introverted—————————————— Extroverted
10. Strong———————————————— Weak
11. Liberal——————————————— Conservative
12. Nervous——————————————— Relaxed
13. Powerful——————————————— Powerless
14. Trusting——————————————— Sceptical
15. Independent—————————————— Conforming
16. Hardworking————————————— Lazy
17. Polite———————————————— Impolite
18. Sensitive——————————————— Insensitive
19. Interesting—————————————— Boring
20. Gregarious—————————————— Solitary
21. Friendly——————————————— Unfriendly
22. Tolerant——————————————— Intolerant
23. Generous——————————————— Mean
```

(See Smith, 1990a, for a similar version of this chart)

In looking at your 'profile', and perhaps using it as feedback, you may find that when you are working you are self-confident and outward-looking but there are going to be times when you and your colleagues are unsure whether you are right and less confident about your relationships with each other. When individuals are uncertain of their status, popularity and happiness at work they may, even if they lack confidence, be able to work efficiently and effectively and strive to succeed. For example, they may be able to meet deadlines early, meetings can be forums for them to state their views reasonably clearly, and relationships with colleagues may help them restore satisfaction and confidence in themselves.

On the other hand, however, some colleagues who feel left out, who might see themselves as unpopular and who lack self-confidence may well become disruptive, arrogant, patronizing and unpleasant in order to prove themselves. Others merely choose not to take part and only work on the fringes of the school, being reluctant to either play any role in the planning processes or even less so in their implementation. It is important to recognize that such negative behaviour usually occurs in people who feel threatened or unsure about their place in the organization of the school (Skynner and Cleese, 1983). Managers need to reverse this as far as possible, and to turn negative feelings into positive and confident ones. In looking at those attitudes that may reduce the effectiveness of a school, it is useful to suggest the kinds of behaviour that will not help, i.e. negative management, and the kinds of skills that may be more successful. If you examine these positive and negative qualities (see discussion on management roles in Chapter 3), it is important to understand that successful and positive managers will certainly try to be objective, take action and accept responsibility. They will delegate, listen to suggestions, offer effective solutions and at the same time learn from colleagues by acknowledging the fact that they cannot know everything and that they need to be able to rely on the knowledge of others. They will also have a positive vision of the future and are able to handle the many problems that will need to be faced. On the other hand, a negative manager might well be much more inactive and will find it easier to talk about problems rather than solve them. At the same time they will be able to offer few solutions to problems and may well see the future as some kind of dark abyss filled with unforeseen issues and problems.

Attempts to categorize ourselves and colleagues will always be difficult, because no one fits neatly into boxes and there is an almost unlimited number of such categories. So far, in looking at yourself and your relationship to others, we have concentrated on recognizing your main attributes together with attempting to suggest some types of positive and negative behaviour that will influence relationships in schools. Another way of looking at these kinds of working relationships is to try and match behaviour to task. One simple way of doing this is to create two characteristics: a person who enjoys the *content* of the work, and a person who enjoys the *processes* and the way jobs are done. While this may be a somewhat forced and not totally adequate dichotomy it is a useful way to begin examining management tasks.

It may be the case that some of the management tasks that need to be completed in school will be more effective if they are taken on by a 'content' person and some will work better if a 'process' person carries them out. If this is the case, it is important within a school that there are colleagues with many different characteristics so that all the jobs that need to be done can be completed by a person or people best suited to the tasks in hand. In developing this point I will suggest two recognizable stereotypical personality types and illustrate this with an example of how they might perform a task.

A content colleague

- Can be single-minded in their approach to an end product.
- Misses important details in the search for an ending.
- Can be very definite about how jobs should be done and solutions reached.
- Gets things done and sees the 'process' as a not too important side issue.
- Can be impatient, intolerant and forceful in order to achieve a final result.

A process colleague

- Is interested in ideas and theories.
- Enjoys talking to people and interacting with them.
- Likes to think about and be involved in complex issues.
- Sees decisions as being dependent on many diverse responses.
- Is not averse to wheeling and dealing if it is interesting and part of the decision-making process.

It will be useful to consider how this dichotomy might work. In considering a management task, for example, controlling the budget, we can examine how both the content and process colleague might deal with it.

In many ways, setting and controlling a budget is a task that has to be completed in detail and to a definite deadline. This means that it is ideally suited to a 'content' colleague because of the very characteristics of the job, e.g. setting figures within budget headings, maintaining spending records, transferring money from one heading to another and supervising the checking of invoices. But, like many tasks in school, this kind of single-minded approach has to be tempered with the knowledge that setting a budget cannot just be part of one person's single-minded and forceful approach. Other people will be involved and this is where the 'process' characteristics will be useful because there will have to be a considerable amount of interaction, careful thinking about complex issues and an interest in many diverse responses. Ideally, both sets of characteristics could be part of one person's management techniques. It is more likely to be the case, however, that in developing a team of managers who will have to work on a number of management tasks, colleagues with both characteristics will have to be carefully considered.

Self-knowledge comes partly from looking closely at how we perform tasks, how we perceive other people and how we work together in teams and groups. It also develops from the clues we pick up from colleagues about our own abilities and how we carry out our jobs. Finding out the views of others is not easy but it is useful if we can identify any obvious differences in how we see ourselves and how others perceive us. It could be that there is a misunderstanding and that we are really closer to a solution than we thought, or it can be because of completely different viewpoints. It is important in all schools to recognize that colleagues have a range of different ideas, abilities, backgrounds, personalities and knowledge. It is thus not surprising that managing schools is difficult and choosing the right person to do a particular job, creating the right mix of people within a team and motivating as many colleagues as possible is essential for success.

Individuals in schools will have to work in teams and groups for many different reasons. These can range from feeling more secure, using matching strengths and weaknesses to create more effective groups, uniting through some common purpose or, in an autocratic environment, forming a group for self-protection. All these groups will function better if the people within them know as much about themselves as possible. As was suggested earlier, individual teachers need to be reflective but becoming more effective and working together might also be as simple as knowing who likes who, who can work better together, who dislikes who and who respects your performance. One way of doing this is for colleagues to create their own staff relationship grid (see Figure 9.1). The vertical axis ranges from *How much you think your colleagues like you* to *How much you think your colleagues dislike you*. The horizontal axis ranges from *How much respect your colleagues have for your professional performance* to *How little respect your colleagues have for your professional performance*.

Two examples are given. Mrs Y likes you but does not have much respect for your professional performance. Mr X does not like you very much but thinks your professional performance is reasonably good. It would be useful to put all your colleagues on to the grid, bearing in mind that this is a sensitive activity and should be confidential. It will help you to learn more about the way colleagues might manage each other and be managed by others.

The grid was developed at seminars held at the Open University Summer Schools for the Reading and Language Diploma (1979–1982).

Another way of managing yourself in relation to your colleagues and hopefully working together more co-operatively and effectively is to look at how you communicate with each other

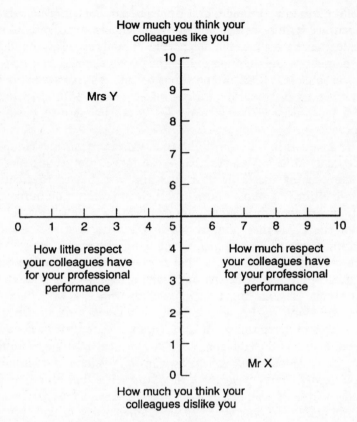

How much you think your colleagues like you

How little respect your colleagues have for your professional performance

How much respect your colleagues have for your professional performance

Mrs Y

Mr X

How much you think your colleagues dislike you

Source: Adapted from Easen, 1985

Figure 9.1 Staff relationship grid

in face-to-face situations. Berne (1967) identified the need that we all have for praise and recognition; he called it 'stroking'. He also developed the idea of how people exchange messages which he called Transactional Analysis (TA). He suggested that our feelings and the way we react to other people depend on the 'strokes' we have received and how we feel about ourselves and other people. Our feelings and therefore how we behave with colleagues can change very quickly when circumstances change. Berne suggested the following three patterns of behaviour:

1. *Parent* ego state (P) where we tell, guide, assert, dominate, criticize, advise and discipline.

2. *Adult* ego state (A) where we behave more in a rational way and reason, listen, suggest, work on problems and collect and sort information. This tends to be objective and rational rather than emotional.
3. *Child* ego state (C) where there is more of a response to feelings and where we behave intuitively rather than rationally and where anger and rebelliousness are close to the surface. This is probably learned during childhood.

Berne noticed the effect that the interaction of the ego states had on two people communicating and trying to work together. He recognized that as well as trying to perform such basic functions as completing jobs, seeking information, or persuading others to accept their views, colleagues may be behaving in more subtle and devious ways. Powell and Solity (1990) suggest that using these descriptions is a way of examining the behaviour of individuals who are interacting together, especially when one party wants and needs an outcome which they conceal. It is a way of looking at strategies that individuals might adopt to get what they want without declaring their intentions. It is important to recognize that if one or both participants are concealing their motives, then the interactions, whether between individuals or during meetings, can become very negative. They may be in agreement or at cross-purposes. This means that working together may be easy or it may become very difficult to achieve any sense of togetherness or team work. When there are interactions in the adult state, which is the assumed starting-point for teachers working together, there should be few problems, but this can be undermined by a series of alternative and hidden motivations.

Transactions or conversations can obviously occur in many ways and this can determine the success or otherwise of the working relationship. Powell and Solity (1990), Easen (1985) and Smith (1990a) describe some of the problems which might arise if participants behave in an adult or childlike manner or assume that their colleague is behaving in such a way. Such interactions effectively block what is happening or conceal a hidden agenda.

In the examples given in Figure 9.2 it is relatively easy to suggest that if the response to the statement is what is expected the interaction is working and moving along lines where everyone knows what is happening and, where appropriate, discussions are fruitful, satisfactory conclusions reached and decisions made. This can happen during transactions between the same ego states and between different states. Where it becomes difficult, however, is when there are crossed transactions and where the responses come from unintended or unexpected ego states. This will mean that there are likely to be communication problems and difficulties are likely to arise. In all the examples both of the participants are teachers and one is behaving in the adult ego state.

● Parallel transactions between the same ego states

P	P	e.g. *Question:* How many meetings have you been
A ←——→ A		to today?
C	C	*Answer:* Oh, about three.
		(This is the ideal kind of interaction between colleagues.)

● Parallel transactions between different ego states

P	P	e.g. *Question:* What do you think you are doing
A	A	shouting like that?
C	C	*Answer:* Sorry, I won't do it again.

● Crossed transactions where the response comes from an unintended or unexpected ego state

P	P	e.g. *Question:* You chaired that meeting well,
A ——→ A		didn't you?
C	C	*Answer:* Don't try and flatter me. I can't
		stand it!

● Crossed transactions used deliberately to control a conversation

P	P	e.g. *Question:* This computer won't go right for
A	A	me, will it?
C	C	*Answer:* Let me try it for you.

Figure 9.2 Transactions between colleagues

Communication that occurs between two 'adults' will obviously be more effective and productive than between any other areas of Transactional Analysis. Because this is not always the case, it is important to know how to handle difficulties. Being successful often means knowing where you are in the structure of power relationships and may determine how assertive you need to be.

POWER IN SCHOOLS

Power as a term is usually related to authority and influence. Power and authority are both forms of influence. If you have authority in school it gives you the right to expect a certain degree of compliance from colleagues. The power that individuals might have is the force that backs up the authority. Conway (1978) suggests that managerial power is in the form of control over pay, promotions, employment, termination of employment, etc. This is not the only kind of power, however. In most schools there are many different sources of power, depending on the relationships that have been established. Some of these sources of power are described here.

Power because of the control of information

If you have information that your colleagues do not possess you have a distinct advantage over them. You are able to make more informed decisions than they, and as a result can take more effective action.

Power because of the control of resources

If you control the budget or the timetable, you have more control over funding and the use of certain teaching spaces than other colleagues. The more 'jobs' you have, the potentially greater the power.

Power because of position

Certain roles within the school will give you more or less authority; for example, a head of department is likely to have more power than a colleague who teaches in that department.

185

Power because of knowledge

If you know more than your colleagues, it is likely that you will have more expertise in certain areas. This expertise, usually gained because of specialist training, gives you more power.

Power because of personality

The force of someone's personality can be a source of power and can influence how colleagues behave towards you.

In order to resist the power colleagues have, it is often necessary to be more assertive within your own sphere of influence. This can be achieved alone but it is often more appropriate in schools to collaborate and work together with colleagues. Collective action is often appropriate when trying to obtain a fair share of the necessary power to work effectively. This can be achieved without having to allow others to dominate meetings and the management structure of the school, without having to accept a passive role in the smooth running of the school and without having to be seen as aggressive. Indeed, aggression and passivity can be a source of inappropriate behaviour which has a negative influence on any kind of team work, and can also act as a source of information on how colleagues are relating to each other. If individuals and managers recognize the presence of aggression and passivity it will be possible to accept that their existence may be causing problems which need to be confronted and solved. This is not easy, and can and will be a considerable management issue until the source of the passivity or aggression is removed. This, in itself, may well be impossible.

Communication, problem-solving, motivating others, effective team work, change and leadership will all be less effective if those participating are either too aggressive or too timid. An aggressive person is likely to become angry easily, to try to dominate meetings, to be volatile and often to become verbally and sometimes physically violent. A timid person who adopts a too passive role will usually be meek, put upon and so mild-mannered that colleagues are able to make them accept and do anything that is required.

In many ways, by being passive and timid or by being angry and aggressive we are not taking responsibility for our behaviour.

Timidity means allowing others to manipulate you and not really recognizing that your own needs are important. By being aggressive you often make others feel worthless and, through your anger, get your own way at the expense of others. Rowland and Birkett (1992) see assertiveness as the key to managing schools more effectively and as an important way of taking responsibility for your own behaviour:

> Being assertive means...having respect for ourselves and others, and being honest. It allows us to say what we want and feel but not at other people's expense. It means understanding the point of view of other people, and being self confident and positive. It is not about winning come what may or getting your own way all the time. Assertiveness is about handling conflict and coming to an acceptable compromise.
>
> (p.6)

Rowland and Birkett go on to state quite clearly that in schools all colleagues have the right to:

- have and express feelings and opinions;
- be listened to and taken seriously;
- set priorities;
- say 'no' without feeling guilty;
- ask for what they want;
- ask for and get information from each other;
- sometimes make mistakes.

By accepting these rights we should gain in confidence and feel more in control of decisions and actions. It is important to assert our rights. Assertive behaviour or assertive dialogue with a colleague does not always come naturally and has to be learned. Smith (1993b) has one way of doing this. By adding appropriate questions or statements to his step-by-step guide to assertion, it becomes easier to see its value as a means to behaving in school.

STEP-BY-STEP GUIDE TO ASSERTION

There are times when everyone needs to be assertive; when it is the only way to behave. In schools, this will usually occur when someone wants you to do something that you are either unable to do because you have no time, or you do not want to do it at a particular time because you are doing something equally important or that you do not want to do it at all because you do not consider it to be part of your job. The kinds of responses you will have to make will only apply when the ethos of the school and the management styles leave you no alternative. The suggestions as to how to cope depend on a series of responses used in a specific order. They are assertive but not aggressive and should invite an adult response without raising anyone's hackles. The responses used as an example are based on the following scenario.

You receive a note from the head/deputy/head of department telling you that because they are unable to attend a particular meeting you will have to go instead. However, you also cannot go at such short notice because of prior commitments.

Step 1: *Summarize* the problem carefully, factually, unemotionally and straightforwardly; e.g. Your memo about the meeting on Wednesday has caused me considerable problems. . . .

Step 2: *State* exactly how you feel . . . *not* how anyone else might feel; e.g. I feel very concerned that although it is an important meeting I will be unable to go.

Step 3: *Describe* clearly and simply why you feel that way and why you are unable to respond in the way that is wanted; e.g. First of all, I have already arranged to have a brief meeting with X and then I am expected home because of a long-standing commitment to go to the theatre. . . .

Step 4: *Sympathize* or *empathize* with the other person's point of view or position; e.g. I can understand the need for someone to go to the meeting but I already have a busy schedule for that evening. . . .

Step 5: *Specify* exactly what you would like to happen. It is important to try and find a solution or compromise in the situation; e.g. If it is not really possible for any of us to be there I will telephone a colleague from another school who should be going and ask her to collect all the information she can. We can collect this at the end of the week.

Step 6: *Decide* what your final response will be. It is important that this does not threaten the other person/other people; e.g. I think that this solution should work reasonably well. I am sorry that I cannot go but as I have already made other arrangements. . . .

It is important to be aware of the 'human relations' side of school management and not to treat it as a tiresome extra. In fact, it is so important that some of the ideas touched on here are discussed more fully in Powell and Solity (1990), where they extend the debate further by citing factors within an individual's family that may lead them to become timid, aggressive, controlling, etc. The idea of pursuing the 'content' of what needs doing relentlessly and at the expense of colleagues' feelings and attitudes will mean that the sharing of views, collegiality, democracy and the support needed from colleagues will be relegated to a side issue. Hall (1972) suggests that good managers need to be interested in the people and the product. Argyris (1970) suggests that individuals are always trying to increase their self-esteem or to enhance their self-conception. They therefore look for psychological success by setting their own challenging goals and meeting them. If this is the case, it is important that in managing ourselves we recognize that we have these needs and that when managing others it suggests that the goals and targets set need to be relevant to an individual's idea of self-conception. Tasks, jobs, meetings, agendas, aims, targets and objectives must be meaningful to all those colleagues who are expected to participate. Transactional Analysis can be taken a step further by simply seeing the child, adult and parent state as being part of a simple polarization of being either OK or not OK.

THE OK AND THE NOT OK COLLEAGUE

The 'OK colleague' is easy to work with and will be co-operative and/or creative in the child state, responsive and analytical in the adult state and will try to bring the best out in people in the parent state. The 'not OK colleague', however, is probably difficult to work with and likely to be immature, forgetful, hostile or over-apologetic in the child state. In the adult state he or she will be obsessed by content in a mechanistic way and in the parent state will be over-protective, indifferent, negative and self-opinionated.

Montgomery (1989) takes this analogy a step further and produces a useful summary of attitudes and relationships that are dependent on one of four positions:

1. I'm OK, you're OK. . . . This means everyone gets along together and should mean that the management of change, decision-making and collegiality are relatively easy to do well.
2. I'm OK, you're not OK. . . . This is the getting people away from you or getting rid of people position. In many ways this is the selfish manager getting his or her own way. There will be little working together and decisions taken in this way where the majority are not likely to agree will be resented. On an individual level it means that one person 'wins' at the expense of another.
3. I'm not OK, you're OK. . . . This is the getting away from people position where an individual can feel isolated because everyone else seems to be achieving what they want and need and that person is not.
4. I'm not OK, you're not OK. . . . This is the everyone getting nowhere with each other position. This is obviously an intolerable position where nothing will happen and decisions will never be taken.

Individuals may adopt very different attitudes towards each other in any one of these states. Complementary positions such as Number 1 suggest sharing, good communications and a feeling of respect and equality. Others such as Number 2 are less effective positions to hold; Numbers 3 and 4 are potentially disruptive and ineffective. In managing yourself you need to make sure that you have a positive influence on colleagues. You have to be able to listen and move through irrelevancies and unhelpful points towards a successful end product. Tasks have to be completed but the process has to allow colleagues to play a leading role. Everyone needs to participate in some area of the school and it is important that colleagues' feelings are taken into account. You need to influence others by assertive persuasion, participation, trust and a common vision and not by your own dictatorial aggression.

CHAPTER SUMMARY

Just as self-evaluation should be a key part of everyone's appraisal process it should also be important in examining an individual's role in the management of the school. If we look at how we relate to what we are expected to do and our relationships with each other, we will recognize strengths and face up to problems and weaknesses. Positive relationships with colleagues are obviously important and can influence the smooth running of the school and the success of any changes that have to be managed. While it is true that different tasks may need different approaches it should be obvious that in Transactional Analysis terms an adult-to-adult approach within a position of 'I'm OK, you're OK' should be able to deal with most relationships and tasks in a sensitive and appropriate way. When this position is not there, and this will be the case at some time in every school, those who manage will have to make sure that relationships are mended and may well have to assert their views and beliefs so that confidence may return and the jobs that have to be done are dealt with seriously. All this takes time and, because in managing yourself you are at the same time managing others, it can be quite stressful. Stress and time management are the subjects of Chapter 10.

FURTHER READING

Berne, E. (1967) *Games People Play: The Psychology of Human Relationships*. London: Pelican.
This book is a good starting-point if you are interested in Transactional Analysis.

Conway, J.A. (1978) Power and participation: decision making in selected English schools. *Journal of Educational Administration*, **16** (1), 80–96.
This contains a useful analysis of how power is used in schools.

CHAPTER 10

STRESS AND TIME MANAGEMENT

CHAPTER OVERVIEW

Teachers often feel a sense of panic about the amount of work that has to be done and the lack of time in which to do it. A certain amount of pressure can be stimulating and allows the individual to draw on reserves of strength and stamina in order to respond in an appropriately energetic way. Too much pressure, however, creates a state where individuals feel incapable of working efficiently. Stress may be caused by many aspects of what happens in school or at home such as the conflicting expectations colleagues have of you, either not being able to delegate or having too much work to do because of delegation, and even poor time management. This chapter will not only suggest ways of recognizing and alleviating stress but should also help teachers manage their time more effectively.

STRESS AND ITS SYMPTOMS

Whether or not we experience stress depends on our own expectations, past experiences, the way we behave towards other people and how they behave towards us. It is difficult to change others but by trying to change ourselves and behaving differently it is possible in turn to make colleagues behave differently. However, relieving tension and stress in this way is not easy because changing our own behaviour is very difficult. We behave in the way we do for many reasons and in some senses it can be argued that we would rather experience stress than change the way we behave. This is because we have good reasons for behaving as we do; it is familiar, comfortable, safe, etc., and to alter this is a challenging, threatening and difficult process. When we feel that we are suffering from stress and finding the situation intolerable we have to decide whether to carry on as we are or try to change. Earlier chapters have discussed such issues as being assertive and recognizing our own strengths and weaknesses but it also has to remembered that some people may be more susceptible to stress than others.

Elliott and Kemp (1983) take the view that the likelihood of succumbing to stress may be determined by the type of person you are. They describe two personality types.

Type A people tend to be aggressive, competitive, impatient and prone to heart disease. If it is suggested that they should relax more, perhaps by taking up golf, they take their aggression and impatience on to the golf course. Such people are likely to be highly stressed.

Type B people tend to be fond of leisure, not particularly hostile or competitive and are generally much more relaxed about life.

It is highly likely that both types of personality exist in every school, and that however the school is managed stress is inescapable in some form or another. In some instances a certain level of stress and tension will help to motivate and create the kind of action that is necessary to achieve results. This is almost certainly the case with footballers, who need a certain amount of tension to perform to optimal level. While Elliot and Kemp provide us with two personality types, it is also useful to understand that there are also those who are able to cope with stress and handle it and those who cannot. Gold and Roth (1993) suggest that when our coping mechanisms are successful the 'distress' is minimized and the individual's self-esteem is not threatened but when coping mechanisms are unsuccessful, negative emotions are experienced and seen as threatening to the individual. Some teachers will obviously cope better than others, but effective managers will make sure that they are able not only to recognize stress in colleagues but that they are sensitive enough to explore both the working conditions and the personality and family background of those suffering from stress.

Alleviating stress is often dependent on making sure that the working conditions in terms of ethos or climate are positive and able to motivate colleagues. In schools where the ethos is one of competitiveness rather than where teachers' jobs are corporate and shared, responsibility will lie with the individual all the time. Any problem which may cause the individual to experience stress will be seen as the individual's fault, and probably be called incompetence. Freen (1983) suggests that where the school ethos is one of shared responsibility and caring for each other, problems of stress can be seen as the responsibility of everyone and positive support can be offered. A caring ethos would also lead to management structures where support would be available to enable staff to function efficiently. This would have the effect of changing the way teachers view the admission of problems that might be causing them stress. In less caring schools teachers learn not to express their problems or anxieties, since this can lead to raised eyebrows and the likelihood of being seen as inefficient and ineffective by colleagues.

Before being able to cope with stress it is important to recognize the symptoms in yourself and colleagues and to relate this to how you manage yourself (see Chapter 9) in terms of your relationship to colleagues and your ability to evaluate your role in the school. Stress, however, does not manifest itself in the same way in everyone and reactions can vary. Whatever symptoms are recognized it is important to begin to take some kind of action because if these symptoms are allowed to persist for long periods physical health can and will suffer. Some of the symptoms of stress suggested by Cooper and Marshall (1978) include: frequent absences from school due to illness; higher blood pressure; being more negative than usual; neglecting one's personal appearance; change in appetite; getting irritable more frequently; drinking more alcohol; making more mistakes; feeling unnecessarily anxious; criticizing constantly; a reduced sex drive; frequent aches and pains; making unrealistic judgements;

smoking more; catching frequent colds; becoming accident-prone; feeling lethargic; changed bowel patterns; becoming aggressive and defensive; and feeling depressed.

If these symptoms affect how individuals feel about themselves, how they manage themselves and how they do their work and relate to colleagues, an important managerial function will be to make sure that something is done. Figure 10.1 indicates the two points at which you need to intervene in order to deal with your own or someone else's stress.

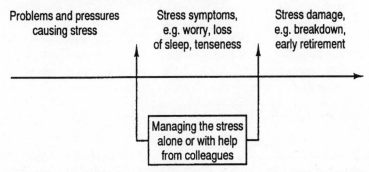

Figure 10.1 Stress intervention points

Using this model, however, involves both recognizing the causes of stress, knowing how to alleviate or remove the problem and reducing the symptoms by doing so. If the situations causing the stress are identified it is possible to intervene by changing these situations. This could include working patterns, work-load or some more personal or private matter that is influencing how the person reacts to the work that has to be completed. On the other hand, the causes of the stress may not be recognized at first and may only become apparent after the symptoms of stress have been diagnosed. Once this has happened it should be possible to begin to alleviate the symptoms by understanding and changing the problems and pressures that are causing the symptoms.

CAUSES OF STRESS

Many arguments about the causes of stress have drawn the distinction between and shown the links with personality and working environment. Cooper and Marshall (1978) argue that stress is directly related to the fit between an individual's ability to cope and the conditions of the work environment in which that individual must function. One way of tracing these links is shown in Box 10.1.

Box 10.1 Stress: symptoms and causes

Environment	Person	Manifestations of stress
Relationships at work • with superiors • with subordinates • with colleagues • inability to delegate • lack of social support	Neurotic tendencies Emotional instability Rigidity Type A behaviour Underachiever Overachiever	*Physical manifestations* • increased pulse • high blood pressure • smoking, ulcers • heart disease
Organizational structure and ethos • lack of participation • no sense of belonging • poor communications • lack of any kind of power		*Emotional manifestations* • low motivation • low self-esteem • anxiety, fear • frustration
Factors intrinsic to the job • too much work and too little time to do it • time pressures and deadlines • working conditions change		
Role in the organization • conflict between several different roles • too much responsibility for 'things' • too much responsibility for 'people' • too little responsibility • too little management support		*Behavioural manifestations* • over-eating • difficulty sleeping • excessive drinking
Career development • Under-promotion • Over-promotion		

While the criteria listed in Box 10.1 are by no means exclusive, they do suggest how and where stress can originate. Since the Education Reform Act, the demands on teachers have increased considerably and the feeling that there is too much to do and too little time is a common complaint in schools. Managing time is important and will be looked at in the second half of this chapter, but as well as having too much to do, having too little, or having to do things that are too easy for an individual's talents can also cause stress. Being bored can produce similar symptoms to those caused by work that is too demanding. Colleagues, together with people who are in authority or those to whom you have to delegate work can be a prime source of stress. It is important to recognize who they are and why they are causing you problems. It could be that by putting too much pressure on yourself and by having unrealistic and unreasonable expectations it is becoming too difficult to both manage and relieve the stress that has developed.

It also has to be recognized, however, that stress can and does arise from personal and individual factors which relate to their own past experiences, expectations and perceptions. Two teachers may react quite differently to the same behaviour from colleagues. One may respond quite well and be more carefree and dismiss unreasonable demands and expectations; the other may take it all extremely seriously and be more likely to feel threatened and under stress. In managing and relieving stress it is important to understand that teachers need to be able to ask themselves whether they actually do feel under stress in a particular situation and if they do, why.

MANAGING AND RELIEVING STRESS

The first thing to do if you are feeling stressed is to reflect on the relationship between your life at work and life outside school. If you manage colleagues, or begin to realize that someone you know is suffering from stress, you can apply these suggestions to them. There must be space for leisure, and suggested ways of coping with stress that combine work and leisure will include such things as: starting off the day properly with time to think and time to eat; occasionally changing routines for starting the day, e.g. with exercise, different breakfast foods and varying times; setting yourself priorities; writing things down; making lists; not trying to do too many things at once; leaving school early occasionally; considering whether it is better to stay later at work and finish or take work home; changing your working environment if necessary by closing or opening doors; cutting down on telephone calls; moving furniture around; taking proper breaks; eating healthily and occasionally changing your lunch patterns; developing wider interests and leisure pursuits, e.g. family, hobbies and interests; being assertive when you need to; taking advantage of the support of friends and colleagues; always listening to what others are saying to avoid any confusion; and feeling positive about your work by making sure you are part of the mainstream ideas in the school.

Figure 10.1 suggested various intervention points when dealing with your own stress or that of a colleague. This is never easy because different people will react to a variety of approaches and some colleagues, despite knowing what they should do, are often unable to act. This is often a result of their own parental messages to succeed, work hard, achieve, etc. and will be extremely difficult to deal with. In any staff training programme, however, there needs to be space for INSET on stress management which, if high-quality trainers are used, could help all colleagues. It may be necessary in dealing with a colleague's stress to distinguish between the types of help that might be appropriate.

Giving advice is really about offering your opinion based on your view of what has happened and what the situation is. For example, if a colleague is concerned about the type and availability of equipment that he or she wishes to use it should be possible to ease any worries by giving advice about the mechanics of borrowing and using school resources.

Teaching can be helping a colleague to acquire knowledge or skills that might help them get out of a specific situation. For example, a colleague who is finding a particular aspect of classroom management stressful may be taught a particular skill which will enable him or her to be more effective in the classroom and less worried about teaching skills.

Changing the organization is making an effort to change the

structure of the organization if it is causing difficulties for colleagues. For example, schools often have entrenched routines
and are organized in such a way that it is hardly ever questioned
why certain things happen in certain ways. Breaks, lunch-times
and how pupils enter and leave the school may be causing tension and stress. These problems could be solved relatively easily
by meeting to discuss changes.

Taking action will mean actually doing something on behalf
of someone else. For example, if it is obvious that a colleague is
becoming increasingly worried about keeping up with his or her
planning documents, someone needs to offer to help or suggest
how there might be an easier way that will save time but be
equally effective.

Giving information will occur when a colleague does not possess the appropriate knowledge to solve a problem. For example,
if colleagues have not received the information they need about
such issues as which sanctions to use against certain kinds of
misbehaviour, they may feel stressed and worried that they are
not following agreed procedures. Information about what action
to take should be readily available.

Counselling is helping someone to solve their problems themselves by exploring the problem and looking at alternative ways
of dealing with it so they can take decisions about helping
themselves. For example, this is a difficult problem to solve and
relies on schools having someone on the staff who is a trained
and skilful counsellor. Time should be made available and
schools need to recognize that counselling is essential in the
case of someone who is obviously very stressed.

Stressed colleagues need to be helped in certain specific ways.
As has already been suggested, how this is done is a matter of
taking the right decision for the right person at the right time.
Many stressed colleagues will tend to be backward-looking and
in finding it difficult to deal with the present they will tend to
see the past as a glorious period of happiness and efficiency. In
order to overcome this obstacle they will need to look to the
future, be positive and plan for the long term rather than the
day-to-day short term.

Social support is crucial. Colleagues can help each other if they
are able to share problems and work together to reach decisions.
This might mean establishing your own strengths and limita-

tions together with the positive elements of the current situation and the strengths of colleagues so that you will know who is likely to need help and who will be able to provide that help. In doing this you should be aware of your own ability to cope with your job and how you can anticipate problems as well as solve them. As a final point in this section it is useful to use some ideas from Gold and Roth (1993) when they suggest that stress can be prevented and relieved by understanding certain fundamental factors related to the job that is being done. They include:

- Recognizing that you cannot control everything.
- Knowing that some things are not easy to understand.
- Being aware that you are only able to change yourself and not others.
- Not expecting to meet everyone's expectations and that you will not always be liked or approved of and not everyone will accept you.
- Realizing that running away from problems will not solve them.
- You can never be right all the time and you can make mistakes, but you can handle them.
- You are responsible for how you react to feelings, situations and other people.
- You are capable of change and while life is not always fair or pleasant it is important to roll with the bad and celebrate the good.

It is useful to compare these factors with the need to be an assertive teacher (described in Chapter 9). By being assertive you are in control and by being in control you are largely avoiding the aggression or passivity that teachers can develop when they feel that classroom events are becoming intolerable. Rowland and Birkett (1992) recognize the importance of using assertiveness to prevent and combat stress when they suggest that by being assertive teachers should feel better about themselves, have more confidence and feel less powerless. A more stress-free and positive image is thus presented to colleagues and pupils and more constructive outcomes are likely to occur because of increased self-confidence and a better developed control of events.

TIME MANAGEMENT

Campbell and Neill (1994) suggest that in looking at teachers of Key Stage 1 children there was an 'initial picture...of teachers spending long hours on work, committed to implementing the policy on curriculum and assessment but finding major obstacles in terms of managing time allocation to the whole curriculum, assessment and testing, and the lack of time in the school day' (p.9). I am sure that teachers of other Key Stages will recognize similar problems over the allocation and use of their time.

Time management is of course a misnomer and, as Smith (1990b) suggests, we cannot really manage time but we can try and learn how to manage ourselves in relation to time, by trying to adopt a more positive and effective attitude to the working day. One point to understand is that the more complex a situation, the more important planning becomes as a means of dealing with it. Every teacher needs to be able to plan: there is a cliché which suggests that if you fail to plan you plan to fail; to control what is happening by keeping to targets and keeping interruptions to a minimum; to follow up by either finishing the task in hand or at least leaving it so that it can be easily picked up next time. Jumping from one task to another is never a very good way to get jobs done. This sounds so easy, and yet we all know that managing the time available in a working day is extremely difficult. Campbell and Neill's (1994) research examines teachers' work-loads in early Key Stages and suggests, for example, that only an extremely small amount of non-teaching time was available, that nine out of ten of their teachers were working beyond what they all considered a reasonable number of hours, and that of the distribution of time, large amounts were spent on preparation and in-service training as compared to teaching. Many of their teachers felt that this shift was likely to produce stress and disaffection. In many ways this research helps to remind us that time is the most valuable commodity in a school's resources and how it is used is important for the quality of pupils' learning. It is reasonable to assume that there will be difficulties in managing the time available. It is also reasonable to assume that Campbell and Neill's suggestion that teachers are having problems at Key Stage 1 is equally applicable to all other Key Stages of the National Curriculum. If this is the case, it is important to prioritize what actually has to be completed in the time available in school. This means that schools and teachers have to recognize and establish important issues so that time is spent on what have been accepted as high and essential priorities.

ESTABLISHING PRIORITIES

It is relatively easy to be unnecessarily busy, and those colleagues who are always rushing around and racing against time are not always the most effective. It is important to establish priorities and then to take decisions about what to do, when to do it and how to finish it. This may seem an obvious overstatement but within the practicalities of schools effective managers of time follow lists of priorities that are constantly updated.

Items on the list that are afforded high priority need to be done quickly and urgently; those that are medium priority can wait for a while but are still quite important; and those that are low priority need to be done by someone eventually. If they are left on low priority for too long, however, they will never get done. By establishing priorities in this way, those items on the low priority list should move up as soon as the urgent matters have been dealt with. It is useful to write a list for each day. It helps establish some kind of order in what can be a situation that often makes unreasonable demands on the time that is available. By not planning, there is the danger that each day will be spent with problems rather than organized opportunities.

There is another cliché: the more time we spend planning a project the less time we require to complete it. Those colleagues who find time management difficult may, as Day *et al.* (1990) suggest, be trying to do too many things at once and fail to recognize what needs to be done, who needs to do it and when it needs to be completed. It is never the total amount of time that is spent on a project that is crucial but the amount of quality or uninterrupted time. Giving all your time to something, however, does not mean working for long periods without a break. If energy decreases and boredom sets in, the work that is being done will be completed in a less effective way. Taking appropriate breaks should increase efficiency and help finish the task more easily. Everyone in schools should strive to create a high-quality service where excellence is the norm. This is not the same as being a perfectionist: this is invariably unattainable, frustrating and bordering on the neurotic. By being largely unattainable it is also a waste of everyone's time. During the search for an excellent service and despite the use of an effective method of prioritizing, there will be times when other people take over your time. All those in school need to be able to say no, tactfully and firmly. If your motivation is not to avoid work but to save time to do a better job on more important things, there will be a good chance that you will find ways of avoiding unproductive tasks. There are a few general rules that will help avoid other people wasting your time in such a way that it prevents you from effectively managing the time available.

Avoiding time-wasting

It may be possible to save valuable time by limiting the number of minutes you will talk to colleagues. This should become quite acceptable and there is no need to be rude or blunt if everyone understands the need to be brief. This may be a slow process with some colleagues, but it may become a necessity. It is also possible to terminate conversations honestly by saying things like, 'Look, I've got to go and deal with something else now', thus limiting professional conversations to a precise length of time. It is often difficult to hold any kind of professional discussion in school because the necessities of teaching leave little room for anything else. If this is the case, it is important to arrange to talk to colleagues at a time when you know that you both have space in your schedules rather than assuming that if the time is right for you it is right for them and vice versa. Remember that if you feel your time is being wasted, it is likely to be caused by valued colleagues with interesting things to say who just happen to want to speak to you when you have not got the same time available as they have. So if you have to say no, try not to fob people off: promise to see them at another time and if possible make a definite arrangement.

Do not delay taking action

Procrastination is often a deeply rooted habit which is difficult to change but which can waste a lot of time. Rather than wait to decide what you are going to do about this area of time management take an instant decision to change as soon as you have finished reading this section. Do not attempt to do too much too quickly but do make sure that you do something instantly. The best start would be to do something that you have been putting off for a long time. The next step – perhaps tomorrow morning – is to start the day by doing something unpleasant that you have been trying to avoid for a long time. Once this is done the day will be exhilaratingly easier.

Cut things out

If you are wasting time on activities that divert you from your real goals, you must do something about it. This applies to personal habits, routines and activities as well as work-associated tasks. Check everything that fails to either give you a feeling of accomplishment or help you work more effectively. If in doubt cut it out.

Delegate

This is inevitable. No head of department, headteacher or deputy head can possibly do all the work themselves. There must be trust in order to delegate and it has to be recognized that other people are able to do an effective and successful job. One golden rule is that once a decision has been made to delegate there must be limited interference. If heads, deputies or heads of department do get in the way by constantly checking and double-checking then several people will be spending time on dealing with part or all of the same job. By avoiding unnecessary interference the delegater is giving others the power, authority and responsibility to do a specific job. Bell (1989) suggests the kinds of questions that need to be asked about what should and should not be delegated.

It is important when delegating to try to identify those tasks that you will be happy about delegating to other people.

Remember that it is no good delegating a task if you cannot really let it go. All this will mean is that you will be looking over the shoulder of the person to whom you have delegated the task. This will waste everyone's time. It is useful to consider the following issues when identifying tasks to delegate:

- Which of my tasks can already be done by some or all members of staff?
- Which of my tasks make only a small contribution to the total success of the school?
- Which of my tasks take up more time than I can afford?
- Which of my tasks are not strictly related to my key targets?
- Which of my tasks are really the day-to-day responsibilities of a colleague?
- Which of my tasks cause problems when I am away because no one else can carry them out effectively?
- Which of my tasks would help members of staff to develop if they were given the responsibility?

(Bell, 1989, p.164)

Delegation will not save time, however, if it is a haphazard part of the time-management process. It has to be planned. Decisions have to be taken about what is to be delegated, who to, how much training they will need to do the job and when they should have time to do it. The tasks to be completed have to be outlined precisely with clear objectives and a relevant and realistic timetable of targets and deadlines. These will be linked to individual job descriptions, the School Development Plan and the appraisal process. Finally, there needs to be a way of evaluating and reviewing any subsequent steps that need to be taken.

GOOD TIME MANAGEMENT HABITS

It is important to realize that no one is perfect. No one will be able to plan their time in such a way that they will work to 'their plan' every minute of the day. It is also important to recognize that as Campbell *et al.* (1991) remind us, time management is a potentially dangerous concept in practice. Faced with absurdly demanding expectations, class teachers who do not meet them all effectively should not be made to feel that the reason for not meeting them is their failure to manage their own time properly. It may be the case that the demands made on teachers' and schools' time is unrealistic and insufficient to enable teachers to complete tasks. Reducing the demands made, increasing the numbers of teachers and the finance available, might enable teachers to feel that they have managed their time reasonably effectively and give them the satisfaction of believing that they have done their work well.

At the same time, however, teachers and schools are working in the present and on a day-to-day basis. There needs to be an attempt to maximize the use of our time and that of everyone else. There are certain criteria which, while not guaranteeing totally effective practice will, if used well, help you and colleagues manage the time that is available without taking the blame for the difficulties that have to be faced. Some of these criteria can be summed up as follows:

- Do not lose sight of your long-term goals but always be aware of the short- and medium-term goals that move everything forward.
- Set aside a specific time for action planning. Set priorities either at the end of the day for the following day or first thing in the morning for the day ahead.
- Make lists in priority order. Try to get everything done. If not, make sure it is added to the next list.
- If you do feel under pressure and begin to feel stressed, check whether you really need to complete the tasks you have set yourself. What exactly would happen if you do not complete them?
- Write things down. Do not rely on an overburdened memory.
- Delegate and always check that what is delegated is correct and whether there are other areas that can also be delegated.
- Set yourself deadlines. Set a time limit for delegated tasks and keep checking whether it is realistic and being followed.
- Always write things down but at the same time try to keep unnecessary paperwork to a minimum.
- Some of your time will be spent dealing with crises and unexpected events. Do not allow this to worry you.
- Keep asking whether you are using your time effectively. If you are not, do something about it.

CHAPTER SUMMARY

Colleagues suffering from stress should begin to look carefully at some aspects of their work together with how they are managing themselves (see Chapter 9). One possible contributing factor is how time is managed. Stress and time, while not being inextricably linked, do, if managed badly, create ineffective ways of working. All those responsible for managing schools need to recognize the causes and symptoms of stress and to have created an ethos and working atmosphere where these are shared problems. If this is the case, the individual will feel less guilty and may well be able to change his or her patterns of working in order to combat the causes of the stress. Colleagues should also be able to offer intervention strategies when and where necessary and to work as a team to solve difficult problems. It is important to understand that time is a scarce resource; like many resources it cannot be saved for a later date, even if it is not used effectively. As a final suggestion: although time needs to be used properly, no one is expected to become a workaholic. Being part of a successful school may mean working long hours but there are other things in life such as family and friends, pleasure and leisure. Some colleagues may be as addicted to work as some people are addicted to drugs. Their symptoms will include refusal to take a holiday, inability to put the school out of their minds at weekends, taking a large amount of work home and the continuous burning of the midnight oil. It might be useful to remember that, as Day *et al.* (1990) suggest, good time management is about being aware that today is all you ever have to work with, the past has always gone, never to return and the future is only a dim, unknown concept.

FURTHER READING

Bell, L. (1989) *Management Skills in Primary Schools*. London: Routledge.
This is a useful general guide to school management and has a useful section on time management.

Campbell, R.J. and Neill, S.R.St.J. (1994) *Curriculum Reform at Key Stage 1: Teacher Commitment and Policy Failure*. London: Longman.
This research presents a disturbing picture of both teachers' working time and the conditions and constraints under which they work.

Elliott, H. and Kemp, J. (1983) The management of stress: figure and ground. *Educational Change and Development*, 7 (2), 19–23.

Freen, A. (1983) Management implications of teacher stress and coping. *Educational Change and Development*, 7 (2).

Misten, M. (1982) Stress management in schools: the organization is the problem and the solution. *Educational Change and Development*, 6 (1).
These three articles are useful in analysing stress in terms of cause and effect.

CHAPTER 11

ACCOUNTABILITY AND THE INSPECTION PROCESS

CHAPTER OVERVIEW

Schools have become increasingly accountable to both professionals and those whose interests lie outside education. This chapter examines the various strands of accountability before concentrating on the way schools are inspected. It begins with suggestions as to how schools can initiate a pre-inspection self-evaluation, before looking at some of the different aspects of the inspection process. These include spiritual and moral development, quality of teaching and the quality and range of the curriculum.

INTRODUCTORY BACKGROUND TO THE CHANGED INSPECTION PROCESS

For most schools, the years before the legislation of the late 1980s were marked by a 'partnership model' of education. This meant that the government, local education authorities (LEAs) and schools worked together to provide high quality education for the community they served. The more recent alternative relies for its success on the idea that if schools were made more 'market'-orientated and more autonomous, the competition between them would increase their efficiency and therefore the standard of education that was offered. Local management of schools, legislation giving more powers to governors and indirectly to parents, the opportunities to 'opt out' of local authority control and the complexity of the administration of schools appear to have changed the nature of the responsibility for achieving high standards. As a result of these factors, views of accountability are changing as well.

This change is reflected in the inspection process. The disbanding of Her Majesty's Inspectors (HMI) and their replacement by the Office for Standards in Education (OFSTED) is designed to change and improve the way school inspections are conducted and, by implication, improve the quality of teaching and learning. There is not the space to expand on the debate which is concerned with the background to these changes, but it is important to realize that as Clegg and Billington (1994) point out:

> The OFSTED approach to inspection reflects government policy. The purpose is not to support and advise . . . Put bluntly, OFSTED inspections are not designed to help individual schools do a better job, they are designed to come to a judgement about the quality of the job they are currently doing.   (p.2)

The cycle of four-yearly inspections which began in 1993 for secondary schools and 1994 in the primary sector will move accountability from the professionals, through the inspectors, including lay inspectors' to the governing body, parents and the public domain.

TYPES OF ACCOUNTABILITY

In defining and analysing aspects of accountability it is important to pinpoint several distinct and separate areas. McCormick (1982) uses the suggestions made in the East Sussex Accountability Project when he identifies three basic types of accountability:

- *Moral* accountability, where the school is answerable to clients, i.e. parents and pupils.

- *Professional* accountability to colleagues and oneself.
- *Contractual* accountability to employers such as the LEA, school governors and the wider political masters.

In breaking these down we need to recognize that certain aspects of accountability are there to 'maintain, preserve or enhance' general levels of performance, while other aspects will begin to solve the problems related to areas of possible weakness.

Moral accountability: maintaining and enhancing levels of performance

This involves written reports to parents and holding parents' meetings to discuss progress and to provide opportunities to see pupils' work. It also means making sure that there is a school brochure and that there are other communications explaining policy and curriculum issues, etc.

Moral accountability: problem-solving

This involves parents knowing how complaints can be made and the action that is taken and seen to be taken when parents use the complaints process. There also needs to be an awareness of the kinds of meetings that will take place between teachers and pupils when pupils have problems in school.

This kind of accountability refers to how a school responds and is seen to be successful in meeting the needs of its clients, such as parents and pupils.

Professional accountability: maintaining and enhancing levels of performance

This aspect of accountability is concerned with how effective the school is in using, managing and developing all those individuals who work in it. This should involve schools evaluating themselves and monitoring internal standards while at the same time making sure that there are regular reviews of staffing, curriculum, teaching methods, assessment results and methods of planning. There is also the need to establish continuing relationships between primary and secondary sectors and to have sound, professional relationships between schools, teachers, LEA officers, advisers and inspectors.

Professional accountability: problem-solving

This includes using appropriate assessments and monitoring procedures to discover needs of individual pupils, providing equal opportunities in terms of the necessary provision for all pupils of whatever ability, being aware of the school's weaknesses and anticipating possible future crises and being able to either prevent them from happening or solving the problem quickly.

Contractual accountability: maintaining and enhancing levels of performance

This will involve observing the instructions of legislation, opening the school to all authorized visits and inspections, being able to explain and justify the curriculum, teaching methods and overall aims and policies as well as to account for pupils' standards of attainment.

Contractual accountability: problem-solving

This involves following agreed procedures for unresolved complaints and grievances and developing an effective management structure to deal with problems. It is also concerned with being able to self-audit and recognize problems that are likely to occur.

If we accept that there are three types of accountability and recognize the different and varied areas which need to be considered, it is important to realize that schools do need to work in partnership with parents and governors rather than try the almost impossible, and certainly the more inappropriate route, of working in isolation. Many headteachers, however, are severely pressured by the enormous numbers of financial and administrative tasks that are associated with LMS. This, according to Pollard and Tann (1993), can 'compromise their vital role as educational leaders' (p.289).

On the one hand, schools are encouraged to work in partnership with their parents and governors and to achieve success they not only have to follow any legislation related to this but they have to make sure that the ethos of the school promotes an atmosphere where this is able to occur. Schools with closed doors and a divide between providers and clients will be less successful. On the other hand, if parents and governors are given more information and increased ownership and choice over what happens in schools they have the chance to create a structure where there is much more accountability to them. The Education Reform Act and the Parent's Charter of 1991 gave parents significant rights. These include: having access to results of school performance; having more freedom to select the school which their children attend; receiving written reports on their child's performance, and an annual report from the school's governors.

Giving increased rights to parents and governors may, in some schools, make a 'real' and positive difference to the teaching and learning process. The more discussions that heads and teachers hold with parents and governors about what happens in the school, and the more knowledgeable all parties are about such issues as teaching styles and the curriculum, the more likely it is that they will be able to use this knowledge to influence what happens. It is equally possible, however, for schools to create an administrative framework which generates lots of documentation but little genuine two-way communication and change that will benefit the teaching and learning process.

Having the fundamental rights which are enshrined in the Parent's Charter and the Education Reform Act may mean that schools that are not successfully accountable will have fewer parents choosing to send their children to them and because the school's budget is dependent on the number of pupils on roll, the school will be less able to meet its needs and could begin a largely unstoppable downward spiral. Fortunately, this rather bleak scenario is unlikely to happen. Hughes *et al.* (1990) have suggested that many parents do not just see their children as consumers within an educational market-place. Most parents value the happiness and security within the community of their local school. Rather than the school being accountable to them with a view to parents exercising their right to transfer their

213

children to another school, parents see themselves as partners in their child's education.

Much of a school's accountability is through the governing body, which has overall control of many areas of school management, even after delegating much of the day-to-day work to headteachers and staff. The market model of education and the increased accountability can be seen as devaluing and reducing the professionalism of teachers. More people are now aware of the cost of education and what teachers do all day, and there have been many more public discussions about teaching styles, classroom management and discipline in schools, e.g. Alexander *et al.* (1992); Elton (1989).

If schools develop an adversarial style of management, it is unlikely that there will be increased effectiveness from its relationship with governors and parents. If, however, the school is able to utilize the expertise and professionalism of its parents and governors the management should be constructive enough to provide procedures and processes, e.g. performance indicators, through which accountability can be expressed.

PERFORMANCE INDICATORS

Schools that are able to self-evaluate on a regular basis will recognize their strengths and weaknesses through the processes they devise. The inspection process, which will be discussed later in this chapter, will add a further professional dimension to what the school knows from its own efforts and that of its parents and governors. It could be argued, however, that an external inspection may prevent schools from deluding themselves about their strengths, weaknesses and successes. Another way of 'measuring' success is by using performance indicators. These are pieces of information that should help schools know how well something is performing or, more controversially, how someone is performing. Cocket *et al.* (1993, p.6) suggest that 'indicators are selected items of quantitative data which help in the evaluation of quality and standards by allowing comparisons to be made or changes over time to be measured'. In *Development Planning: A Practical Guide* (1991) which was funded by the DES and directed by David Hargreaves and David

Hopkins, it is suggested that performance indicators have so far only been used for factual information such as exam results, class sizes, attendance figures, costs per pupil, etc. This is quite simple to obtain and to process in statistics and figures that are 'easily' understood. For example, a school's exam results measure the standards pupils have reached in public examinations and, as performance indicators forming part of the accountability process, they might provide clues to the quality of teaching in a particular subject and the success of the school as a whole.

There are, however, other important issues which these kind of quantitative performance indicators do not measure.

It is easy to over-value what is measurable but it does not tell those interested in quality such things as how far pupils have progressed, how hard it is to get from where they started to where they finished and whether pupils benefited from school more than it is possible for rigid and simple performance indicators to measure. However, in the context of accountability, schools that are looking at their own effectiveness and who are planning for the future need not only see performance indicators as part of any criteria for success, but to recognize that they can exert a positive influence on ways of thinking and working. They do this by promoting desirable goals for the school, suggesting appropriate standards which can be linked to desirable goals, recognizing the type of action that is needed to achieve agreed standards, knowing what evidence is needed to judge success and assisting in reporting success to parents, governors, the community and visiting inspectors.

SCHOOL INSPECTIONS

The new system of inspections will bring a further dimension to accountability and the way a school looks at its successes and failures and plans for the future. The abolition of HMI and the creation of OFSTED has changed the face of school inspections. Whereas before OFSTED, whether your school was inspected was a fairly random decision with some schools never having any kind of inspection, now it is a certainty. Inspections are also different in the sense that they are not solely the property of professionals within the school. They now have a wider range of participants in the inspection process as well as a wider and more public audience for the inspection report and any subsequent developments in the school arising from what the inspection report said in its judgement of the school.

This new and four-yearly cycle of inspections will, according to OFSTED (1992), concentrate on four broad areas:

- The quality of education provided by schools;
- the educational standards achieved in schools;
- whether the financial resources made available are managed efficiently;
- the spiritual, moral, social and cultural development of the pupils in the school.

As the inspections will be judgemental in nature it will be necessary for schools to prepare thoroughly and carefully for the inspection so that all teachers are aware of the process and that they carefully evaluate their own strengths before beginning to plan the action that is necessary as a result of the inspection report.

The following sections are based on *Framework for the Inspection of Schools* (1992), which summarizes most of the areas inspectors will concentrate on during an inspection. Individual schools will manage the process of inspection in different ways but it will help everyone if individuals, teams, departments and whole schools self-audit in a way that allows them to recognize their needs, strengths and weaknesses and what areas they may need to develop.

The inspection process begins with the governors and parents and ends with a public report. It is argued by OFSTED (1993) that the initial meeting gives parents the opportunity to express their views about all aspects of the school. The inspectors are able to note these views and assess their validity against the evidence collected during the inspection. The inspection itself is carried out by a team of registered inspectors and lay inspectors in close liaison with the governors and headteacher. A wide variety of documents will have to be made available, including planning records, assessment procedures, policy statements, minutes of meetings, budget forecasts, etc. This will be complemented by the bulk of the inspection which will comprise classroom observation. As well as looking at pupils' work, talking to them and listening to their views the team will comment on accommodation, resources and resource levels and how the school relates to the community. It is important to understand that this kind of structure has its flaws. Inspections are carried out quickly. There will be very few opportunities for inspectors to engage in meaningful dialogues with those teachers they have observed. It is also questionable whether it is possible for inspectors who are strangers to have an accurate picture of where schools are coming from and where they are going.

Smith (1994) suggests that the public document that is made available at the end of the inspection will list 'good' and 'bad' points together with a comparison of standards between the inspected school and similar schools in the area. He goes on to raise the important point that although there will be discussion between teachers, governors, headteacher and inspectors during the inspection there will be no debate allowed about the content of the report on the school. Under no circumstances will there be any modification of the report or negotiation of the findings. The only response is: 'for the governors to state how they are going to form an Action Plan to meet the needs of the inspection report and to suggest the time span in which they are going to do it' (p.4).

There are, however, constraints on how long it should take before an Action Plan is made public. What could be even more daunting is that schools that are deemed to be 'failing' may have their management taken over by specially constituted bodies whose sole concern will be to make improvements if the school has been unable to make sufficient changes in the time allowed. In reaching a decision as to whether a school is failing or is likely to fail to provide an acceptable standard of education, the registered inspector will consider various characteristics. Cocket *et al.* (1993) identify the following areas which could be used to identify failure: achievements of pupils and the curriculum, behaviour and welfare, staff and teaching and the ineffectiveness of senior management.

Inspection will be totally divorced from advice and development. In many LEAs advisers have been replaced by inspectors who are OFSTED trained and both they and what used to be teams of advisory teachers will, because of their changing role, not be where schools go to for advice. This is unfortunate because there are disquieting reports suggesting that school inspections do not necessarily mean that schools will improve. Brimblescombe *et al.* (1994) in an unpublished paper from Oxford Brookes University suggest that in a study of thirty-five schools inspected by OFSTED only 38 per cent of the total staff intended to change their practice as a result of the inspection. If these findings are supported by further studies as OFSTED continue their cycle of inspections, it will be a damning indictment of a system that is especially designed to be judgemental (and by implication critical) and yet has as one of its central aims the improvement of educational 'standards'. It is perhaps important for all inspectors to consider Handy's (1976) conclusions when he suggested that criticism only improves performance when 'It is given with a genuine liking for the other person and the subordinate trusts and respects the superior' (pp. 267–8). In the kind of inspections conducted by OFSTED there will certainly be little trust and, I am convinced, a feeling of superiors making judgements on subordinates.

Before any school is inspected it is important that there is considerable self-evaluation by individuals, teams and departments. In evaluating what the school does well or does less well, the areas examined must, in order to make the inspection a worthwhile activity, match up to the issues to be addressed by an OFSTED inspection. There is obviously too little space here to consider fully all the areas OFSTED will examine and the evaluation criteria they will use. However, it is useful to summarize that these areas will include: standards of achievement; quality of learning; efficiency of the school; pupils' spiritual, moral, social and cultural development; behaviour and discipline; attendance; subjects of the curriculum and other curricular provision; quality of teaching; assessment, recording and reporting; equality of opportunity; provision for pupils with special educational needs; resources and their management; and links with parents and other institutions.

Basically, the inspection process will recognize quality in terms of teaching and learning. By using the above headings, together with such publications as *A Framework for the Inspection of Schools* (OFSTED, 1992) as part of a reflective process, it is possible to identify areas of the schools' organization and structure that will be looked at by inspectors. The section on 'The efficiency of the school' (OFSTED, 1992) suggests that the report should include. 'An evaluation of the extent to which school programmes and procedures are carried out efficiently, making best use of staff and material resources, and of time' (p.6).

Planning effective procedures and motivating and developing human resources is certainly one of the keys to successful management. Making sure all these aspects happen is part of the pre-inspection process as well as being part of the continuing daily pattern of management. An inspection will delve into all aspects of a school's work and it is relevant to end this chapter by briefly considering a few key areas (Wylie, 1994) where inspectors are likely to ask searching questions. By examining these areas in more detail it should be possible to look at your own school in such a way as to understand more about standards, quality and ethos as well as knowing the kinds of plans which need developing. At the same time, as Wylie (1994) suggests, looking in detail at important aspects of the school will 'help clarify the evaluation criteria on which an inspection team base their judgement and the evidence on which they draw' (p.1).

CURRICULUM CO-ORDINATORS

Most schools employ teachers who are paid above the 'normal' pay spine. Inspectors will expect to see them being used effectively, not only in their knowledge of their 'subject' but in the overview they have of the teaching of that subject throughout the school. They must therefore have time to work alongside colleagues, offer advice and gain an overview of future developments. This can of course, cause problems. To effectively monitor what is happening inside classrooms and to have an overview of the continuity of a particular subject will mean having non-teaching or non-contact time. This is far from easy in primary schools and yet it is impossible to perform the duties of a subject co-ordinator properly without such time.

The core of most advice about the teaching and learning of a specific subject will come from the National Curriculum statutory guidelines and the school's own policy. The concept of 'ownership' is important here. For a policy to be effective it must reflect what actually happens in the school. An appropriate way for the co-ordinator to 'write' such a policy would be to share knowledge with his or her 'team'. Sharing common knowledge should produce an agreed working document. For one such as a co-ordinator to go away and write a policy and then present it as a *fait accompli* would be to invite dissent and lead to teachers not wanting or being unable to follow such a document. This leads us to the wider issue of the ethos of the school. Sharing knowledge, working together to reach decisions and acting corporately on decisions already taken will be more appropriate than a management structure which is largely if not totally hierarchical and where decisions are handed down from supposed 'superior' to supposed or accepted 'inferior'.

BEHAVIOUR, DISCIPLINE AND THE COMMUNITY

Ethos, culture, aims of the school and the atmosphere in which pupils work together and learn underlie another aspect of what an inspection report will include. By observing standards of behaviour and the quality of relationships within the school, Cocket *et al.* (1993) suggest that the inspection team will be able to issue a statement as part of their report on behaviour, discipline and pupils' responsibilities. OFSTED (1992) suggests that there will be

> A comment on the extent to which the school functions as an orderly, safe, and corporate community, with an evaluation of the effectiveness of the governor's policy on discipline and the school's arrangements for promoting good behaviour and relationships. (Pupils' and parents' response to any system of rewards and sanctions should be noted. (p.7)

There seems to be a continuing emphasis on a management style where the school as a whole has common goals and where everyone works together to achieve those goals. The words 'corporate' and 'community' both point to a shared responsibility to act for the common good. It seems to me that this concept of shared responsibility might be one that OFSTED should be attempting to foster between itself and schools in order for there to be a link between their judgements and school improvement.

Unfortunately, as Clegg and Billington (1994) make clear, this will not happen because OFSTED inspections are designed to judge the quality of the job which a school is currently doing. Once these judgements have been made and the report has been written it is the responsibility of the school and the governors to plan for any necessary improvements. There is a marked division of responsibilities.

Discipline and good relationships obviously have to be part of an agreed system and whatever this system is must have been devised by heads, deputies, heads of department and teams, etc. The OFSTED statement on p.313 takes this aspect of school management a step further and involves parents, teachers and pupils. This can be linked to some earlier analysis of behaviour in schools. Elton (1989) suggested that in order to improve what he called 'discipline', schools can involve parents in at least five ways:

- Maintaining high-quality channels of communication including both written information and opportunities to meet teachers.
- Providing a welcoming environment which could, where space allowed, include facilities for a parents' room.
- Ensuring that there is effective liaison between the school and individual families. This home–school liaison might also involve educational social Workers as well as teachers.
- Using parents as helpers in the classroom to work with individuals and small groups of pupils.
- Encouraging parents to take part in home learning schemes which involve them in reading, helping with mathematics or watching television programmes.

By being involved in the school's aims statement, the content of the school's prospectus and the details of the School Development Plan, teachers, parents and governors should feel that they have a share in the processes involved in the management of behaviour and discipline in the school. Once again, however, it does have to be a whole-school policy with all teachers adopting a consistent approach.

SPIRITUAL AND MORAL DEVELOPMENT

The inspection report will contain an evaluation of the pupils' spiritual and moral development and of their responses to what the school provides. This includes such issues as religious education, development of a moral code, and the ways in which beliefs influence behaviour. The criteria suggested by OFSTED (1992) are that the quality of social development can be judged in terms of: relationships in the school; the extent to which pupils show respect for individuals and property; their understanding of the structures and processes of society; the opportunities for them to exercise responsibility; and their attitudes to work, to the school and to the wider community.

This is obviously a huge management task and again will have to involve the whole school, parents, pupils and governors. The aims, ethos and policies will be the starting point and will have to suggest the kinds of moral attitudes expected from pupils. If it is part of the school's expectations that pupils will develop as autonomous adults able to work co-operatively to solve problems, the school's aims must support this. For example, it would be inappropriate if such a school were authoritarian to such an extent that all pupils were policed and controlled, with classrooms where individuals worked on isolated tasks. The mismatch between what exists and the school's expectations would be such that aims could not possibly be met. The curriculum and pastoral life of the school would also have to be managed in ways that met the aims of the school. A rigidly 'formal' curriculum linked to a *laisser-faire* pastoral system would once again create a mismatch that would not promote the required results.

QUALITY OF TEACHING

The inspection process will identify the strengths and weaknesses which occur in the quality of teaching and at the same time will recognize the range of techniques, their fitness for the purpose they are used for, pupil groupings, teachers' command and coverage of subject content, the degree to which work is matched to pupils' individual characteristics, needs and abilities, the effectiveness of lesson planning, classroom organization and use of resources. Clegg and Billington (1994, p.31) suggest that

> teaching is good where there is a clear explanation of the task, pupils are given examples of what is expected of them, work is well matched to pupils' needs and teachers' expectations are high. It is frequently unsatisfactory where the whole class is set the same task, often involving copying from the blackboard or completing worksheets which are inappropriate for many pupils.

During any self-audit or school evaluation process most if not all of these areas will have been examined. Where weaknesses were found in schools with effective management, efforts would have been made to provide training programmes through INSET, either from within the school or from outside providers. There should also be discussions about teaching quality within departments, working parties and teams. There are certainly key texts available that should help schools take decisions concerning teaching styles and the quality of teaching. An interesting example of this is Appendix B from *Curriculum Organisation and Classroom Practice in Primary Schools: A Follow Up Report* (Alexander *et al.*, 1993), pp. 22–3.

QUALITY AND RANGE OF THE CURRICULUM

Schools will also be judged on the quality and range of the curriculum and its organization including cross-curricular themes and the way the curriculum meets the needs of all pupils within the requirements of the National Curriculum. There are separate sections in *Framework for Inspection* (OFSTED, 1992) on special needs, equal opportunities, use of accommodation, and resources, but the key issues are the processes of teaching, i.e. the quality of teaching and learning and the content of the curriculum. The inspectors will judge this by the extent to which its content, structure, organization and implementation contribute to the achievement of high standards. The effective school will have policy documents available representing the school's views on each subject area. The National Curriculum documents will join the internal policies to create the school curriculum. All teachers need to know the content of the curriculum either for their own subject(s) in secondary schools or in a generalist way in primary schools. They will also need to be able to assess, record and moderate material within their own subjects or across the whole range of levels and subjects. Many of these areas of the curriculum and related documentation can be found in *The National Curriculum from Policy to Practice* (DES, 1989).

ASPECTS OF A BROAD AND BALANCED CURRICULUM

Finally – and perhaps as an appropriate end to the penultimate chapter of this book – we look at the need to develop a curriculum with a content that is both broad and balanced and at the same time relevant to the needs of each pupil. This is of course an extremely difficult task which, if it is ever completed, has to be taught through all the processes which have been developed and managed in the school to promote and satisfy the individual pupil's abilities. Inspectors will be looking at the quality of teaching and learning and at the quality and range of the curriculum and the extent to which the content, organization and planning contribute to high standards of achievement and quality in learning (Wylie, 1994). It will need to promote the spiritual, moral, cultural, mental and physical development of pupils both in school and society, prepare pupils for the opportunities, responsibilities and experiences of adult life and serve to develop the pupil as an individual, as a member of society and as a future adult member of the community with a range of personal and social opportunities and responsibilities.

In an effective school, successful headteachers will have a 'vision' which will be at the heart of the school curriculum. That vision will influence those who manage the school and how planning, teaching and evaluation will be undertaken in order to ensure that the aims and objectives of the curriculum are translated into pupil learning (Alexander *et al.*, 1992). Inspectors will recognize these 'visions' and will be looking for their translation into practice. Good management will ensure that they will see whole-curriculum planning as a reality where a substantial proportion of the staff appreciate the necessity of a high-quality, broad and balanced curriculum (Weston *et al.*, 1993).

CHAPTER SUMMARY

Schools are more open to public scrutiny than ever before. The market economy within which they are being forced to operate has attempted, probably less successfully than central government would have liked, to create a competitive system with increasing rights and choices being given to parents and governors. Schools need to be managed in ways to enable them to develop their own performance indicators that combine accountability in the sense of involving pupils, parents, governors and the community together with the kind of professional accountability that increases the quality and excellence of the services offered to pupils and all other interested parties. The inspection process itself, however, will create its own criteria. The documents that the inspection teams will use are freely available, and well-managed schools will use them in self-evaluation exercises to gain a detailed picture of the school's successes and failures.

FURTHER READING

Alexander, R., Rose, J. and Woodhead, C. (1992) *Curriculum Organisation and Classroom Practice in the Primary School: A Discussion Document.* London: DES.

Assuring Quality and Standards in Education (1992) London: OFSTED.

Framework for the Inspection of Schools (1992) London: OFSTED.

DES (1989) *National Curriculum from Policy to Practice.* London: HMSO.

These are all key documents in the debate about quality and excellence in schools.

Cocket, P., Milroy, E. and Phillips, S. (1993) *Inspection and Beyond: A Professional Development Package for Primary Schools.* Manchester: Manchester Metropolitan University, Didsbury School of Education.

This is a useful summary of what an inspection will be like and it also includes some interesting and relevant ways in which schools can prepare for an OFSTED inspection.

Smith, R. (1994) *Preparing for Inspection.* Lancaster: Framework.

This is full of practical activities that teachers and schools can carry out prior to an inspection.

CHAPTER 12

CONCLUSION

CHAPTER OVERVIEW

Successful schools do not just happen. They are effective and popular because all those who work in them have a commitment to making them so. Leadership, team work and sound management structures all go together to promote an attitude where constant professional effort helps to move schools forward at a time of rapid, frequent and seemingly never-ending change. While much early research has suggested that external factors such as social and economic conditions had the greater effect on pupils' learning, there is now enough evidence of differences of achievement between schools in similar catchment areas to point to management performance as an important factor (e.g. see Rutter *et al.*, 1979; Reid *et al.*, 1987; Mortimore *et al.*, 1988).

If we accept that the principal focus of a good school is effective learning, then it must be the task of management to create the conditions which enable pupils and teachers to achieve this objective. Each chapter in this volume should have added to the debate and helped provide information which will assist effective management. As a conclusion it is important to try and summarize all those issues that are important in helping us to recognize all the factors which lead to effective schools.

LEADERSHIP AND THE MANAGEMENT TEAM

Schools need the sense of direction provided by strong leadership. Leaders need beliefs and values that can shape the culture and ethos of the school and encourage high-quality teaching and learning. This does not mean, however, an autocratic, dictatorial figure who takes decisions and passes down edicts and instructions that have to be obeyed. Being decisive, forceful and yet consultative is one way of accessible leading from the front and at the same time being recognized as a leader. Many leaders – and it is important to remember that although this automatically applies to headteachers, it also means all staff members who lead, chair meetings, manage change and take decisions – have qualities that go beyond taking decisions and being forceful. To be effective, leaders have to be capable of motivating colleagues. They have to be enthusiastic, and able to express appreciation and encourage professional growth and expertise. They should also be able to support colleagues and, while accepting the necessity for taking ultimate decisions, must also be capable of making colleagues feel secure by virtue of their ability to be prepared for new developments and by not leaping on any or all of the latest and current bandwagons without thought and consultation. The one attribute, however, that is an absolute necessity is the ability to work with colleagues as a team.

Any leader should consult, work for a negotiated solution and involve colleagues who will, because they have been part of the decision-making process, feel that they have a sense of ownership. Leaders in school who work together in this way must set out broad strategies for change but at the same time encourage open discussion within a framework of reassurance, sound knowledge, openness, honesty and integrity together with a sense of mobilizing everyone's talents so that the school can take positive steps forward.

DEVELOPING THE SCHOOL'S AIMS

The aims of the school must be shared within a development plan that is constantly reviewed. This shared sense of purpose needs to be understood and supported by all the staff and in all important senses has to be written down clearly and prominently. The successful school must have as its aims the intention of helping all pupils achieve their potential by devising a curriculum and using teaching styles that are sufficiently differentiated to satisfy every individual's needs. It is equally important to develop the ability to meet pupils' social and personal needs and to help every individual pupil acquire moral values by having in place a process which ensures that there is a secure, welcoming environment where all pupils are happy, feel valued and can co-operate with each other.

By planning efficiently, thinking ahead, paying attention to long-, medium- and short-term plans and goals, the aims of the school should be entrenched in such a way that they are relatively stable, can still be modified and fine-tuned, but will form the rock that the school is built on so that the calmness and security of the environment prevents any frenzied, rushed and ill-conceived crisis management.

THE ETHOS OF THE SCHOOL

There needs to be an open atmosphere in the school and a sense of community where colleagues trust each other and are able to discuss professional matters freely. As well as this openness, there needs to be a relaxed but purposeful working atmosphere where pupils and staff can feel secure and are able to understand that teaching and learning are given high priority. This ethos will not be one of hidebound complacency but one where there will be a sense of change because a questioning, critical attitude will be actively promoted in order to encourage a striving for improvement and growth. Such schools should have few discipline problems and pupils' attendance will be high, vandalism low and parental expectations met.

RELATIONSHIPS WITHIN THE SCHOOL

Effective leadership that is well thought out together with a positive ethos will be reflected in the quality of professional relationships that the school fosters. There should, as has been mentioned many times before, be a feeling of team spirit where new colleagues are welcome, co-operative working is the norm and support is available for those experiencing problems of stress. Within such an environment there should be the idea of the 'thinking school', where building a learning environment for staff is seen as important. In this kind of supportive school professional development will be seen as an important part of the job and there will be regular educational discussions together with shared ideas, experiences and advice.

LINKS WITH PARENTS, GOVERNORS, LEA AND THE COMMUNITY

It is extremely important that staff and governors maintain good relations. Governors are key figures in policy-making, recruitment and the financial management of the school. The relationship between teachers and governors needs to be harmonious and positive or problems will arise which will use up valuable managerial time. These good relationships also apply to parents, the LEA and the community. They will not just happen but will need to be developed. The school ethos has to reflect a welcoming atmosphere where everyone feels able to meet, discuss and learn about current developments and key issues. The presence of an active PTA will help this process but must function within a wider concept of support and encouragement throughout the school and the community it serves.

MANAGEMENT STRUCTURES AND DECISION-MAKING

It is important to remember that effective schools are dependent on an appropriate organizational structure that meets the school's aims. Not only does this structure define staff roles, recognize areas of responsibility and fix routines and policies for the day-to-day running of the school, but it is also flexible enough to react to different circumstances and pro-active enough to develop change. This suggests that successful schools will have documentation as well as accepted routines which enable the monitoring and evaluation of current practice. The written policies will be easily accessible to all those who need them and there will be effective meetings that discuss major policy issues, take decisions and reflect the efficiency of communication between all colleagues in the school.

MANAGING CHANGE

Change is inevitable. It will not go away or lessen its impact on what happens in schools. Effective management will ensure that there is a largely receptive attitude to change and that innovation is part of the school's agenda in terms of discussions, meetings and the allocation of resources.

The rapid changes of the late 1980s and 1990s have meant that in order to absorb and deal with the changes, schools that are the most successful have been able to work collaboratively and, while it takes more time, made efforts to reach consensus because they recognize that this method of working will produce long-lasting and shared improvements.

CHAPTER SUMMARY

There are many ideas which can contribute to the debate on what 'good' management is. This book has tried to use as many sources as possible in introducing those issues of which effective school management has to be aware. While it is impossible to agree on what an effective school is, they do seem to share most if not all of the characteristics set out in Box 12.1. (Many of these are suggested in School Management Task Force (1990).)

A tall order? Perhaps. But if we are to promote and ensure high-quality learning, the management of schools has to build on its current expertise and develop effective strategies for the future. I hope that this final summary may help to encapsulate part of the debate that is necessary in order to do just that.

Box 12.1 Characteristics of an effective school

- Good leadership offering breadth of vision and the ability to motivate others.
- Appropriate delegation with involvement in policy-making by staff other than the head.
- Clearly established and purposeful staffing structures.
- Well-qualified staff with the appropriate blend of experience and expertise.
- Clear aims and associated objectives applied with care and consistency.
- Effective communications and clear systems of record-keeping and assessment.
- The means to identify and develop pupils' particular strengths, promoting high expectations by both teachers and pupils.
- A coherent curriculum which considers pupils' experience as a whole and demonstrates concern for their development within society.
- A positive ethos: an orderly yet relaxed working atmosphere.
- A suitable working environment.
- Skills of deploying and managing material resources.
- Good relationships with parents, the local community and sources of external support.
- The capacity to manage change, solve problems and to develop organically.

FURTHER READING

NDC/CREATE Project, Summary Report, (1993) *Effective Management in Schools*. London: HMSO.

School Management Task Force (1990) *Developing School Management: The Way Forward*. London: HMSO.

Both these short papers offer some interesting summaries of school management.

BIBLIOGRAPHY

ACAS (1986) *School Teacher Appraisal: A National Framework.* London: ACAS.

Adair, J. (1983) *Effective Leadership.* London: Pan Books.

Adam Smith Institute (1984) *Omega Report: Education Policy.* London: Adam Smith Institute.

Alexander, R., Rose, J. and Woodhead, C. (1992) *Curriculum Organisation and Classroom Practice in Primary Schools: A Discussion Paper.* London: DES.

Alexander, R., Rose, J. and Woodhead, C. (1993) *Curriculum Organisation and Classroom Practice in Primary Schools: A Follow Up Report.* London: DES.

Argyris, C. (1948) *Personality and Organization.* London: Chapman & Hall.

Argyris, C. (1970) *Intervention Theory and Method.* London: Addison-Wesley.

Baginsky, M., Baker, L. and Cleave, S. (1991) *Towards Effective Partnership in School Governance.* Slough: NFER.

Beare, H., Caldwell, D. and Millikin, R. (1989) *Creating an Excellent School.* London: Routledge.

Belbin, R.M. (1981) *Management Teams.* London: Heinemann.

Bell, L. (1989) *Management Skills in Primary Schools.* London: Routledge.

Bennett, N., Desforges, C., Cockburn, A. and Wilkinson, B. (1984) *The Quality of Pupil Learning Experiences.* London: Lawrence Erlbaum Associates.

Bennis, W. and Nanus, B. (1985) *Leaders.* New York: Harper & Row.

Berne, E. (1967) *Games People Play: The Psychology of Human Relationships.* London: Pelican.

Bishop Grosseteste/NFER Consortium (1990) Report on SATs in *Times Educational Supplement,* 16 November.

Boydell, D. (1980) The organization of junior school classrooms: a follow-up report. *Educational Research,* **23** (1), pp.31–9.

Brand, T. (1993) The first week and how to survive it. *Child Education,* September, pp.58–9.

Brehony, K.J. (1992) Active citizens: the case of school governors. Unpublished paper given to Westhill Sociology of Education Conference, Birmingham.

Brighouse, T. and Moon, C. (1990) *Managing the National Curriculum: Some Critical Perspectives*. London: Longman.

Brimblescombe, N., Ormston, M. and Shaw, M. (1994) Unpublished paper from Oxford Brookes University, presented to BERA conference, September.

Bruner, J.S. and Haste, H. (1987) *Making Sense: The Child's Construction of the World*. London: Methuen.

Busher, H. and Saran, R. (1990) Teachers' morale and their conditions of service. Paper delivered at the Annual Conference of Bemas, Reading University. In Preedy, M. (ed.) (1993) *Managing the Effective School*. London: Paul Chapman.

Campbell, R.J. (1993) A dream at conception, a nightmare at delivery. In Campbell, R.J. (ed.) *Breadth and Balance in the Primary Curriculum*. London: Falmer.

Campbell, R.J. and Neill, S.R.St.J. (1992) *Curriculum Reform at Key Stage 1: Teacher Commitment and Policy Failure*. London: Longman.

Campbell, R.J., Ridley, K. and Saunders T. (1987) *The National Curriculum: Primary Questions. A Report of the National Primary Conference*. Leamington: Scholastic.

Campbell, R.J., Evans, L., Packwood, A. and Neill, S.R. St. J. (1991) *Workloads, Achievement and Stress*. London: AMMA.

Carrington, B. and Troyna, B. (1988) *Children and Controversial Issues*. London: Falmer.

Clegg, D. and Billington, S. (1994) *Making the Most of Your Inspection*. London: Falmer.

Cocket, P., Milroy, E. and Phillips, S. (1993) *Inspection and Beyond: A Professional Development Package for Primary Schools*. Manchester: Manchester Metropolitan University, Didsbury School of Education.

Conway, J.A. (1978) Power and participation: decision making in selected English schools. *The Journal of Educational administration* **XVI** (1), pp. 130–9.

Cooper, C. and Marshall, J. (1978) Sources of managerial and white collar stress. In Cooper, C. and Payne, R. (eds) *Stress at Work*. New York: John Wiley & Sons.

Coulson, A. (1986) *The Managerial Work of Primary School Headteachers*. Sheffield City Polytechnic: Department of Educational Management.

Coulson, A. and Cox, M. (1975) What do deputies do? *Education 3–13*, **3** (2), pp. 100–3.

Day, C., Johnston D. and Whittaker, P. (1985) *Managing Primary Schools*. London: Paul Chapman.

Day, C., Whittaker, P. and Johnston, D. (1990) *Managing Primary Schools in the 1990s: A Professional Development Approach*. London: Paul Chapman.

Deal, T. and Kennedy, A. (1983) Culture and school performance. *Educational Leadership*, **40** (5), pp. 14–15.

Dean, J. (1987) *Managing the Primary School*. London: Routledge.

Dearing Report (1994) *Implications for Teacher Assessments, Record Keeping and Reporting*. London: SEAC/NCC.

Deem, R. (1992) Educational reform and school governing bodies in England 1986–92. In Preedy, M. (ed.) (1993), *Managing the Effective School*. London: Paul Chapman.

Dennison, W.F. (1990) Performance indicators and consumer choice. *International Journal of Educational Management*, 4 (1), pp. 8–11.

DES (1986) *The Education (No.2) Act*. London: HMSO.

DES (1987) *Financial Delegation to Schools: A Consultation Paper*. London: HMSO.

DES (1988) *Task Group on Assessment and Testing Report*. London: HMSO.

DES (1989) *The National Curriculum from Policy to Practice*. DES/Welsh Office. London: HMSO.

DES (1990) *Developing School Management: The Way Forward*. London: HMSO.

DES (1991) *Development Planning: A Practical Guide. Advice to Governors, Headteachers and Teachers*. London: HMSO.

DES (1992) *Assuring Quality and Standards in Education*. London: HMSO.

DFE (1993a) *Parent's Charter: Publication of Information About Performance*. London: HMSO.

DFE (1993b) *School Teachers' Pay and Conditions of Service Document*. London: HMSO.

DFE (1993c) *Curriculum Organization and Classroom Practice in Primary Schools; a Follow-up Report*. London: HMSO.

Downes, P.A. (1990) Costing the curriculum. *Managing Schools Today*, 1 (3), pp. 14–20.

Easen, P. (1985) *Making School Centred INSET work*. London: Croom Helm.

Elliott, H. and Kemp, J. (1983) The management of stress: figure and ground. *Educational Change and Development*, 7 (2), pp. 19–23.

Elliott, J., Bridges, D., Ebbutt, D., Gibson, R. and Nias, J. (1981) *School Accountability: the SSRC Cambridge Accountability Project*. London: Grant McIntyre.

Elton Report (1989) *Discipline in Schools: Report of the Committee of Enquiry Chaired by Lord Elton*. London: HMSO.

Eraut, M.E. (1977) Strategies for promoting teacher development. *British Journal of In-Service Education*, 4 (1–2).

Everard, K.B. (1986) *Developing Management in Schools*. Oxford: Blackwell.

Everard, K.B. and Morris, G. (1985) *Effective School Management*. London: Harper & Row.

Fayol, H. (1930) *Industrial and General Administration*. New York: Pitman.

Franck, M.E. (1982) What is learned in inservice education. *British Journal of Inservice Education*, 9 (1), pp. 28–35.

Freen, A. (1983) Management implications of teacher stress and coping. *Educational Change and Development*, 7 (2), pp. 12–19.

Fullan, M. (1985) Change processes and strategies at the local level. *The Elementary School Journal*, **85** (3), pp. 391–421.

Georgiades, N. and Phillimore, L. (1972) *The Myth of the Hero Innovator and Alternative Strategies for Organizational Change*. London: Department of Occupational Psychology, Birkbeck College.

Getzels, J.W. (1969) A social psychology of education. In Lindzeyg, G. and Aronson E. (eds) (1972), *The Handbook of Social Psychology* (second edn), Vol. 5, *Applied Social Psychology*. London: Addison-Wesley.

Gilbert, C. (1990) Local management in schools: an introductory summary. In Gilbert, C. (ed.), *Management of Schools: A Guide for Governors and Teachers*. London: Kogan Page.

Gipps, C. and Stobart, G. (1993) *Assessment: A Teachers' Guide to the Issues*. London: Hodder & Stoughton.

Gold, Y. and Roth, A. (1993) *Teachers Managing Stress and Preventing Burnout: The Professional Health Solution*. London: Falmer Press.

Goodworth, C.T. (1984) *How to be a Super Effective Manager*. London: Business Books.

Greenfield, R. (1990) *Handling Headship*. Leamington Spa: Scholastic Publications.

Hall, R. (1972) *Organization, Structure and Process*. London: Prentice Hall.

Hand, G. (1981) First call on your adviser: the INSET role of advisers. In Donoughue, C. (ed.) (1982), *Inservice, the Teacher and the School*. London: Kogan Page.

Handy, C. (1976) *Understanding Organizations*. London: Penguin.

Hargreaves, D. (1984) *Improving Secondary Schools*. London: ILEA.

Hargreaves, D.H. and Hopkins, D. (1991) School effectiveness, school improvement and development planning. In Hargreaves, D.H. and Hopkins, D. (eds), *The Empowered School*. London: Cassell.

Harlen, W. (1979) Making the Match. *Primary Education Review*, Spring, No. 6.

Havelock, R.G. (1973) *The Change Agents' Guide to Innovation*. Englewood Cliffs, NJ: Educational Technology Publications.

Hersey, P. and Blanchard, K. (1982) *Management of Organizational Behavior: Utilizing Human Resources*, 4th edn. Englewood Cliffs, NJ: Prentice-Hall.

HMI (1927) *Handbook of Suggestions for the Consideration of Teachers and Others Concerned in the Work of the Public Elementary School*. London: HMSO.

HMI (1977) *Ten Good Schools*. London: HMSO.

HMI (1978) *Primary Education in England*. London: HMSO.

HMI (1985) *The Curriculum from 5–16*. London: HMSO.

HMI (1990) *The Implementation of the National Curriculum in Primary Schools: A Survey of 100 Schools*. London: HMSO.

Hughes, M., Wikeley, F. and Nash, T. (1990) *Parents and the National Curriculum: An Interim Report*. Mimeo. University of Exeter.

Hurst, V. (1992) *Planning for Early Learning in the First Five Years*. London: Paul Chapman.

ILEA (1985) *Improving Primary Schools: Report of the Committee in Primary Education*. London: ILEA.

Kogan, M., Johnson, D., Packwood, T. and Whittaker, T. (1984) *School Governing Bodies*. London: Heinemann.

Landers, T. and Myers, J. (1977) Organizational and administrative theory. In Bush, T., Glatter, R., Goodey, J. and Riches, C. (eds), *Approaches to School Management*. London: Open University/Harper & Row.

Levacic, R. (1992) Coupling financial and curriculum decision making in schools. In Preedy, M. (1993) (ed.), *Managing the Effective School*. London: Paul Chapman/Open University.

Lewin, K. (1947) *Human Relations*. Chicago, III: University of Chicago Press.

Macbeth, A. (1989) A minimum programme and a signed understanding. In Macbeth, A. (ed.), *Involving Parents: Effective Parent–Teacher Relations*. Oxford: Heinemann.

McCormick, R. (ed.) (1982) *Calling Education to Account*. London: Open University/Heinemann.

Macdonald, B. (1974) Quoted in Walker, R. (1980) The conduct of educational case studies: ethics, theories and procedures. In Dockrell, W.B. and Hamilton, D. (eds), *Rethinking Educational Research*. London: Hodder & Stoughton.

Maychell, K. (1994) *Counting the Cost: The Impact of LMS on Schools' Patterns of Spending*. Slough: NFER.

Miles, M.B., Saxl, E.R. and Lieberman, A. (1988) What skills do educational change agents need: an empirical view. *Curriculum Enquiry*, Ontario Institute for Studies in Education. **18** (2), pp. 24–36.

Misten, M. (1982) Stress management in schools: the organization is the problem and the solution. *Educational Change and Development*, **6** (1), pp. 11–20.

Montgomery, D. (1989) *Managing Behaviour Problems*. London: Hodder & Stoughton.

Montgomery, D. and Hadfield, N. (1989) *Appraisal in Primary Schools*. Leamington Spa: Scholastic.

Moon, B. and Shelton-Mayes, A. (eds) (1994) *Teaching and Learning in the Secondary School*. London: Routledge/Open University.

Mortimore, P., Sammons, P., Stoll, L., Lewis, D. and Ecob, R. (1988) *School Matters: The Junior Years*. London: Open Books.

NCC (1989a) *GRIDS: Guidelines for Review of Internal Development*. London: NCC.

NCC (1989b) *A Curriculum for all: Special Needs in the National Curriculum*. London: NCC.

NDC/CREATE Project, Summary Report (1993) *Effective Management in Schools*. London: DFE/HMSO.

Nias, J. (1979) Leadership style and job satisfaction in primary schools. In Bush, T., Glatter, R., Goodey, J. and Riches, C. (eds.) (1980), *Approaches to School Management*. London: Open University/Harper & Row.

NUT (1991) *Appraisal: Your Rights and Expectations*. London: National Union of Teachers.

OFSTED (1992) *Framework for the Inspection of Schools*. London: HMSO.

OFSTED (1993) *Curriculum Organization and Classroom Practice: A Follow up Report*. London: HMSO.

Pease, A. (1984) *Body Language*. London: Sheldon Press.

Peters, T.J. and Waterman, R.H. (1982) *In Search of Excellence*. New York: Harper & Row.

Plant, R. (1987) *Managing Change and Making It Stick*. London: Fontana Collins.

Playfoot, D., Skelton, M. and Southworth, G. (1989) *The Primary School Management Book: A Practical Handbook for Heads and Teachers*. London: Mary Glasgow.

Pollard, A. and Tann, S. (1993) *Reflective Teaching in the Primary School: A Handbook for the Classroom (second edn)*. London: Cassell.

Pondy, C.R. (1978) Leadership in a language game. In McCall, M.W. and Lombardo, M.M. (eds), *Leadership: Where Else Can We Go*. Durham, NC: Duke University Press.

Powell, M. and Solity, J. (1990) *Teachers in Control*. London: Routledge.

Purkey, W.W. (1970) *Self Concept and School Achievement*. Englewood Cliffs, NJ: Prentice-Hall.

Reid, K., Hopkins, D. and Holly, P. (1987) *Towards the Effective School*. Oxford: Basil Blackwell.

Rogers, C. (1980) *A Way of Being*. Boston: Houghton Mifflin.

Rowland, V. and Birkett, K. (1992) *Personal Effectiveness for Teachers*. London: Simon & Schuster.

Rutter, M., Maughan, B., Mortimore, P., Ouston, J. and Smith, A. (1979) *Fifteen Thousand Hours: Secondary Schools and Their Effects on Children*. London: Open Books.

SEAC (1989) *A Guide to Teacher Assessment*, Pack C, *A Source Book for Teacher Assessment*. London: Heinemann.

Schon, D. (1983) *The Reflective Practitioner*. New York: Basic Books.

Shipman, M.D. (1979) *The Sociology of the School* (second edn). London: Longman.

Sikes, P.J., Measor, L. and Woods, P. (1985) *Teachers' Careers*. London: Falmer Press.

Skynner, R. and Cleese, J. (1983) *Families and How to Survive Them*. London: Methuen.

Smith, R. (1988) What makes a good teacher. *Child Education*, reprinted in Moon, B. and Shelton-Mayes, A. (eds) (1994), *Teaching and Learning in the Secondary School*. London: Routledge/Open University.

Smith, R. (1989) The good, the bad and the effective. *Business Education Today*, March.

Smith, R. (1990a) *The Effective School Vol. 1: Teachers Working Together: The Whole School Approach*. Lancaster: Framework Press.

Smith, R. (1990b) *The Effective School Vol. 2: Classroom Techniques and Management*. Lancaster: Framework Press.

Smith, R. (1990c) Effective time management. *Business Education Today*, December, pp. 13–14.

Smith, R. (1991) Effective appraisal. *Business Education Today*, October, pp. 10–12.

Smith, R. (1992a) Effective motivation. *Business Education Today*, December, pp. 8–9.

Smith, R. (1992b) *The Heads and Deputies Handbook: Managing Schools in the 1990s*. Lancaster: Framework Press.

Smith, R. (1993a) Elusive ethos. *Managing Schools Today*, **2** (6), pp. 39–41.

Smith, R. (1993b) *Preparing for Appraisal: Self Evaluation for Teachers in Primary and Secondary Schools*. Lancaster: Framework Press.

Smith, R. (1994) *Preparing for Inspection*. Lancaster: Framework Press.

Socket, H. (ed.) (1980) *Accountability in the English Education System*. London: Hodder & Stoughton.

Solity, J. and Bull, S. (1987) *Special Needs: Bridging the Curriculum Gap*. Milton Keynes: Open University Press.

Southworth, G. (1990) Leadership, headship and effective primary schools. *School Organization*, **10** (1), pp. 25–37.

Stenhouse, L. (1975) *An Introduction to Curriculum Research and Development*. London: Heinemann.

Stogdill, R.M. (1974) Personal factors associated with leadership: a survey of the literature. *Journal of Psychology*, **25** (3), pp. 35–71.

Stott, K. and Parr, H. (1991) *Marketing your School*. London: Hodder & Stoughton.

Suffolk LEA (1985) *Those having Torches*

Tannenbaum, S. and Schmidt, T.L. (1973) How to choose a leadership pattern. *Harvard Business Review*, **36**, (2), pp. 95–101.

Trethowan, D. (1987) *Appraisal and Target Setting: A Handbook for Teacher Development*. London: Harper & Row.

Weston, P., Barrett, E. and Jamison, J. (1993) Review and reflection: the quest for coherence. In Weston *et al.* (eds), *The Quest for Coherence: Managing the Whole Curriculum 5–16*. Slough: NFER.

Wragg, E. (1987) *Teacher Appraisal: A Practical Guide*. London: Macmillan.

Wragg, E. (1994) Unpublished report of the Leverhulme Teacher Appraisal Project. *Times Educational Supplement*, 9 September.

Wylie, E. (1994) *Guidelines on Partnership Review*. Warwickshire County Council.

INDEX